BRANCHING OUT

VOICES FROM SOUTHEAST ASIA
The Refugee Experience in the United States
by John Tenhula

DISTANT MAGNETS
Expectations and Realities in the
Immigrant Experience, 1840-1930
edited by Dirk Hoerder and Horst Rössler

BRANCHING OUT
German-Jewish Immigration to the
United States, 1820-1914
by Avraham Barkai

Ira Glazier and Luigi de Rosa,
series editors

BRANCHING OUT

German-Jewish Immigration
to the United States
1820-1914

Avraham Barkai

HM

HOLMES & MEIER
New York/London

Published in the United States of America 1994 by
Holmes & Meier Publishers, Inc.
160 Broadway
New York, NY 10038

This book has been printed on acid-free paper.

Library of Congress Cataloging-in-Publication Data

Barkai, Avraham.
   Branching Out : German-Jewish immigration to the United
States, 1820–1914 / Avraham Barkai.
      p.   cm. — (Ellis Island series)
   Includes bibliographical references and index.
   ISBN 0-8419-1152-5
   1. Jews, German—United States—History. 2. Jews—Germany—
Migrations. 3. Immigrants—United States—History. 4. United
States—Emigration and immigration. 5. Germany—Emigration and
immigration. 6. United States—Ethnic relations. I. Title.
II. Series.
E184.J5B34   1994
973'.04924031—dc20   93-10833
                                                              CIP

Manufactured in the United States of America

The lords of the nations have struck
down its branches, which reached to Jazer
and strayed to the desert. Its shoots spread
abroad and passed over the sea.

Isaiah 16:8

Contents

Illustrations follow page 112

Preface

The many thousands of Jews from Bavaria, Württemberg, and other parts of Germany, Austria, and Bohemia who, in the early nineteenth century, came to the New World have been rightly regarded as "the pioneers of a migration overseas that knows no parallel in Jewish history . . . and was materially to transform the Jewry not only of Germany but of the whole world."[1] These immigrants played a decisive role in the formative period of American Jewry; a great part of what to this very day constitutes the social character, spiritual essence, and institutional framework of American Jewish society was created by German or German-speaking Jews and their descendants, who remained the dominant group long after they had been outnumbered by Jewish immigrants from Eastern Europe.[2] In more than one sense, American Jewry of the nineteenth century, up to the 1880s, can be regarded as a branch of German Jewry, at various stages along its route toward defining its own identity.

Despite the achievements of recent studies on the "German period" in American Jewish history, one important aspect of the process has been largely neglected: the impact of mass emigration on those German Jews who stayed behind. It is not unusual for a society to underestimate the significance of an ongoing emigration and to ignore its possible influence on the country of origin. In the case of German Jewry, which was at the time preoccupied with a process of social and spiritual evaluation, legal emancipation, and acceptance by—as well as identification with—German society, this underestimation was all the more understandable. Today we know, however, that at least in demographic terms the effect of the emigration was of considerable importance.

In this book I have therefore tried to follow the development, in immigrant society, of a continuous interaction between German Jewry and its American branch. This is not only the story of an emigrating group and the process of its "Americanization," if only for the simple reason that emigration to the United States was a prolonged process. Considerable numbers of German Jews took part in it, up to the turn of the century. Mutual and multifaceted contacts with the homeland were kept alive over a long period of time, between families and friends as well as in both groups' common social, cultural, and religious interests and developments. These relations and exchanges, similarities and differences, can be traced throughout the nineteenth and early twentieth centuries, and they had important and lasting influence on both sides of the ocean. Another aspect of this phenomenon is the impact of events in the "old fatherland" on the changing relations between Jewish and Gentile German immigrant groups in America.

It is mainly in view of this interaction that, after having spent most of the last ten or more years studying the economic and social history of Jews in Germany, I agreed to write this book. After some hesitation I was glad to accept the invitation of the editors of the Ellis Island Series to contribute a volume "written for the general reader but based on the most recent research." Some aspects of American Jewish life I deliberately decided to mention only in a cursory way, as was especially the case regarding religious and spiritual developments; illuminating scholarly studies have recently been published, to which I willingly refer the interested reader for more information.[3]

From the first draft of this volume I found myself confronted with the serious problem of selection. Time and again I had to remind myself that this is not a history of American Jewry, but only of one of its components: German-Jewish immigrant society. Actually, until 1880 the two are very hard to separate. Years ago Oscar Handlin referred to exactly this problem when he placed the immigrant experience at the very center of American history. Like other ethnic groups, the German Jews—up to 1880 the overwhelming majority among America's Jews—had to grope their way through the immigration process, in which "danger and insecurity [were the] other words for freedom and opportunity."[4] Separately and individually, they—or a substantial part of them—realized and at the same time fulfilled their need and desire for an integrating and supportive community. In doing so they unknowingly laid the religious, cultural, and institutional foundations of modern American Jewry. Keeping this in mind, I have nevertheless tried to remain, as far as possible, within the limits of the project as initially defined.

This book would not have been possible without the assistance of many people. The editors of the Ellis Island Series trusted me, a relative newcomer to this field, with the task of writing this volume. A Bernard and Audre Rapoport Fellowship from the American Jewish Archives in Cincinnati made possible several months of intensive research for my wife and myself; at these archives we enjoyed the helpful assistance and expert advice of Dr. Abraham A. Peck and the archives' staff. The friendly and informal atmosphere and hospitality at the archives, and at the Klau Library and everywhere on the campus of the Hebrew Union College, remain a delightful memory of our first close acquaintance with American Jewish academia. Professors Jacob Marcus, Michael Meyer, and Jonathan Sarna spent many hours guiding my steps and providing valuable advice. My publishers and their readers and editors, through rather strenuous efforts, made possible the publication of this volume in readable English. During our stay at the library and archives of the American Jewish Historical Society, Dr. Nathan Kaganoff and his staff were very helpful in filling in some gaps in my sources. I am also deeply indebted to Jonathan Sarna, Marion A. Kaplan, and Lloyd P. Gartner for reading drafts of the manuscript and for correcting my data on many issues.

Even with all this much appreciated assistance, as well as that of many unmentioned colleagues and friends, I am aware that many omissions and misconceptions may have remained in the following pages, for which I alone am responsible.

Last but not least, my thanks belong to my wife, Shoshanna, who as always efficiently assisted in my research and helped me in endless table talks to organize and evaluate the sources and data.

A. B.
Lehavoth Habashan

BRANCHING OUT

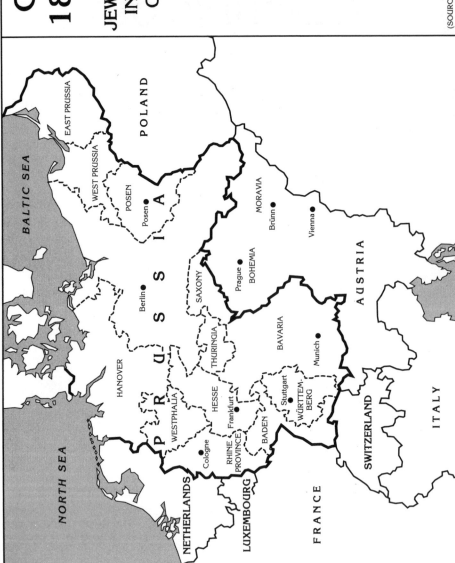

GERMANY 1815 - 1848

JEWISH POPULATION IN MAIN REGIONS OF EMIGRATION

WEST PRUSSIA
1825 - 15,350
1871 - 26,632
1910 - 13,954

POSEN
1816 - 51,960
1871 - 61,982
1910 - 26,512

BAVARIA
1822 - 53,402
1840 - 59,376
1880 - 53,526
1910 - 55,065

(SOURCE: JÜD. LEXICON, BERLIN 1930, VOL.V 639f)

NORTH SEA

BALTIC SEA

EAST PRUSSIA

WEST PRUSSIA

POLAND

POSEN

Posen ●

SILESIA

MORAVIA

Brünn ●

Vienna ●

Berlin ●

SAXONY

THURINGIA

BOHEMIA

Prague ●

AUSTRIA

P R U S S I A

HANOVER

WESTPHALIA

HESSE

Frankfurt ●

BAVARIA

Munich ●

Cologne ●

RHINE PROVINCE

BADEN

Stuttgart ●

WÜRTTEM-BERG

SWITZERLAND

ITALY

NETHERLANDS

LUXEMBOURG

FRANCE

Introduction: The Old World and the New

German Jewry in the Nineteenth Century

At the end of the Napoleonic wars, about a quarter million Jews lived in German "Länder." Half of them lived in Prussia, some 53,000 in Bavaria, and about the same number in Posen, which had been annexed to Prussia in 1815. The legal, social, and economic position of the Jews in both regions, as elsewhere in Germany, was anything but favorable. In Bavaria, by a notorious law of 1813, no Jew was allowed to marry, to live permanently in any region, or to pursue any economic activity without being inscribed in the so-called "Matrikel," which fixed the number of "settled" Jews for every township and village. Once fixed, the list could not be expanded, not even to include descendants of the local Jewish families, to whom right of settlement was granted only after some place in the "Matrikel" became vacant because of death or migration. The declared policy was "not to enlarge the number of Jewish families in places where they exist, but on the contrary to gradually decrease it where it is too large."[1] In this aim the policy was quite successful: despite a remarkably high birthrate, Bavarian Jewry declined by emigration not only in relative

1

but also in absolute terms. It counted about 50,000 in 1871 and slightly less in 1925, and its proportion in the total population fell from 1.23 percent in 1852 to only 0.7 percent in 1925.

The Jews of Posen, the second important source of emigration to America, did not enjoy even the restricted emancipation granted to Prussian Jews. In the annexed province, as in neighboring West Prussia, rights of citizenship or free movement were not granted until 1848, and Jews were generally not allowed to live in small villages. In contrast to Bavaria and other western parts of Germany, where at this time most Jews were living in small communities, the Jews of these territories lived mainly in towns, constituting in some places the majority of the local population. In the first years of Prussian rule many Jews crossed the border from Poland, and in 1846 the Jewish population of the Posen "Grand Duchy" had increased to over 81,000, that is, to 6.4 percent of the total population. Emigration took its toll in this region as well: 100,000 Jews lived in Posen and West Prussia in 1852, 89,000 in 1871, and only 66,000 in 1910.[2]

The situation in Bavaria and Posen represents the differences between the main regions of Jewish settlement in Germany: the west and southwest (Bavaria, Baden, Hesse, Württemberg, the Prussian provinces Rhineland and Westphalia, and Alsace-Lorraine), and the east (Posen, West and East Prussia, and Silesia). In the western territories the French conquests under Napoleon had for a short period granted the Jews varying degrees of legal emancipation, which were restricted again by Napoleon's "décrét infâme" of 1808 according to which local officials could determine Jewish rights of settlement and economic pursuits. After Napoleon's defeat and the Congress of Vienna, all centralized legislation regarding the Jews was abolished. In the newly established German kingdoms and duchies the legal status of the Jews was regulated by variously discriminatory legislation. In Prussia, where the Enlightenment and the French Revolution had left their mark, the Emancipation Law of 1812 had granted the Jews rights of citizenship and settlement while excluding them from civil service and some professions. But even this law did not apply to the new Prussian territories like Posen. Here restrictive legislation remained valid until 1869, when the *Norddeutsche Bund* (the North German Federation) granted the Jews at least formal civil rights in all its member states.

These legal and juridical differences influenced the social and economic situation of Jewish communities in German countries. By general opinion, the legal equality of the Jewish population was to be conditional on their economic and moral "betterment," that is, by replacing their traditional commercial activities with more "honorable" occupations in agriculture and handicrafts. Only after the Jews had abandoned their traditional activities of petty trade, peddling, and money-changing would they be considered worthy of full civil rights. The way to achieve this goal, to which even the liberal "emancipators" adhered, was to have Jews "educated" by allowing them to enter handicrafts and other occupations, while at the same time withholding essential legal reforms so as to encourage them to choose these "more honorable" economic pursuits.[3]

These and other historical developments left their mark on Jewish communities. Economic differences resulted from environmental conditions and the legal situation of the various Jewish communities. Among the formerly Polish Jews of Posen we find a relatively high percentage of artisans. In Bavaria and the Rhine provinces, Jews worked primarily as peddlers, cattle, grain, and wine dealers, and small shopkeepers. The urbanization of the German Jews occurred much later than is generally assumed. Until the late nineteenth century, German Jewry was dispersed over more than 1,700 small communities, and even in 1852 less than 9 percent lived in towns of over 50,000 inhabitants.

Despite these differences, the economic position of German Jews everywhere was far from comfortable. In 1800 most were poor people who had to work long, hard hours to eke out a frugal living for their families. By some estimates, close to one-fifth still belonged to the twilight zone of unsettled *Betteljuden* (begging Jews), where vagrant beggary and small trade, often in stolen goods, merged occasionally with organized crime. True, the economic ascent of the German Jews had begun around 1815, but their social position at mid-century was still quite low. Around 1848 only 15 percent of all German Jews belonged to the upper and middle bourgeoisie, and 35 percent to the lower middle class; the remainder continued to live at a bare subsistence level.[4]

On the cultural and religious level, the diversity was quite remarkable. In eastern Prussia, with the exception of Berlin, the traditional way of life and the Yiddish language persisted longer than in the west and southwest, where it was replaced by "Jüdisch-Deutsch," "Western Yiddish" in current philological terms. Jüdisch-Deutsch was more similar to the local vernacular than Yiddish was, but was still written in Hebrew letters. These east Prussian Jews had been living for generations in the same environment. Despite the territorial fragmentation of Germany, and even repeated evictions from towns or principalities, the ancestors of these Jews remained clustered in the same locality, or nearby in towns where they were more welcome. Over time this segment of German Jewry assumed a distinctly autochthonous German-Jewish group mentality quite different from that of their Eastern European or even Posen coreligionists.

As long as they remained in Germany, there was little contact and therefore almost no friction between these two groups of Jews. Still, both groups were aware of their differences. The southwesterners were initially better-situated and had gained a greater number of economic and legal advantages from the French conquest. Their general education was hardly more advanced than that of the Eastern European Jews; the latter were better versed in traditional Jewish learning. Although a condescending attitude toward "Polacks" appeared quite early among the Bavarian and other western Jews, this was not yet a major problem of inter-Jewish relations. With regard to religion, the Eastern European Jews were generally more traditional, but early differences of religious ritual were not strictly on geographic lines. Reform had started in Berlin in the eighteenth century; it continued in Westphalia and finally put down some roots in Hamburg.[5]

Despite these differences, the constitutional framework of Jewish community life around 1830 was everywhere still intact. Even in the German regions where piecemeal emancipation was relatively advanced, local Jewish communities remained corporate bodies by law, and no Jew was free to leave there without renouncing his or her religion. When in 1876 a special law of the German Reich made it possible for individuals or groups to declare their withdrawal or secession from existing communities, the act had to be performed by a positive legal procedure. Jews could, of course, attend or refrain from religious services at will, but in any case they were obliged to pay community taxes according to the assessment of the community's administration, taxes that were endorsed, and if necessary collected, by the local government. On the other hand, they retained certain communal rights, such as the rights to elect synagogue boards and functionaries, to determine religious services and education, and to be buried in the Jewish cemetery.

These legal arrangements reflected the seclusion and semi-autonomous nature of Jewish self-administration, which continued since the Middle Ages, and which had changed only gradually in the process of emancipation and acculturation. Even though both emancipation and acculturation were taking place, the lives of German Jews were still guided to a large extent by the religious law and behavioral norms of a closed Jewish society. During the nineteenth century, the influence of the Enlightenment, secular education, and religious laxity were to undermine many of these traditional constraints. In a sense, the very decision to emigrate, to leave familiar and communal ties and obligations behind, was an early sign of this development and its influence on the younger, less conservative, more enterprising elements of German-Jewish society. This may explain, at least in part, why Jews from economically and socially relatively advanced parts of Germany had emigrated to America one or two generations earlier than did their coreligionists from eastern Germany and Europe.

In general, expectations that emigration would mean economic improvement and a more secure future undoubtedly prevailed among most German Jews. A purely economic rationale alone would not have initiated mass emigration. Only the combined effect of legal, social, and economic situations at home, and the promise of a better life across the ocean, could convince the younger, unmarried, and more enterprising Jews to leave Germany at a time of general economic expansion.

The "push" of a frustrating existence in Germany sometimes justified a Jewish exodus even in the eyes of sympathetic Gentiles. "The Jews of Bavaria," wrote the *Allgemeine Augsburger Zeitung* in August 1838, "have well-founded motives for exchanging the dear hearth of the homeland for the trans-atlantic shores, . . . to defy the perils of the sea in order to find an asylum where their civil rights and honors are less humiliated than in their fatherland. . . . Nobody should be surprised that so many Jews choose the one and only honorable way . . . to live in a country where all citizens are equal."[6] The later emigration of the Jews from Posen was similarly explained, in the *Vossische Zeitung* in March 1853, as an understandable reaction to the discriminating practice of the administration, a reaction taking place despite Jewish loyalty to the German cause and culture in this multinational province: "Who would blame the more prosperous Jews for preferring the democratic institutions of America and leaving a province where . . . they cannot disregard their feelings of insecurity about their present and future?"[7]

Add to this the "pull" of the New World, reflected in a letter of November 25, 1846, written by Max Lilienthal from

New York, from the God-blessed country of freedom, the beautiful ground of civil equality! The old Europe with its restrictions lies behind me like a bad dream. . . . At last I breath in liberty. . . . Jew or Christian, Christian or Jew—this old strife is forgotten, and only the man as such is respected and loved. . . . Shake off the centuries-old dust of Jew-pressure . . . become a human being like everybody else. . . . May my oppressed brethren in old Europe . . . not be frightened by the many victims of previous emigration! Those times are past. . . . Jewish hearts are open in welcome, Jewish organizations ready to help anyone. Why should you go on carrying the burden of legal exclusion?![8]

The American Scene: "Sephardic Grandees" from Bavaria

According to Wolf and Whiteman, "Before American Jewish history began to be written there had already grown up a myth of the predominance of Spanish and Portuguese Jews in colonial America. As a matter of fact, by the time of the revolution there were far more Ashkenazi Jews in North America than Sephardim."[9] There was, of course, a kernel of truth in this myth. Most of the first Jews to settle in North America in the seventeenth century were Sephardic. Some of them had settled in Brazil, and later established new communities in Cayenne and Curaçao. After the Portuguese conquest, according to tradition, twenty-three Sephardic Jews came to settle in New Amsterdam in 1654. Peter Stuyvesant, who governed the colony for the Dutch West India Company, tried to expel them, but he had to yield to pressures from Amsterdam, where the wealthy Sephardic community wielded some influence. Still, his unconcealed hostility induced a part of the new Jewish settlers to leave for Newport, Rhode Island, which was known for its more liberal attitude. This first Jewish community in New England did not last for long, however, and it was reestablished only in the 1740s.[10]

Until 1740 the population of American Jewry grew steadily but was confined almost entirely to New York. From 1740 on, however, probably as a result of the imperial naturalization law by which England had offered its American Jewish subjects full civil equality, new communities sprang up in Philadelphia and in the south. The first Jewish settlers to choose a site other than New York arrived in Savannah, Georgia, as early as 1732. These seem mainly to have been poor German Jews shipped off by the London Jewish community after it tired of supporting them. Some evidence indicates that in the eighteenth and early nineteenth centuries quite a few Polish and German Jews found their way to the New World as indentured servants. But, at the same time, some men of substance arrived. Many of the most prominent persons appearing in the records of this "Sephardic period" came indeed from Germany, in some cases via London: merchants and shipowners like Moses Levy or Samson Simson; the most important Jewish importer and exporter in New York in the mid-eighteenth century, Jacob Franks; and the merchants Aaron Hart and Michael and Barnard Gratz.[11]

Not all of the successful immigrants who in America became well-known entrepreneurs came from the rich German-Jewish families of the conspicuous elite of the Court Jews. On the other hand, in America as in Germany these large-scale traders, importers, and bankers were no more than a small, visible, and therefore historically recorded minority of American Jewry. As Jacob Marcus states: "It may be fairly maintained that all but an infinitesimal number of North American Jews were to be included in a broadly conceived middle class. Some Jewish merchants were even wealthy by contemporary standards; practically none of the Jews were paupers, very few were proletarians, and a substantial number were lower middle-class petit bourgeois shopkeepers and middle-class storekeepers and merchants."[12]

Early in the nineteenth century the majority of American Jews—estimated to have numbered about three thousand souls in the seven congregations recorded in 1799—were foreign-born and mostly from German-speaking countries. From the early nineteenth century onward, however, the term "Sephardic Period" is correct only in the religious sense. The new arrivals were readily accepted and integrated into the existing Jewish community. In all existing congregations the Sephardic ritual regulated the services, and this remained the rule after newcomers from Germany, Poland, and London had joined. And so we find many of the prominent German Jews of the colonial and early post-revolutionary period, the Sheftalls, Gratzes, Harts, or Franks, serving on the boards of Sephardic synagogues, burial societies, and philanthropic institutions. In later years, David Einhorn, one of the most "German-conscious" Reform rabbis, referred to these people somewhat contemptuously as "Portugiesen aus Schnotzebach" (Portuguese people from Schnotzebach).[13]

The first Ashkenazi synagogue, Rodeph Shalom of Philadelphia, which was started in 1795 and formally dedicated in 1802, was clearly an exception. Only much later were similar congregations founded in New York and elsewhere. All early synagogues were founded by men of Sephardic ancestry, and the ritual they followed was accepted by later arrivals. There seems to have been a kind of social status attached to Sephardic practice and Sephardic society. Sephardic Jews from Amsterdam or London were leaders of the community, "the established, the cultured, the integrated Jews. So it was that in America it seemed better to begin at this level of society, at leat as far as form of worship was concerned, and throughout the country Sephardic synagogues were joined and founded by Yiddish-speaking Jews."[14]

This process of assimilation was by no means one-sided. Although the small Sephardic-Jewish minority had rapidly adopted English and been well integrated in the Gentile society, they had still preserved their orthodox Judaism and ethnic self-consciousness. They were also aware that their knowledge of Hebrew and Jewish ritual was meager, and they welcomed reinforcement from the new arrivals from Germany, Jews better grounded in their cultural heritage. True, as Naomi Cohen states, "the aristocratic pretensions of the Sephardim, who would not permit the masses of the 'boorish' Germans to ride [on] their coattails, antedated their American experience," but in America this attitude was slowly but effectively undermined prior to the massive influx of German Jews. The earlier arrivals "were accepted by the original congregations and easily shaped to fit the Sephardic mold."[15]

There may have remained some tensions between Ashkenazi and Sephardic Jews, but thanks to their collective integration, American Jewry on the eve of the revolution was a small but unified, generally prosperous and generally accepted, group. There may be some exaggeration and even an element of myth in some earlier laudatory descriptions of the Jewish participation in the War of Independence. Haim Salomon, the legendary "financier of the Revolution," certainly fulfilled an important function, as did other Jews; but it seems evident that the American Jews at that time already felt they were an integral part of the emerging society, and as such most, but by no means all, identified with the reigning political sentiments and aims of the period. Like other Americans, they fought and suffered for the common cause—for example, Mordecai Sheftall and his son of Savannah, Georgia, who were taken prisoner by the British and exiled to the West Indies; and David Salisbury Franks, who went to Europe on several missions for the Continental Congress, from 1775 to 1786 served the United States without any pay, and finally found himself impoverished. There were also, however, a number of loyalist defectors to the British who went to England or Canada.[16]

The Emigration and the Emigrants

Surprisingly, no generally agreed-on estimate of the number of German-Jewish emigrants to America exists, and diverging figures are found even in recent publications.[17] Contemporary Jews and Gentiles alike had quite unrealistic ideas about the numbers of Jews in America. For instance, the German American Dictionary of 1871 "counted" no less than 600,000 German Jews living in America at that time.[18] Even this sounds modest compared with the number that appeared in the *New York Herald* on July 23, 1879. When questioned about his reaction to the notorious Coney Island Affair (an attempt to exclude Jewish patrons from a Brooklyn seaside resort), Mr. Edward Lauterbach, a prominent German-Jewish lawyer, spoke of "the 2,500,000 Jews in America." Likewise, one of the "poorer class of Jews in Chatham Street," when interviewed by the *Herald's* reporter, declared his conviction that "we shall soon have done forever with this sort of thing. There are in this country about two million and a half of Jews. Most of these are engaged in commerce, and at least one-fourth have accumulated riches." The conclusion to be drawn was that such a number could be relied on to take appropriate action.[19]

These estimates are, of course, curiosities. The entire Jewish population of the United States in 1880—that is, just before the East European mass immigration started—is by now more or less reliably estimated at around 280,000, and most of these Jews were of German or German-speaking origin. Based on demographic data, statistical calculations arrive at an "emigration loss" of close to 140,000 Jews, within the boundaries of the later German Reich alone, between 1840 and 1870.[20] Not all came to America, but most of them did. We also know that emigration from Bavaria and other areas in southwest Germany had started before 1840. It is less known that after 1871, and up to 1910, emigration from the German Reich continued in remarkable dimensions; the number is estimated by a recent study to be no less than 70,000 to 80,000 Jews.[21] The greater part immigrated to the United States; German-speaking Jews also continued to arrive from Austria, Bohemia, and Hungary. All together, the estimate that in 1914 some 250,000 American Jews had come from these countries can be considered cautious and even conservative.

Jewish emigration from Germany was, of course, a part of the general population movement that in the course of the nineteenth and early twentieth centuries transplanted around 5.5 million Germans to the New World. But general emigration alone cannot sufficiently explain Jewish emigration. German Jewry was at this time not only a religious group that was legally discriminated against, but also a socially and economically distinct minority. Compared with the general German population, Jews had a different occupational structure and diverged from the general population as much in average income and property as in their reactions to economic, social, and political change. With all these differences, they had to deviate also in patterns of migration, in their direction, motivation, and composition. Once in America, the Jews' adaptation to the new homeland was connected with the general German immigrant population only for a short while. How German Jews and Gentiles lived together in America, and how and when their paths parted, is another important aspect of our story.

During all its stages, Jewish participation in the emigration from Germany exceeded their proportion in the general population. The general German mass movement started with the "emigration fever" of 1816 in Baden and Württemberg. It gained momentum during the 1840s and 1850s, and reached its first peak in 1854, when close to a quarter million Germans—0.7 percent of the total population—left their homeland in one single year.[22] Fluctuating from 40,000 to 140,000 per year, the emigration-curve reached a new apex of 221,000 in 1881 and 204,000 in 1882. Between 1880 and 1893 over 1.5 million people left Germany, almost all of them for the United States.[23] The over 200,000 Jewish emigrants from the boundaries of the German Reich between 1830 and 1914 constitute close to 4 percent of total emigration, whereas the average for Jewish population in this period was only around 1.1 percent of the general population (or, more accurately, 1.3 percent in 1852 and 0.9 percent in 1910). These calculations are corroborated by some piecemeal data from Bavaria and Württemberg that contain information about the emigrant's religion.[24]

Jewish mass emigration started several years later than that of Gentiles, and was concentrated mostly in Bavaria. Later, when most of the general emigration originated from the northeastern parts of the country, Jewish emigration also increased from Posen and West Prussia and at the same time continued in quite considerable numbers from the South and West of Germany. The reasons for these differences are to be found in the different motivations and differing demographic and social composition of the two groups of emigrants.

By all existing evidence, non-Jewish emigration from Germany was predominantly a middle-class phenomenon. The greater part consisted of small freeholders and peasants or their second- and later-born sons, who intended to settle on the free land in America. Only 20 to 30 percent were small craftsmen or of other occupations. Until mid-century, 70 to 80 percent emigrated with their families, and even later, when more poor farmhands were included, married emigrants were in the majority.[25] In contrast, Jewish emigration was mainly a movement of young, unmarried, and poor people. And although economic motivation played an important role in the decisions of Jewish emigrants, it does not seem to have been of the same crucial importance to the Jews. As long as Jews were not allowed to set up families and had no right of settlement, legal and social discrimination would be a far stronger incentive. But other reasons for emigration, such as the wish to escape military service, were by no means exclusively Jewish.

For all these reasons we have to regard Jewish emigration as an autonomous and unique phenomenon. From the point of view of German population movements it was, of course, a part of a general trend. Contemporaries and later historians, dedicated to proving that the hoped-for integration of Jews into German society had indeed occurred, were inclined to overemphasize the common background and cultural heritage of the emigration, and to ignore differences and conflicts. I can see no reason to continue today in this tradition. To its very end in World War II, German Jewry was a distinctive minority group and so, too, were those German Jews who left to put down new roots in America.

Sources and Methods

The German emigration of the nineteenth century has been tentatively conceived as a kind of "substitute revolution."[26] Be this as it may, there can be little doubt that, for the German Jews who left their country at this time, emigration was a substitute for emancipation. In the New World they immediately found what the Jews who remained in Germany would not see for several decades: equality, at least before the law, and freedom of movement, settlement, and economic enterprise everywhere. But what constituted a relief for them has created a problem for the historian of our own times, who must hunt for reliable quantitative information: banned in America from the sphere of the state, religion remained unlisted in most public records.

Most earlier works dealing with the history of congregations and institutions seem to have been little aware of, or concerned with, the fact that they were working with highly selective sources. In almost all of these studies, a dozen or so prominent families are more or less extensively investigated under the evident underlying assumption that the activities of a visible elite reflect the experience of the whole community. Although congregational records are available and have been explored, as in some of the more recent local studies, we remain in the dark as to what proportion of the Jewish population belonged to any existing congregation at any given time. Even our secondary sources, indispensable in an effort to register a greater part of the Jewish residents, are in most cases of only limited value: city directories often list the more prosperous and publicity-conscious firms and individuals and can ignore the transient and less prosperous ones. The local Jewish press kept rather exclusive records of activities of the prominent and successful Jews, as, for example, in the case of Columbus, Ohio, where the local *Jewish Chronicle* of the whole year 1918 contained information on no more than 9 percent of the Jewish residents.[27] And when a meticulous historian tries to examine tombstones and burial registers of the past, he or she sometimes discovers, as in the case of New Mexico, that many Jews were laid to rest in the Masonic cemetery.[28]

In the absence of more reliable indicators, many historians have tried to identify Jews by the family- and given names recorded in manuscript census, taxation, and other official lists. This method can be regarded as a passable expedient, the more so if its results can be at least partly corroborated by additional sources. We may assume that in this way one can discover a greater part of the Jewish population than that included in the congregational records, especially those of the later nineteenth century, when religious indifference and the disaffiliation of Jewish individuals was pervasive. But the shortcomings of the procedure are evident. In the United States, biblical names among Gentiles are even more usual than in Europe, and the "Anglicization" of names was widespread not only among Jewish immigrants. When individuals proven to be of pure Christian stock are known under the name Israel Israel, and when German-born Jews appear as Bennett King, Henry Jones, and John Middleton, caution is in order.

Only the combined and cross-referenced use of cemetery surveys, congregation records, directories, official census data, and supplementary sources can hope to achieve a more or less full identification of the total Jewish population of any locality. Understandably, where such success has been claimed, in recent studies profiting from modern data-processing techniques, they have mostly dealt with smaller communities.[29] A comparable effort for cities like New York or Los Angeles is still awaited, and is probably impossible at the present state of preliminary local and regional research.

If such are the trials of a purely quantitative demographic investigation, any attempt to obtain specific data on the social and economic stratification and development of the Jewish population of any given place must appear to be an almost Sisyphean task. Some recent attempts in this direction—by authors who are somewhat uneasily aware of the fact that "the economic history of the nineteenth-century German Jewish community in America has been described far too long in facile rags-to riches terms"[30]—have found only partial and palliative solutions. Even careful scrutinies of lodge-membership lists or the reports of credit-rating firms like Dun and Bradstreet supply us with information of only those German-Jewish immigrants who "made it." Although we have no quantitative estimates, we find enough indirect evidence to enable us to assume that a good part never did join a lodge and never did set up independent business firms, providing for their families through blue- or mostly white-collar jobs.

The probable fallacy of selective sampling may be even more aggravated by what in my opinion appears to be geographic selectivity in American Jewish historiography. Most of the not too numerous studies that may be considered as adequate by the standards of modern social and economic history concentrate on the regions of Jewish settlement in the West, Midwest, and South of the United States. As far as I could discover, only a few satisfactory works of this kind deal with the Jewish communities on the East Coast. But in 1877, before the start of the mass immigration, over one-half of the estimated total Jewish population of the United States resided in five large eastern communities. No less than 35 percent lived in New York, mostly in New York City (whose numerical predominance in U.S. Jewry was already well established in the 1860s), and another 19 percent in Philadelphia, Baltimore, Boston, and New Jersey combined.[31] Historians' prevailing preoccupation with the enterprising Jewish peddlers and merchants and their reform-oriented religious congregations in the Midwest has, to a great degree, distorted the real picture of Jewish life in the United States in the nineteenth century.

(A general review like the present one cannot, of course, pretend to overcome these shortcomings, let alone replace them with better or more comprehensive data. It has to base its conclusions on the effort of previous scholars, mainly on a local or regional level. But neither can we neglect to mention what has yet to be achieved in order to know the full and true story. What remains is the hope that forthcoming work and the effective exploitation of new data-processing techniques by a younger generation of historians will fill out the many remaining lacunae. Meanwhile, we have to take refuge in the proviso that these future efforts may either confirm or—perhaps more probably—revise some of the more hypothetical contentions offered here.)

One rather innovative hypothesis is reflected in dividing the integration and acculturation process of immigrants in America into two stages, roughly separated by the Civil War. I believe that German-Jewish immigration of the later stage, and up to 1910, was indeed distinctively different from the first wave in demographic and social composition, as well as geographic origins, and so was the process of these immigrants' integration into communities in their new homeland.

All that said, some doubtful reflections refuse to be suppressed: to what extent does our study really represent the main body of German-Jewish immigrants? Like others of its kind, and like the secondary literature extensively used here, our study is based mostly on published and unpublished sources in central and local Jewish archives. The main body of these records are personal reminiscences and letters, family histories, and the preserved records of congregations and other Jewish associations. All this material originates with individuals who chose to remain inside the Jewish community, as well as inside the organizations they created or belonged to, and who chose to write about their community. It was this group of immigrants and their descendants who were known to, and approached, by historians.

What segment of the German-Jewish immigrants of even the earlier wave of immigration do these records really represent? Shortly before 1880, secular Jewish associations attracted about 40,000 members, and synagogue membership less than 13,000, of a total Jewish population in the United States of 250,000 souls.[32] If this is true, we are bound to be skeptical. Second, one has to assume that it was mainly those who "made it" who wrote memoirs, and whose papers were posthumously deposited in the archives. What about the less successful Jews, those who returned, disillusioned to Europe, or who were submerged in the American maelstrom without leaving traces?

These are long-standing dilemmas, well-known to everyone interested in modern social history, especially cases where reliable quantitative data are missing or incomplete. It should, of course, not discourage attempts like the present one to make the best of those sources that are available, always keeping in mind the limitations of their endeavors.

1

The First Wave: A Substitute for Emancipation

1820–1860

Leaving the Old Home

Individual Jews or occasional Jewish families were leaving Germany for America—directly or after some transit period in England—already in the late eighteenth century. The real mass migration, however, did not begin until the 1820s. In purely demographic terms this emigration was a part of the German migrations that had started with the "emigration fever" of 1816 in Baden and Württemberg.[1] Nevertheless, we have to deal with Jewish emigration as an autonomous phenomenon. Jewish emigration was different from the general movement even in its starting points: Bavarian Jews, principally those from the Franconian districts, were the real pioneers of the mass exodus to the New World, followed closely, and probably in no lesser numbers, by Jews from Bohemia (see map, p. xvi).

Statistics for the early nineteenth century are scarce and not very reliable, but from existing evidence the Jewish emigration from Bavaria for the period 1820–40 has been estimated at around 10,500 people, with some 15,000 Bohemian Jews leaving their homeland at the same time. During this twenty-year period, the total Jewish population of each country numbered on the average around 55,000 to 60,000, and we may safely assume that the greater part of the emigration came to America. (The Bohemian Jews have been somewhat overlooked in most studies of the "German Period" in American Jewish history, but there can be no doubt that in language and cultural heritage they were an inseparable part of

the group of German-speaking Jews in the United States. They will therefore be treated as such throughout this book.)

Jews from Württemberg and Baden arrived in America more or less
at the same time, although in smaller numbers, and adapted easily to
their former neighbors from Bavaria.[2] Actually, there was little difference
between them with regard to cultural background or socioeconomic situation: in both kingdoms, as in the Grand Duchy of Baden, most Jews
were living in small rural communities. Most of them were small-scale
cattle dealers, peddlers, and storekeepers; the rise into the middle classes
had hardly begun. Legislation regulating the status of the Jews of Württemberg and Baden was less restrictive than in Bavaria, but economic
motivation served everywhere as a powerful incentive to induce enterprising youths to try their luck in the land of freedom and unlimited
opportunities.

Contemporary Jewish observers were concerned about the future of
small and even larger communities as a result of the emigration: "Many
a small community may be compelled to give up public worship and
its school, because it may be unable to pay the teachers and religious
functionaries. . . . From certain places, in which there are 30–40 Jewish
families 15–20 persons or more are leaving, and, at that, mostly young
and hard-working people."[3] The emigration movement introduced a new
element into German-Jewish history, an element that would spread, one
or two generations later, to other parts of Europe: the transplantation of
a significant part of the young generation of Jews to a new continent.
Jewish community life in Bavaria and elsewhere was seriously affected,
in the demographic as well as in every other sense, by this loss.[4]

Jewish emigration from Posen started in the 1830s and reached a
peak in later decades. These immigrants usually appear in contemporary
records as having come from Prussia, including Posen and the province
of West Prussia, but, at the time, in language and cultural background
they were actually more similar to the Polish Jews. The exact number of
immigrants to the United States from these parts is hard to estimate. A
considerable percentage of the emigrants settled in Berlin and elsewhere
in the old Prussian kingdom, where the emancipation edict of 1812
granted them greater freedom of settlement and trade. On the other hand,
data of net migration movements in this region are inconclusive because
of the compensating influence of Jewish in-migration from Poland. All
this taken into account, we may estimate that close to 20,000 Jews from
Posen and West Prussia arrived in America between 1840 and 1860, most
of them during the 1850s. As a result of the emigration, the Jewish population declined, resembling the Bavarian development, in both territories:
in Posen from an annual average of 80,000 between 1844 and 1848 to

73,500 between 1854 and 1858, and in West Prussia from 25,000 in 1855 to only 14,000 in 1871.[5] Contemporary reports from Hamburg and Leipzig noted the transient stream of "Polish Jews" on their way to America, but these must have come mostly from the Prussian provinces.[6]

The Immigrants: Young, Single, and Poor?

A popular account of the immigration of what later became the German-Jewish elite describes them as arriving "for the most part poor, soiled-looking and underfed."[7] The adjectives are well chosen to perpetuate a current myth, but they do not paint a true picture. Neither did the mostly young and poorly educated people who emigrated from Germany in the early decades of the last century arrive in rags, nor did their greater part "make it," to amass great riches in a few short years. They may have been poorer than most German immigrants, who came mostly with their families and at a more mature age, and they may even have been soiled-looking and underfed after a long sea voyage as third-class or steerage passengers, but this was hardly the way they looked when leaving home.

Actually, German Jews emigrated to America some time after the process of their economic advancement had already begun. Most of those who decided to leave their homeland did not belong to the lowest social strata of German Jewry, the still abundant vagrant *Betteljuden* at the fringes of the underworld. The greater part was composed of young sons and daughters of "settled" Jews, in villages and small towns, who were emerging as the dominant middle class of nineteenth-century German Jewry. Many of them had taken the various regulations of the government's "education laws" at face value and had taken care that their young sons acquire the prescribed training in "useful" handicrafts. Soon they learned that their efforts had been in vain: even a concluded apprenticeship did not secure the right of settlement. This explains the relatively large number of artisans among the emigrants. As we read in a newspaper report from Hamburg, dated June 1836: "A caravan of German emigrants passing [through] here last week included 70 Israelites from Bavaria who had all learned handicrafts, but were unable to perform them in their homeland, where the number of Jewish families is not allowed to increase."[8]

The high proportion of craftsmen, mainly young apprentices and journeymen, among the early emigrants from Bavaria and Württemberg has been established in previous studies by some fragmentary statistical evidence. For instance, of 385 adult male emigrants from the Kissingen district of Bavaria between 1830 and 1854, 109—that is, over 28 percent—registered as craftsmen. The situation with Württemberg was similar: in records of 332 adult male emigrants between 1848 and 1855, 93 are stated as being "artisans."[9] In the light of more recent research, these data appear somewhat exaggerated. We have to take into account the prevailing tendency of the Jews, and of some of the registering officials, to meet government expectations through statistical manipulation. Cattle-dealers who owned a cowshed and a small plot of land could be registered as farmers or, probably more often, as butchers. Nevertheless, the predominance of at least partially trained craftsmen among the emigrants, as compared with all Jews gainfully employed, is clearly established. As we shall see, only a few of them engaged in their learned trade after their arrival in America.

Table 1.1

**Jebenhausen, 1825–1870: Family Status and Occupation
of Jewish Emigrants**

| | | | | | | Occupation | | |
| | | Family Status | | | | Peddler, | | |
Years	No. of emigrants	Single	Married, widowed	Children	Artisan	tradesman, etc.	Cattle dealer	Other
1825–29	9	9	—	—	1	4	3	—
1830–34	8	8	—	—	1	3	—	1
1835–39	53	13	15	25	6	9	3	—
1840–44	19	11	4	4	2	2	2	2
1845–49	91	37	15	39	20	6	7	—
1850–54	73	47	14	12	13	11	5	3
1855–59	19	12	2	5	4	3	—	—
1860–64	16	14	2	—	1	5	—	1
1865–70	26	18	4	4	—	6	5	—
1825–70	314	169	56	89	48	49	25	7

SOURCE: Stefan Rohrbacher, "From Württemberg to America," *American Jewish Archives* 41 (1989): 148.

Most of the arriving immigrants of this period were certainly young and unmarried, but here also the picture has to be somewhat revised. Even among the first arrivals from Bavaria or Württemberg we can find quite a number of married couples in their forties and fifties, sometimes with more than a few small children. Depending again on the quoted sources, the percentage of married or widowed emigrants was close to

30 percent.[10] Evidence from Jebenhausen (table 1.1) shows that while the emigrants of the first stages of the exodus in the years 1825–35 were indeed mostly single males, families with children followed very soon and constituted no less than 47.5 percent in the period 1825–1870.

Jebenhausen in Württemberg may, of course, have been an exceptional case: some of the more well-off families, "whose fortunes were well known in the community," seem to have been among the emigrants. It has been suggested that these families were the exceptions that prove the general rule,[11] but how much of an exception is hard to decide. There exist quite a number of family histories in the collections of American Jewish memoir literature and in unpublished archival sources that record cases of immigration with families in the 1850s and early 1860s. Even earlier, a passenger list of the ship *Howard,* sailing from Hamburg in 1839, contains 46 identified Jews out of a total of 114 emigrants, including three families with five children all together. Almost all of them came from Bavaria, and, among the given nineteen occupations, ten were registered as craftsmen: six weavers and tailors, two butchers, and two soap-boilers.[12]

A recent study of the demographic composition of Bostonian Jews who had come to the United States between 1845 and 1861 indicates similar trends. The picture there is of "a small but growing community of young married couples and single brothers, the majority of whom were from either Southwest or Northwest Germany and most of whom were in the process of raising large families."[13] Families were indeed large, averaging 3.8 children per family. Although most of these children of 1860 were native-born, the community contained forty-six families who had immigrated as families, and eighteen of them also had children born abroad. Approximately two-thirds of the Jewish immigrants to Boston between 1840 and 1861 came from Prussia, Poland, or Posen. They seem to have immigrated at the same age, and in similar types of marital status as the Bavarians who had preceded them by one or two decades.

The Jews remaining in Germany demonstrated mixed feelings toward the emigration, at least in its early stages. Reporting the departure of a large group from Ichenhausen the *Israelitische Annalen* of Frankfurt am Main regretfully explained:

> Emigration is, of course, nothing new among us, . . . but now North America . . . has become the sole goal for everybody who wishes to say goodbye to the homeland. . . . The confidence that one will find there a secure subsistence is such that not only young and engaged couples who wish to get married, but even elder married people and families with many children, are confident to prepare their voyage, sell their property, and pin their hopes on the ocean and the far continent.[14]

The *Allgemeine Zeitung des Judenthums* reported an earlier exodus from the same place in a more elegiac tone:

> Today was the day of deepest sadness, of bitterest heartache for the local Israelite congregation. Six fathers of families with their wives and children, all told 44 persons of Mosaic faith, left home to find a new fatherland in far-off America. Not an eye remained dry, not a soul unmoved, when the bitter hour of parting struck. Such departures leave a visible void in the local community, from whose midst 100 persons have left so far, and have already settled or will settle in the free United States of America.[15]

A similar occurrence was reported from Meiningen on the Bavarian-Saxon border:

> On May 6 the Israelites emigrating from the neighboring parts . . . gathered . . . and almost 100 strong entered together upon their journey. They will betake themselves jointly to one ship and they intend to found a small Jewish community together in America. They are carrying a *Sefer Tora,* as well as a *Megilla,* a *Shofar,* etc., and have taken along likewise such persons as are qualified for the exercise of religious functions, as slaughtering, circumcision, . . . religious teachers, cantors, etc. They have made the necessary arrangements in Hamburg in advance so that they may live during the voyage undisturbed in their religion. May now also God's blessing attend them and may they settle happily in the land of their new domicile.[16]

The *Matrikel* laws induced many young couples who were unable to found a family in the place of their birth to emigrate. In a letter from New York dated 1841 we are told of the consecration of a new synagogue, whose congregation were "German immigrants driven from Bavaria, the duchy of Baden, etc., by oppressive laws. One of these laws forbade Jews to marry; and among the immigrants were many betrothed couples, who married as soon as they landed at our shores, trusting their future support to the God of Jacob."[17] We do not know how widespread this procedure of traveling together as an unmarried couple and marrying immediately at arrival actually was, but marriage was certainly one main motivation for emigration. Here again we gain important information from the records of the Jebenhausen emigrants: in 1834 Juettle Ottenheimer, the 25-year-old daughter of one of the prominent families, emigrated alone, taking along her dowry of 400 florins. Not much later she was followed by more and younger single women, who in many cases were recorded as taking along similar or larger amounts for the same purpose. It appears quite probable that some of them married the young men from Jebenhausen who had arrived with them or somewhat earlier.[18]

However, most of the first wave of immigrants were single, more of them men than women. If they did not all arrive in rags, they were certainly not rich. Many of them possessed some small amount of initial capital to help them to get started in the new homeland, as borne out by many personal memoirs and family histories. The Jebenhausen records, which are unique in providing full and detailed information about almost all emigrants over a period of 45 years, corroborate this. As can be seen in table 1.2, ninety of the recorded 165 adult emigrants declared that they had taken with them more than 100 florins in addition to their fare. That Jebenhausen was, after all, not so exceptional is proven by Adolf Kober's research on all recorded Jewish emigrants from Württemberg between 1848 and 1855. According to his figures, the average sum taken along by emigrants ranged from 150 to 400 florins, but some of them brought more, up to 15,000 florins.[19] In the case of Jebenhausen, the largest amount was 2,800 florins, which was carried by Gedalye Moses Arnold, a 51-year-old cattle dealer who emigrated with his spouse in 1870.

Table 1.2
Jebenhausen, 1825–1870: Property of Jewish Emigrants

Years	Less than 100 florins	101–500 florins	501–1,000 florins	Over 1,000 florins
1825–34	7	6	—	—
1835–44	19	43	1	—
1845–54	53	63	19	3
1855–70	4	33	7	4
1825–70	83	145	27	7

SOURCE: Stefan Rohrbacher, "From Württemberg to America," *American Jewish Archives* 41 (1989): 148.

One hundred florins in addition to the fare was, of course, not a large sum of money even for a young and single person, and it was chosen here rather arbitrarily to differentiate between the poorer and the somewhat better-off emigrants. For many of them, even mobilizing the needed funds to pay for passage was not easy. This may have been one reason why Jewish emigrants, in contrast to Gentile Germans, were at first mainly not whole families. Few Jewish immigrants possessed sufficient soluble assets to finance the emigration of the whole family. Diligent saving could at best provide funds for only one family member to start life in the New World. Non-Jewish emigrants, however, "were mostly peasants who, by selling their farmsteads, could realize enough to take a whole family."[20] For Württemberg we have some indication that, in addition to the usual contributions from parents, relatives, or the Jewish communities, the cost of transportation was at times paid by the State Treasury, but these were exceptional cases. Jewish charities played some role in some places. *"Pattern ist Geld wert"*—"Riddance is worth money"—was a typical attitude of Jewish communities eager to get rid of transient migrants. But most of the young emigrants paid their fare through their own efforts or those of their families, and they sometimes worked their way toward the ports, earning their transportation in stages.[21]

Most of the emigrants of this period came from lower-middle-class families whose economic ascent had already started to transform the socioeconomic structure of German Jewry. The ambitions, thrift, and enterprise that had spurred on this emerging class of shopkeepers and tradesmen must also have induced their emigrating children and grandchildren to try their luck overseas. It was probably even the more enterprising and dynamic elements among them who dared to undergo the hardships and dangers of emigration, "blazing the trail" for siblings and relatives. Given the opportunities of unlimited economic pursuits under the conditions of America's expanding economy, these qualities offered them every chance of success. As has been quite rightly concluded, "it was not so much a radically different life that they sought as it was an improved version of the old one." Once in America, however, "the selectivity of the emigration, which tended to leave behind the most well-educated and wealthiest, as well as the poorest and least ambitious, militated against the duplication of old patterns, while the American environment was bound to induce change."[22]

This does not, of course, imply any kind of uniformity. Social differences obviously existed, and they were in part the result of the different means and capabilities that each individual had brought with him or her from home, of the way each of them adapted to the new country, or even of sheer luck, pure and simple. There remains nevertheless a strong impression that the German Jews in America constituted, at least in the first, formative period up to the Civil War, an ethnic group that was, socially, highly homogeneous and cohesive. Important intragroup differences came to the fore early enough, but they were not sufficient to break this general pattern of collective German-Jewish identity.

At both ends of the social ladder we can find, at all times, individuals or small groups that deviated a good deal from the general pattern. Among the early immigrants of the eighteenth century were many poor and destitute people whose later fate seems to have left no trace in our sources. The group of Ashkenazi Jews who had been sent away to Georgia by the Sephardic congregation of London has already been mentioned.[23] In 1791, Rebecca Samuel, the wife of a competent Virginia watchmaker from Hamburg, was writing informative letters in Yiddish about a whole group of early Jewish immigrants, who apparently had fought in the ranks of the mercenaries hired out to the British forces by the duke of Hesse. She writes: "You cannot imagine what kind of Jews they have here [in Virginia]. They were all German itinerants who made a living by begging in Germany. They came to America during the war, as soldiers, and now they can't recognize themselves." There seem to have been quite a number of Jews among the deserting Hessian soldiers, especially in Richmond, Virginia, where in 1788 they founded a mutual aid society of their own.[24]

In the upper social strata we find, early on, some rich and conspicuous Jewish bankers and merchants. The brothers Armand and Michel Heine, cousins of the famous poet, arrived in New Orleans in 1842, and in 1854 their banking and commission business was estimated to be worth as much as $600,000. Like most of the rest of the family in Europe, however, both of them had by this time severed all their ties to Jewry. Other scions of a famous German-Jewish banking family were Frederick and Daniel Warburg. The first was born in Hamburg in 1796 and arrived in Florida in 1821, where he worked with Moses Elias Levy, a Sephardic businessman and landowner, on one of the earliest settlement projects.[25]

Daniel Warburg had a more illustrious career. Born in Hamburg in 1789, he made quite a fortune in New Orleans before he went broke in 1839–41. In addition to some unfulfilled political ambitions, Warburg appeared on the public scene in 1836 with a sensational announcement of his own scientific genius: he possessed "the true knowledge of what is termed the quadrature of the circle." For the revelation of his discovery he asked for "ten Millions of Dollars of the American nation and government, or of the British nation and government Five Million pounds sterling . . . , but a trifling sum, for, if the genius that governs me, should teach me the secret art of ship building . . . the nation I shall instruct in that secret will govern on the seas of the world." When none of these governments came forward to purchase his secret, Warburg published a couple of tabled mathematical pamphlets. Bertram W. Korn, to whom we owe this amusing story, quotes "a professor of mathematics who has examined these communications [and] thinks that Warburg was an early member of 'the International Clan of Assorted Nuts.' Perhaps his family was aware of his ambition . . . and therefore shipped him off to the United States where he would not embarrass them."[26]

August Belmont in New York was far better known and less eccentric. Born in Alzey, Hesse, in 1816, he started work with the Rothschilds early on and in 1837, after a short stay in Naples, arrived in New York City as a representative of their bank. After setting up his own banking business, Belmont became one of the more illustrious figures of New

York City's high society. But by then he had almost no connection with Jewish community life, be it religious or charitable. This tendency of the established Jewish economic elite to disaffiliate from the Jewish community at large was at that time characteristic of Jewish life in Germany as well. It seems to have been transplanted to the New World, although in a diluted fashion, by some of the immigrants originating from the Jewish elite in Germany.

The Push and the Pull

What else should they do but seek a new fatherland, where they could exercise the profession they had learned, to show off their wares, their knowledge and their learning? A young man, capable and a professional, applied to his district court . . . for a certificate of protection [i.e., for right of settlement]. It was denied to him at the first tribunal as well as repeatedly at the higher ones. He made a last attempt to obtain it, but simultaneously annexed his position to have his passport permitting him to go abroad, . . . received the latter and emigrated.

This is but one of the frequent attempts to explain why young, often well-trained youths were emigrating. "What else should they do?" is the general tenor of publications or rabbinical sermons, for example, in *Der Orient* in 1847: "A silk-embroiderer emigrates because his fatherland has no tolerance for his political views; the poor *Schelm Moses* must seek his salvation in America because he is a homeless Jew, . . . and it is, as a rule, the younger generation in particular that emigrates. . . . On inquiring as to the motives, one usually hears the answer: We can no longer withstand the pressure and the disdainful treatment and the disgrace of isolation." In another article these pressures were explained in more detail:

As it is known, the [*Matrikel*] makes it little short of impossible for young Israelites to set up housekeeping in Bavaria; often their head is crowned with gray hair before they receive permission to set up house and can, therefore, think of marriage. Once having learned their profession, whereby they can hope to gain their livelihood everywhere, why should they not transfer their desires and power to hospitable North America, where they can live freely alongside members of all confessions? In addition [there are] alien-taxes, goose-taxes, horse-taxes, etc., etc., taxes re-introduced everywhere by the Bavarian estates and recently once more left to their sweet will, obsolete imposts that are a great burden on the Jews, . . . all this tends to cause young, strong men and even those of more advanced age to seek their salvation in other regions of the earth, where at least they don't have to bear this.[27]

These and other, similar accounts confirm two important features of this emigration: (1) it was indeed conceived by the emigrants of that period as a "substitute for emancipation," and it actually fulfilled this function in practice; and (2) economic need and political oppression should be regarded here as necessary, but by no means sufficient, conditions for emigration. Almost fifty years ago Jakob Lestschinsky, one of the outstanding pioneers of Jewish social and economic history, explained this very coherently:

> Every emigration is caused by many motives. The first is, of course, distress, but distress alone is not enough. At mid-nineteenth century the Russian Jews were by far poorer than the German. Politically also they were much more persecuted. . . . But the Russian Jew was at the time still not advanced enough even to know of America, let alone to leave his homeland and to risk the long journey to a strange country. Finally, you also need some means to pay the fare. In other words, emigration becomes possible only at a certain stage of cultural development and economic advancement that [had] become disproportional to the existing opportunities.[28]

We may add that the indispensable prior achievement of at least some elementary education and monetary income explains not only the fact that Jewish emigration to the United States started first in the more advanced parts of Western and Central Europe but also the composition of this early emigration.

An additional motive of Jewish emigration, one that was often repeated in the German press with anti-Jewish undertones only slightly concealed, was to escape military service. Understandably, these allegations usually evoked the excited protest of Jewish spokesmen: "Did it ever happen in Prussia that a Jew should leave his fatherland to avoid service in the army? This is a brazen lie!"[29] In 1839, when this was written, emigration from Prussia had just begun, or else this writer would have been more careful not to lean on the Prussian experience. Notwithstanding all this patriotic fervor, avoidance of conscription was a very real—and, under the circumstances, quite justified—reason for young Jewish men to expedite their departure. Of this we have manifold evidence in published and unpublished sources. For example, Henry Frank, born in 1836 in Obbach, Bavaria, came to America at the age of eighteen for, among others, just this reason. At the age of thirteen, after finishing elementary school, he had started working as a peddler of his own, and "was happy when I sold my goods and could assist my dear parents, and made enough money toward creating a sinking fund, which in a few years was to be used for my journey to a New World." In 1854 Frank decided to leave, together with his sweetheart and a group of young men of the same age, "for if I remained at home it would mean military service for four years in time of peace and more in time of war." He left Bavaria with the help of a fictitious pass and went on to Leipzig:

> There I was stopped by the police. They had been notified to look out for young men from across the border who were leaving without government permission. I had worked hard, saved every penny that I could and with the assistance of relatives and friends had enough money, with some extra Dollars, to pay for my transportation to New York. With some of this precious extra money it proved very easy for me to be set free. The unscrupulous Gendarme even went so far as to buy my railroad ticket to Hamburg, where our party had agreed to meet after travelling over different routes.[30]

After the first wave of immigration had gained a foothold in America, optimistic reports in the Jewish and general German press began to add an ever-growing "pull" factor, inducing further and increasing emigration. Some obscure *Dorfzeitung* in 1839 informed its readers that "in America nobody is accepted more willingly than the German Jews and nobody is doing better. They bring with them four things that are most helpful there: obedience, level-headedness, thrift, and enterprise."[31]

Most enthusiastic were the early correspondents of Ludwig Philippson's *Allgemeine Zeitung des Judenthums*. In May 1842 six full pages of this weekly were dedicated to an extensive essay by Dr. Max Wiener. Following a short review of the early Jewish communities in America, he praised the conditions of the Jews in the North of the United States

> who, as is well known, are politically absolutely equal to the Christian population. Therefore no material advantage can be gained by converting to the Christian faith . . ., and the convert will not obtain any more respect [from the side of the Christians] that he was not considered to be worthy of before. . . . In the Old World live very few Christians that have not absorbed anti-Jewish prejudice and Jew-hatred from their earliest childhood. . . . But the native Christian of the United States . . . is used to judging every man by his behavior, not by the way he prays to God.

Elaborating on many examples to prove this contention, the author admitted that during his stay there did occur "one attempt to arouse Jew-hatred in New Orleans," which originated in the political ambitions of a candidate for the Louisiana state legislature, a Christian German immigrant running against a Jewish opponent. In the end the Jewish candidate was elected almost unanimously, "mainly because every voter who would have voted against the Jew was afraid to be suspected of ridiculous prejudice." After all this enthusiastic praise of America, this author was nevertheless so concerned about the religious laxity of the congregations he had visited that he concluded his long report with the remark that "the religious Jew cannot feel happy in America and the new Zion of the people of Israel does not lie in the New World."[32]

With increased emigration and the establishment of stable German-Jewish communities in the United States, the connections with the old homeland and its Jewish establishment became both more frequent and more complex. Although reports were now more objective, the general tenor remained favorable. In November 1846 Dr. Max Lilienthal, from his arrival in 1845 rabbi of the first three "German" congregations of New York, presented another six-page report focusing on the internal Jewish situation and the economic achievements of the immigrants. His call to the German Jews to come and join the freedom and blessings of the new continent already sounded, however, much more cautious:

> My description will certainly not fail to evoke the desire for emigration, . . . but in order to call hither only the right people allow me these comments: America is a young and blessed country. . . . Whoever is willing and able to work, ready to overcome the first hardships that meet everyone coming to a strange country, and ready to leave old, pompous dreams behind will certainly find an existence [here] and all the chances on his side. . . . One may answer me that whoever is able and willing to work can achieve something also in Germany. This would be true were the Jews there not hampered by thousands of discrimination laws. . . . . If families send their young and unmarried men ahead, knowing them to be industrious and courageous . . ., these will quickly find their foothold, bring over the elder people and their siblings, and all will be happy. But this summer we have received here people who in the old home had shown neither the will nor the ability to work . . ., people who were sent [here] to be gotten rid of. How could their relatives not have been afraid to send people like these and expose them to limitless distress? Many had to be sent back by the voluntary contributions of the communities, but what will become the fate of these unfortunates if these [communities] should tire of [their] efforts?[33]

Before long, "chain-migration" of siblings following the first emigrants only a few years after their departure became the most decisive "pull" factor of increased emigration. In most cases, boys in their early teens were the first to join their elder brothers, who in many cases provided at least part of the fare and arranged the necessary formalities. Usually these younger brothers also started to work with them as partners shortly after their arrival, at least for some time. Unmarried sisters followed in many cases only after the death of parents, for whom they had cared in the old country, with financial assistance sent from America as the usual means of support. The emigration of aged parents was rather exceptional. Mostly only after a longer period, when the emigrants had already settled and obtained secure economic standing, or after a mother or father had been widowed, did parents emigrate to join the younger members of the family.

"Beloved Brother," wrote Menko Stern in May 1838 to his brother Julius in Philadelphia, who had left from Karlsruhe four years earlier:

> Next summer I hope, if God wishes . . ., to start my voyage to you. I regret not being able to respond to your demand to come without delay, as I also do not want to leave before the fate of our sister [i.e., her planned marriage] is finally settled. . . . She deserves everything. What she has suffered can never be repaid, she can never be rewarded enough for taking care of our late parents. . . . At the moment I am still lacking the money to prepare for the voyage, to buy clothes, etc., and the fare. . . . I am aware of your kindheartedness, . . . but do not wish to burden you with the care of my provision. So I hope to be able to work with you in friendship or to find something else.

In a postscript Menko asked if he could bring a friend along with him.[34]

In March 1847, Menasses Hirsch, writing from New York City to his "dearly beloved sister Babette," expressed his and the entire family's joy that "you, my dear sister Babette, and dear [brother] Sheiver are well enough to make the journey to join us. It will gladden our hearts to have you here with us." He was sending them $75: "Along with the money you receive for the house, this should give you sufficient funds for the journey." As we learn from the letter, three brothers were already in America and some siblings had remained in Germany. In a note to his "Dear uncle Leib Hirsch," Menasses acknowledged receiving a letter, which "has made us very happy, because we know that you and your family will be able to be with us soon. . . . Dear uncle, please be of material assistance to our unfortunate relative—treat her as a father and help her in her daily needs. If we are unable to repay you later ourselves, then surely God in Heaven will repay you." As is apparent from this communication, this family was bringing over their needy relatives before they themselves had achieved a secure economic position. Even the $18 for the entry permit is described as a "great effort . . . but we did it all with the greatest of pleasure and with the best of intentions. What one does in spite of great difficulty is later rewarded by the good Lord."[35]

The influence of relatives who had already gone to America appears time and again as the single most important inducement for emigration, as in the memoirs of Julius Weis, written in 1908 in New Orleans:

> In the latter part of 1844, a cousin of mine . . . who had emigrated to America in 1837, at the same time with my brother, came home on a visit to his mother . . ., and his arrival created quite a stir among our people, as he was one of the first from that section who ever returned from America.

He was located in Natchez in the dry goods business and during his stay I listened to his accounts of this country and made up my mind to come here.

Weis was nineteen years old at the time, an only son (after his elder brother died of yellow fever in America). His parents were therefore reluctant to let him go, but "I became very restless, and finally told my parents that as I saw no prospects [in Germany] either for them or for myself, if they did not give their permission I would find a way to go without it."[36]

Ernst Troy of Cincinnati arrived in America at the age of seventeen. Writing his memoirs in 1909, he described how his oldest brother, with a visiting aunt, had been the first to leave for America:

My brother Ludwig, a robust and bright youth, made so favorable an impression on Aunt Zilly that she suggested to my father that she take Ludwig with her to America and look after him. . . . My father gave his consent. Although he hated to part from his first-born child, he would not stand in the way of the prospective fortune offered under Aunt Zilly's protection. Aunt Zilly, although not rich, was sufficiently wealthy to take not only my brother but also the entire family of her sister Emmy, including her brother-in-law . . . the teacher, and his four children.

In September 1856, after they had not heard from the brother for two years, the family received a letter from Keokuk, Iowa, where Ludwig had returned after working at accompanying mail coaches across the Nebraska prairies. Now he

was about to open a store; he wanted me to join him in America in order to become his partner. At that time it was believed at home that all "Americans" were rich, for most of the emigrants who returned to their homeland for a visit were, or appeared to be, wealthy. The sums of money sent to their poor relations in Germany helped corroborate this evidence. From those who led a toilsome life in America, however, one rarely heard anything.

Still, Ernst Troy was not the youngest Jewish boy who traveled alone on this voyage: "En route from Leipzig to Magdeburg I became acquainted with an elderly gentleman, whose twelve-year-old son was about to go to his uncle in New York. His father wanted to accompany him to Bremen, and asked me to care for his son on the voyage."[37]

The "Forty-Eighters" and Other Intellectuals

In July 1853, almost seventeen years after he had started his weekly and some thirty years after the start of the Jewish mass emigration, Rabbi

Ludwig Philippson wrote, in somewhat ambiguous terms, his first lead article on the emigration. He was not positive about the life in America. In his opinion, Jewish participation in the great European exodus had been delayed because the German Jew proved his

> greater moral background when he hesitated in his decision to emigrate; it showed that his love for the homeland is greater, that he regrets to lay the ocean between himself and his parents, his brothers and relatives, that his heart is not jubilant to "sever all ties" and sail to a "New World." . . . Still, no sentiment can resist the general stream.

Philippson admitted, however, that it was in the general interest of Judaism that "in the midst of this great development taking place in the New World, a broad foundation for Judaism should already now be created." If this had to be at the cost of many German-Jewish communities that could no longer carry on, he felt compensated by the many new communities coming to life across the ocean. Day after day, "synagogues, schools and benevolent societies, fresh blossoms and fruits sprouting from the tree of Jacob" were emerging. He regretted that "the New World is still no place where literature may find remarkable ground," but found consolation in the religious institutions that flourished there: "Life has always been more important . . . for the masses of the Jewish people . . . who with all their admiration for the books were never great friends of them, and are now even less so."[38]

Less than a year later Philippson returned to his subject, this time reprimanding German-Jewish intellectuals for staying behind: "You, the learned men among the Jews, the physicians, jurists, philologists, mathematicians, natural scientists . . ., why do you waste away in Europe or betray your religion? . . . Learn to make practical use of your knowledge and you will have bright careers before you in America."[39] The reproach was not unfounded: most of the emigrants had received no more than an elementary education, if any at all; Jewish professionals, eager to gain entrance to academic or public offices, showed a higher rate of conversions, and preferred to remain in their old cultural and professional milieu. This is somewhat in contrast to the traditional picture of the emigration, Jewish or Gentile, as a movement allegedly led by enlightened liberals, democrats, and socialists who were fascinated by the winds of political freedom blowing from across the ocean.

Some Jewish intellectuals had shown an early interest in emigration to America. When Mordecai M. Noah published his first project for the founding of a Jewish colony in the United States, his appeal received remarkable approval in certain circles of young German intellectuals. The *Verein für Cultur und Wissenschaft des Judentums,* founded by Eduard

Gans and Leopold Zunz, elected Noah as its "Extraordinary Member and Correspondent-General for the United States of North America," informing him of the nomination in an address from Berlin dated June 1822:

> Amid the general distress and public calamity of the European Jews . . . it was indeed no small consolation . . . to hear the noble voice of a most excellent partaker of our faith, animating the abject spirits of the members of an oppressed nation, by summoning them from an ungrateful and unjust country, to that part of our globe which they style the new, but would yet, with greater reason, name the better one. . . . The more enlightened and respectable portion of European Jews are looking with eager anxiety to the United States of North America—happy to exchange the miseries of their native soil for public freedom, which is there granted to every religion.[40]

The poet Heinrich Heine, who was at the time in close contact with the association in Berlin, also showed interest in the project and proposed the name "Ganstown" for the colony in America. But Noah published this communication only in October 1825, as "evidence of the fact that . . . Jews abroad have been alive to the project." But by the time his "Proclamation to the Jews" summoning them to "Ararat" (which was published in September 1825), together with his letters appointing, among others, Eduard Gans and Leopold Zunz as his "Commissioners for Emigration," reached Germany, the association had in fact been dissolved.[41] Gans was already a converted Christian on his way to a brilliant academic career, while Zunz remained dedicated to the modern scientific exploration of Judaism as one of the founders of the *Wissenschaft des Judentums* in Germany.

Emigration was taken up by "the people" who, as Philippson contended in the article mentioned above, "had been more astute [than the intellectuals], to let themselves be guided by their instincts." There was to be another short revival of intellectual interest in emigration, however. Just as the reaction to Napoleon's defeat had caused young and disappointed Jewish intellectuals to cast their eyes—but, for the most part, *not* their lots—to America, so did the reaction after the revolution of 1848 cause German Jews to look across the ocean, but this time with more practical results.

This influence should, however, not be overestimated. If 1848, the "Year of Freedom," did indeed fuel new emigration, it was not so much by its failures as by the pogromlike anti-Jewish riots that preceded and accompanied the revolution. "From Amsterdam to Rome, from Lombardy to Galicia, and from France to Serbia . . urban and rural Jews suffered alike, and the rioters made no [distinction] between . . . support-

ers [and] opponents of the revolution, because both sides were represented in the ranks of the rioters themselves."[42] As before 1848, those
who, most affected by these developments, decided to leave or to hasten
their emigration were young lower-middle-class people departing from
the villages and small towns of Alsace, Bavaria, Baden, and Westphalia.
Emigration from Bohemia, Slovakia, and Hungary—where anti-Jewish
excesses had been particularly vicious—increased.

This mood is reflected in the words of one of the many who arrived
at this time in the United States:

> In March 1848 people started to think in Germany that a free man is better
> than an oppressed one. With whom do you think the revolution in Bavaria
> started? With no one else but the Jews. In many places their windows
> have been smashed and their belongings stolen. These events intensified
> my desire to emigrate. . . . I found that it was not such an easy step to
> leave my fatherland, to depart from my loved ones, whom I might never
> see again . . . , but I thought [about it] and decided, in the end, that it would
> be better to give pleasure to my parents from a far distance than to stay
> here and be killed by the Revolutionists.

The writer, Morris Stern from Maroldsweisach, was seventeen years old
at the time, and had behind him six years of "German and Hebrew school"
and two years' work as an apprentice in his uncle's business in a nearby
town.[43]

As Jacob Toury states, the German-Jewish reaction to the revolution
of 1848 as reflected in the various utterances of its spiritual and intellectual leadership was something of a paradox:

> Not only did the revolution end in general disappointment, but from its
> very start it was accompanied by anti-Jewish riots that should have con-
> vinced the Jews that the slogans of *liberté, égalité* and *fraternité* were lead-
> ing to deadlock, and that a unified Jewish position was badly needed, in
> order to avoid the worst. Instead the . . . principal common Jewish reaction
> was just the opposite: It claimed that no united Jewish position was to be
> presented, and each and everyone was to be left to take his stand according
> to his own opinion and conscience.[44]

Jewish students and intellectuals mostly chose to identify with the fight
for democratic reform, and some of them fought actively on barricades
in Vienna and Berlin. But the cumulative reports of anti-Jewish excesses
in the wake of the revolutionary uprisings did not pass unnoticed. The
best-known, and often quoted, reaction was the "On to America" movement that a group of young Austrian and Bohemian Jews started long
before the general impasse of the revolution had become evident. Its
main initiator was Leopold Kompert, a young poet and publicist who had
dedicated his work to the description of life in the Bohemian ghettos.

Together with the first reports of anti-Jewish riots in Prague on May 6, 1848, his first appeal appeared on a prominent page of the *Oester-reichisches Central-Organ für Glaubensfreiheit,* a paper published and edited by Isidor Busch, another young Jewish intellectual who himself emigrated to America at the end of that year. Kompert dramatically denounced the

> slavish hordes . . . that did not and do not understand the spirit of freedom, and let us pay for it! God forbid that we held our head ready for every blow. . . . In the hour that has brought freedom to the land there is no other desire in us than to get out of the way of *this* freedom. . . . For centuries our history has been nothing but mute assent to every affliction, torture and coercion. . . . For once we want to lose our temper, with the permission of the "sovereign peoples," jack up—and then get out of the way . . . to America![45]

The call for emigration met with some very passionate and hostile resistance, from various quarters. In a communication from Vienna of June 21, 1848, the Jewish conservative *Der Orient* attacked "the Jewish counselors who urge the cowardly emigration to America upon the Jews" as traitors to their fatherland, "the Jews, and Judaism. . . . You eternal Jews and arch-separatists, do you ask for more of the special Jewish accusations?"[46] This was a sharp rebuke to Kompert and others and to the emigration committees being established at this time. Although the editors of the *Central-Organ* had openly come out in favor of emigration, they also lent space to a long "Open Letter" by David Mendl opposing the initiative:

> What great calamity has befallen Israel that you wish to break the ties that bind you to your fatherland? . . . Have they staked pyres for us as for heretics? Have they thrown our babies to drown in the streams? Nothing of this all. ["Many thanks for that!" the editors could not refrain from interpolating.] Is this the time to desert fatherland, friends and brothers and selfishly seek your own well-being far from here? . . . If indeed the Jews are in danger it is your sacred duty to remain with your brothers, to fight and to struggle, to win or to fall with them![47]

The discussion for and against the emigration continued throughout 1848, reiterating these same arguments in different forms. On the whole, discussion mainly reflected the dilemma of young Jewish intellectuals in the Habsburg empire, who remained more closely attached to Judaistic values, and probably also more idealistically engaged, than were their more assimilated peers in Germany. The practical effect of this short-lived movement, in terms of increased emigration of intellectuals, seems to have been quite negligible, and those who followed the appeal came indeed mostly from Vienna, Prague and the Habsburg empire. A meticulous investigation detected only some forty Jewish immigrants who could be considered real "Forty-Eighters," that is, active revolutionaries.[48] Generally, the emigration from Germany, and not only that of the Jews, increased quite remarkably in the 1850s; as before, however, Jewish emigration was still for the most part economically motivated, and the "pull" of family members already in America was gaining in importance.

If the number of professionals who emigrated in the wake of 1848 was not impressive, their impact on the life of the young Jewish communities in America seems to have been even less so. The alienation from Jewish religion and society that characterized many of the more educated and politically active among young German Jews went on in America. Here, most preferred to seek, and find, entrance into the cultural and political circles of German—rather than German-Jewish—society. The two milieus were growing farther and farther apart. Many of these Jews opposed the separation of Jewish education and social associations from mainstream life, and their "ambivalent loyalty to German culture on the one hand and American life on the other did not leave much room for Judaism."[49]

There were, of course, exceptions, and these were regarded as such by contemporaries. One of them, Moritz—or, as he was known in America, Maurice—Mayer, was a real "Forty-Eighter": he had fled from Kaiserslautern to escape a long prison term. After some years as a "minister," that is, leader of a Jewish congregation, in Charleston, Mayer, an accomplished jurist from home, started a law practice in New York, "but did not follow the example of so many . . . who had given up all interest and activities for Judaism. He continued to contribute to it with all his heart, particularly in his office as president of the B'nai B'rith lodge." The fact that he had also translated one of Philippson's tracts may have gained him the special attention of the editor.[50]

Like the futile attempts of the early 1820s, the "On to America" movement of the revolutionary year and its limited influence once again demonstrated that "the movement which began in the 1830s did not owe its spontaneity and drive to the spur of the intelligentsia, but to other causes and impulses."[51] The same is undoubtedly true for the later waves of the emigration as well. The split between their Jewish and German loyalties and identity continued to torment many of those intellectuals who, voluntarily or by compulsion, found their way to America.

Crossing the Ocean

If a Jew emigrates from the country with his family and belongings he is obliged to pay the emigration tax, e.g., in Silesia it is ten percent. . . . In the other royal states those Jews who desire to leave the country and must then surrender their letter of protection are exempt from the emigration tax if they do not possess any large property of five or more thousand taler . . . but in the case that they have to take an inheritance out of the country, they must pay an emigration tax on that, as well as on the sum they had previously received as a dowry.[52]

The emigration tax mentioned above in an encyclopedia of 1784 continued to exist in most German lands. Despite the agreement of free emigration concluded between the United States and most European governments, we learn that in 1839 "the princes are entitled to demand every tenth florin of the entire property to be carried away, so that a family which is taking away some 4,000 florins must pay 400 florins to the prince. . . . [M]any obstacles are thus set in the path of the emigrants."[53] For most of the young and unmarried, the obstacle may not have been of great consequence; but for families and the more prosperous who, as we have seen, increasingly joined in the emigration as it gained momentum, the tax must have played some part in their decision making.

In any case, all emigrants needed a permit releasing them from their present nationality, or as it was then called, "the community of subjects" *(Untertanenverband).*[54] This seems to have been more than a formality, for in 1846 it is again sarcastically mentioned, in connection with the still outstanding reform of the "Matrikel" laws in Bavaria, that "according to such a law . . . , it should be of little concern to the government if the Jews are leaving the country *en masse.* But this does not seem to be the case, judging by the many obstacles they have to overcome before they are granted permission to emigrate."[55] The young and unpropertied emigrants probably had to pay no tax at all, but in some lands they had difficulties in getting permission to leave before they had fulfilled their military service or been granted a release from it. We have seen how some of them found illegal ways to evade these regulations. The Bavarian authorities must have been aware of these methods, for in 1854 we learn of a new regulation obliging everyone who applied for emigration before conscription to deposit 800 florins as a security, and this was "a real blow for the unpropertied classes who are most of the emigrants."[56]

After emigrants had concluded these formalities, liquidated their affairs, and taken leave of parents and relatives, they would start on their way to the various ports of departure. Here we have to turn back to the earlier years of the emigration, when sea travel was still a very strenuous affair. Until the 1860s Le Havre was the most important port of departure, at least for the emigrants—Jewish and Gentile alike—from south and southwest Germany. Le Havre apparently remained far ahead of Bremen or Hamburg for Jewish emigration even after 1860, for it was easier to reach via the French border and offered less danger of discovery *en route* by officials searching for deserting conscripts. It also spared the emigrants the crossing of the stormy English Channel, and seems to have been less expensive.[57]

The costs of passage did play an important role for most of the first wave of emigrants. Up to the 1820s the least expensive route was to travel as an indentured servant, in what is called "white labor servitude." Enterprising shipowners or captains would induce emigrants to sign contracts obliging them to pay their fare after arriving in America. When they were unable to do so at the port of arrival, emigrants were kept on ship until their contract was "sold" to competing patrons. In this way the immigrant was "indentured" to pay for his or her passage by working for the patron during a fixed time. These servants were in fact sold, bought, and kept—not unlike slaves, with the difference, of course, that they were considered to be free people and were allowed to move freely after the time of servitude had been met. Meanwhile, they were obliged to work for food, lodgings, and some clothing. Sometimes they also received some small compensation. Escapees were at first liable to be sentenced to death, later mostly to an extension of the contracted work-period. Although some of the existing evidence does not show that many Jewish emigrants arrived in this way, other sources indicate that there were quite a few of them in the late eighteenth and early nineteenth century.

One of these was Wolf-Baer Samuel from Brachenheim in Württemberg. In a letter to his parents in June 1819, Wolf-Baer recounts his arrival in Baltimore after five months at sea with ninety-six other passengers, six of them Jews: "Now the market begins. The Americans arrive and ask the captain how much they have to pay for one or another man. Some have to serve three years for their passage, others four. Then comes a Jew from Holland who is already 17 years in America, a million rich." There follows an idyllic story of how rich he had struck it, working as an overseer for this imaginary "Dutch Jew," getting the same food and tobacco as the patron, a whole wardrobe of new clothes, and so on.

These obvious lies, written in "Jewish German" with Hebrew letters, were apparently intended to set his parents' hearts at rest. The following documents tell an entirely different story. In February 1820 "Wolf Samuel, servand by Esra Boyd" filed a complaint against Stephen Boyd of York County, Pennsylvania, with the Justices of the City and Borough of York, accusing his master of maltreatment, and not abiding by the terms of the contract, not giving him any clothes and giving him the worst of food. Next we read of "William Samuel who . . . calls himself William Samuel Verrend" in an announcement of Stephen Boyd in the *New Recorder* of May 24, 1820, offering a $5 reward "to any person for securing the said runaway in any jail so that I get him again, or for delivering him to the subscriber."[58]

White labor servitude was abandoned in the early 1830s, and most German-Jewish emigrants were soon in a less destitute position. Most of them could only afford to cross at the lowest cost, preferring sailing ships to the more expensive steamers. Seafaring was at the time improving rapidly, and the time of passage was becoming shorter and shorter. In 1840 Sarah Hammerschlag, a young girl traveling alone from Bremerhaven to Baltimore on board the *Ferdinand,* needed only forty-seven days for the trip, and her extensive and detailed travel diary makes for rather boring reading in that it lacks any unusual or untoward incidents.[59]

In 1853 the anonymous author of a hotly debated pamphlet embarked from Hamburg, together with some three hundred passengers, for a six-week journey to New York. His description of the passage is a lively account of both traveling conditions and the Jewish emigrants on board:

> There were twelve Jews out of three hundred aboard. . . . A varied group, thrown together by chance, they are a reflection of the Jews back on land. The image that [some] Christians have that only wealthy Jews are aboard isn't true. . . . In first class there was a woman with four boys, aged six through ten, who were following husband and father to America. . . . He went to America shortly after the revolution [of 1848] and soon earned enough money to bring his family—and first class yet! . . . A young dressmaker from the same place, who helped out with the children, was seasick. She cried in fear of an early death at sea . . . , [of] becoming food for the fish. . . .
>
> A young Gymnasium student aboard was being brought over by his parents. . . . In second class was a young woman and her sister from Posen. Her husband, a poor tailor, had gone to America two years earlier. He paid for his sister-in-law as well, because his wife didn't want to travel alone. They seemed to be getting along quietly and nicely. This was not the case with their good-natured classmate, also from Posen, who was harassed by a German-Frenchman and German-American in next-door cabins.

The rest were traveling in mid-deck, and they were mostly young tailors, apprentices, and journeymen. One of them "had a youthful 'happy-tailor' temperament [and] seemed [to be] content: 'It's really lucky that I haven't the money to travel second class. There you have to pay extra for the privilege of being beaten up.'"[60]

Julius Weis, a lad of nineteen years, departed in 1845 from his home in the Rhine Palatinate. He describes his travels thus:

> My father went to an agent in Landau and made a contract for my passage from Weisenburg, which was about ten miles from my native village, via Paris and Havre to New Orleans, paying for the entire trip 125 gulden

(equal to 50 Dollars), part of which was paid from the money I had saved up, and the remainder of which we were obliged to borrow. . . . As there were no railways from there to Paris the trip was made by stage, taking us twelve days. . . . We remained in Paris two days, and then went to Havre, traveling partly by rail and partly by stage. There were about twelve young men from our surrounding country in the party, and also six young ladies and one family with small children. . . . We sailed on the 21st of September on the sailing vessel "Tackalione," there being in all 400 deck passengers and only three cabin passengers. The voyage lasted forty-two days, and we had a pleasant passage. . . . Mr. Bernard Haas and myself cooked our own victuals, which consisted of rice, Irish potatoes, sausages and coffee, I attending to the cooking, and my companion washing the dishes.[61]

Julius Weis needed "only" forty-two days to arrive in America, but traveling as "deck passenger" was in those days anything but a pleasant cruise. Many tell of the miserable conditions of the people crowded on deck or in huge storerooms, left to look after themselves under lamentable sanitary conditions:

The position of the poor emigrants—men, women and children, Jews, French and Germans, stowed amidships—was at the best unpleasant. As long as the weather was fine, matters went on tolerably smoothly, and we had them chirping and singing enough; but a gale set them all at loggerheads, and rumors of fights and feuds not unfrequently came aft. Three Frenchmen (Jews and sharpers if they were not maligned) seemed to be just as much of a stumbling-block to the honest Germans, and even the quality in the great cabin took spite against them . . . and it was whispered that they had conjured up bad and adverse winds. The majority of the steerage passengers were Alsatian and Bavarians, and were rushing with their little all collected around them, to settle in a new land.[62]

All reports on traveling and passage reflect and corroborate the general picture we have already gained of the social and demographic composition of the emigrating German Jews. They were by no means destitute, and did not arrive totally unequipped; many of them had learned trades and crafts before leaving their homes. Most had acquired some elementary education and had brought with them at least some small amount of money to help with getting started. Generally they were a group of healthy and industrious young people, full of hope and enterprise, and ready to work hard in order to make the best of the opportunities offered by an expanding economy and a democratic political system.

No profound cultural or emotional crisis seems to have burdened the minds of most of these youngsters, whose eyes were cast forward, not backward. Any yearning they may have felt for what they had left behind was compensated by their satisfaction at being relieved of the social discrimination and legal restraints of their homeland. At the same time, emigration was not conceived by most emigrants as the absolute and final severance of all old ties. Contacts with families and friends in Germany were continuously kept up through letters, financial support, and soon repeated visits as well. In many aspects these young emigrants considered themselves to be—as they often actually were—the pioneer vanguard that was clearing the way for the transplantation of whole families, clans, and even communities.

2

Exploring the Territory

Having left behind the often stifling, but protected, framework of families and organized communities, immigrants set out on their own and had to rely on their own resources to find a way to survive on foreign ground. They may have nourished the hope that they would find some assistance from earlier immigrants, family members, friends, or neighbors, and often enough help was indeed given on arrival. But this could not last long, at least in the first years of mass immigration, given the hardships and limited means with which most of the early immigrants had themselves to cope.

First Steps

The first wave of immigrants of the 1820s and '30s came ashore in Philadelphia, New York, and other eastern ports and met there not only the old established Sephardic community, but already some German coreligionists who had been in the United States, as we have seen, since the end of the eighteenth century. The first German-Jewish congregation, Rodeph Shalom of Philadephia, was established in 1795. Most of the early German-Jewish immigrants disembarked there, and many of them decided to stay there. Many had found their place inside the Sephardic congregation and society. Isaac Leeser, one of the dominant personalities of nineteenth-century American Judaism, arrived in 1824 and served as minister of the Sephardic Mikveh Israel for over twenty years.[1] In New York and New Orleans, the other gateway cities of the German-Jewish immigration, German-Jewish communities had been present since the start of mass immigration.

Although the majority eventually settled in East Coast cities, the historiographic focus on the pioneering westward move, as the most outstanding phenomenon of the German-Jewish immigration, is not entirely unjustified. Many immigrants settled down at their final place of settlement, be it New York or another coastal city, after years of exploratory ventures around the country. The story of the German Jew's economic adaptation and settlement was one of considerable movement from place to place and from occupation to occupation.

Isaac Bernstein, who arrived in 1852 in New York, for six years tried his luck in at least eight different locations, from New York City and Elmira, New York, to Cincinnati, Savannah, and New Orleans, to back east in Bedford, Massachusetts.[2]

Hyman Spitz left his native Posen to live for five years in London. In 1840 he arrived in New York, for which he found he "had no liking"; he then went by sailing vessel to New Orleans. Finding out that he did not like "city life in the way it was conducted at that time—too much fun and devilment for me"—he set out for Natchez, Mississippi, bought a horse, and traveled throughout rural Mississippi and Louisiana. During 1841–46 he kept traveling from New York and Boston to New Orleans, took part in the Mexican War, and turned up in Bangor, Maine, where he stayed for a decade, only to move finally to settle in Baltimore.[3]

Henry Seessel, an immigrant from the Rhineland in 1843, arrived in New Orleans via Paris and Le Havre. He went north to Natchez and before finally settling down for life in Memphis in 1857 had worked and done business in Vicksburg, Cincinnati, Lexington, Kentucky, and New Orleans, and in Richmond and Milliken's Bend, both in Louisiana. In between he had fought for a year in the Mexican War. Seessel was in many respects

> the typical Jewish émigré from Central Europe. . . . For years he was an itinerant merchant, peddling clothes and jewellery. . . . He was a trunk-maker, a storekeeper, a stock raiser, a saloonkeeper and a butcher. The yellow fever struck his family and his employees, . . . making it difficult for him to keep what money and possessions he had acquired by dint of hard labor and great effort.[4]

Even people who in the end were more successful than Seessel knew periods of hardship and despair. One of them was Abraham Kohn, who later became a friend of Abraham Lincoln and a prominent Republican Chicago politician. He arrived in September 1842 from Bavaria via New York, and his diary is a lively and authentic description of the first steps of the immigrants in the New World. Peddling all over New England, and being a well-educated man, he kept reflecting about the "American way of life," comparing it with what he had left behind, with sometimes quite surprising conclusions:

> America consumes too much, produces too little. Her inhabitants are lazy and too much accustomed to providing for their own comforts to create a

land which will provide for their real and spiritual needs. . . . O youth of Bavaria, if you long for freedom, if you dream of life here, beware, for you shall rue the hour you embarked for a country and a life far different from what you dream of. This land . . . offers harsh, cold air, great masses of snow, and people who are credulous, filled with silly pride, cold towards foreigners and toward all who do not speak the language perfectly.

Kohn goes on to lament the excessive freedoms of too much democracy: "So goes it with the masses of the people which governs itself . . . in a country where each man is allowed to talk and write about anything whatsoever. It reminds one of the French republic and its Rousseau, who wanted to restore the world to a state of nature, remote from art, science, and civilization."[5] Kohn finally settled in Chicago, became one of the founders of a congregation, and, judging by his later political career and social prestige, adjusted somehow to American standards.[6]

Those family members who arrived first and lacked relatives or friends to help certainly had a hard time. Writing from Philadelphia in October 1834 to his parents in Miltenberg, Julius Stern described his arrival in New York on the eve of the Sukkot holiday:

Immediately after disembarking I went to the synagogue, to thank the Almighty for arriving safely. I believed that among my coreligionists I would find some whom I could ask for advice. But what I found was a temple full of heartless people. Not a single one wanted to know of me, let alone do something for me. Even some meals for the *Yom-Tovim* [holidays] I could not get for my money. One can hardly believe this to be possible in a place where 8,000 *Yehudim* live.

After he had tried in vain to get work as the skilled weaver he was, and after traveling two hundred miles along the Hudson River, he returned to New York only to learn that

all my efforts to find some place, and all my letters of recommendation were useless. Seeing no prospects at all, I went to Pennsylvania, . . . but here also my recommendations are fruitless. People receive them with the remark; "You have to see how to help yourself," not even adding some humanitarian piece of advice. . . . Thank God I have no more of such recommendations, so I shall take my last few *Groschen* [pennies] to buy some goods and go peddling. . . . Here you have to do every kind of work, if you have no capital and don't want to starve.

Stern also considered returning home, but was apparently discouraged by his brothers' warnings not to return "to our lamentable situation. . . . Even if you could bring along some capital I would advise against your returning, as long as the money is not enough to live on its interest." His position must finally have stabilized, for in 1838 we learn that he had married and was making arrangements to bring his brother over to America.[7]

Henry Frank, whom we have met before, was to learn that even relatives who had earlier immigrated were not always eager to help the new arrivals. After arriving in New York in 1854, and after passing the physical examination and other formalities at Castle Garden, he first visited an uncle, "Herr Sachs, my mother's brother, who had been living in New York City for several years and was established in the cigar business." He

> had quite a large family, and was evidently not very prosperous, for his reception was cold and indifferent. He said to me: *"Heinrich, sei willkommen. Warum kommst Du, Lieber?*—I welcome you, but why did you come to America? What do you expect to do here?" I looked him straight in the face, and answered him promptly and courageously: "Well, uncle, I came here to better my condition, like all foreigners. Thank God I am young, strong and brave . . . , and I shall not be a burden to anybody." After a meager meal was partaken of, I took leave of my dear old uncle and never saw him again.[8]

Still, even without connections, immigrants were not entirely abandoned to their fate. Benevolent societies and other philanthropic institutions, which had been established early in every larger city, lent some help. Although their main purpose was to support the local poor, providing care for widows, orphans, and other people in need, they often also gave assistance to new immigrants. A report from Baltimore in December 1849 informs us of the existence of two separate voluntary associations; the "Assistance Society" established years before "whose funds benefit solely the local poor. Another aid-society *'Va'chai Achicha It'cha'* [Hebrew: "May your brother live with you"], founded only half a year ago by Dr. Guenzburg, is aimed to give assistance to poor new immigrants."[9]

The older established Jewish communities in New York and Philadelphia naturally had the first and best-equipped philanthropic organizations. Being also the main gateway cities of the immigration and the starting point of the immigrant's movements across the country, they must have been of vital importance for many of them. When an economic crisis erupted in 1857, these associations went out of their way to grant every possible help. Arnold Fischel of New York's Congregation Shearith Israel blamed "man's recklessness and arrogance" for the disaster, but at the same time he did not consider "the panic sufficient to sour the immigrant's dream of economic freedom in the New World." He called for a renewal of faith in God, "a commitment to the principle of brotherhood of man, and an outpouring of charity."[10]

The Saga of the Peddler

The German-Jewish immigrants took part in the general westward movement of the time. But they did so mostly in a different and idiosyncratic way, according to traditional occupations and abilities. "The saga of the Jewish peddler was woven into the drama of the burgeoning American economy."[11]

In Germany, as we have seen, peddling was considered at the time to be an inferior occupation. German legislators and even well-disposed officials, as well as Jewish emancipators, ardently demanded the "normalization" of the Jews' economic pursuits as a condition for emancipation. Everywhere Jewish peddlers tried to exchange the pack for more "honorable" trades, or to have at least their sons learn some craft. When these youngsters arrived in America, they found an entirely different atmosphere. In the absence of the restrictive guild structures that were still strong in Germany, they faced a rapidly expanding market economy. The Yankee peddler, a romantic figure, although somewhat suspect for his shrewd business practices, was a respected distributor of retail goods in the new western territories. But by the time larger numbers of German-Jewish immigrants were arriving, many of these pioneering New England peddlers had settled down. "As the mantle of the westward travelling Yankee was discarded, it was snatched up by the Jewish immigrant."[12]

This is not the place for an in-depth investigation of the economic function of the Jewish peddlers to establish their important role in the American economy. What we are concerned with here is the role of peddling in the process of the immigrant's economic and social adaptation. Even if it were true, as is "reasonably concluded" by Rudolf Glanz, that most of the 16,000 peddlers who wandered across all parts of the United States on the eve of the Civil War were Jews, they could have constituted, by the most liberal estimate, no more than a third of all gainfully employed Jews at that time.[13]

There can, however, be little doubt that Jews were concentrated in the commercial sector. By mid-century diversification was already taking place, but this was happening mostly *within* the commercial sector. In the port cities, Jewish importers sold to wholesale distributors from the interior. There were some workers and artisans, but only a sprinkling of professionals and intellectuals. In major distributing and manufacturing centers such as Buffalo and Rochester, New York, Cincinnati, Chicago, and St. Louis, Jewish resident wholesalers supplied local retail stores and itinerant peddlers. Some had already ventured into the manufacture of clothing for sale through the same outlets. In smaller townships all across the continent, Jewish retail stores sold clothing, textiles, dry goods, and groceries. "Finally there were the rural areas from the New England states to Michigan, Wisconsin and Minnesota in the north; Mississippi, Alabama, Texas in the south; Colorado and Utah in the west, where itinerant peddlers continued to eke out a precarious livelihood."[14]

In recent years this general picture has been borne out and corroborated by local studies of the social and economic history of Jewish communities. As more reliable information of this kind is unearthed, it becomes evident that peddling was no more than a transitory, and sometimes very short, stage in the economic career of only a segment of the immigrant population. A meticulous inspection of peddler license registers in Cincinnati establishes some common characteristics: The ages of the peddlers ranged from eighteen to twenty-five years, and their average peddling term lasted from one to five years. They specialized in so-called Yankee notions, dry goods, and clothing, cheap jewelry and German silver, neglecting the tin- and copper-wares that had been important in Yankee peddling.[15]

The reason that this kind of economic endeavor overshadows all other occupations in the voluminous literature on the German-Jewish immigration of the time is probably more literary than historical. The success stories of the Strausses, Seligmans, Rosenwalds, Bloomingdales, and other illustrious families are much more suited to catching readers' imaginations than this rather gray reality of the many thousands of immigrants toiling in all parts of the country. A few of the German Jews did indeed start from scratch as itinerant peddlers to evolve in a remarkably short time into the financial aristocracy of American Jewry. Naturally, those who "made it" also left more traces than those who did not. Few of the less fortunate who populated the crowded ghettos of New York and other cities or who, disappointed, gave in and went back to Europe wrote diaries and memoirs. "The story of the mass of peddlers, those who merely reached the first rung of success or attained none at all, has been overshadowed by the grandeur of the rags-to-riches story, and by the half-truth that identifies the peddler as the builder of the American department store system."[16]

Nevertheless, peddling was certainly of importance at this stage of our narrative, in which we accompany immigrants on their first steps in new and foreign surroundings. Many of those who in 1860 were already settled, well-established heads of families had started as peddlers. Arriving without capital, or with only a small sum, and unable to find immediate employment in whatever craft he may have learned at home, "taking the pack" was the most obvious way for the young and unmarried male immigrant to earn some money. Already settled earlier immigrants, relatives or not, were eager to take a risk and provide him with a few dollars' worth of merchandise on credit, not only because they had the good intention of helping him on his way, but also out of self-interest, to expand their own market. As long as the transportation system lagged behind the demographic and territorial expansion of the country, the peddler did indeed fulfill an important economic function. He worked hard, but his toil was well-rewarded.

As mentioned above, the colonists of New England had preceded the German-Jewish peddler. "There are three Christians in a Jew and three Jews in a Yankee" was the current contemporary evaluation. As a German observer of the American scene wrote in 1780 from New York: "The New Englanders . . . , who have the nickname *Yenkies* since many years, . . . are a merry and—under the mask of sanctity—deceitful folk; their ways became proverbial and, in business, they were trusted with being just as much honest as the Jews." Even later, the first German-Jewish arrivals were regarded as "clever traders, but in the Yankees they have found their masters." Rudolf Glanz concluded that "at first, when the Yankee had not yet given up peddling and the German-Jewish immigrant was beginning to resort to it, the two must have been on the same economic level. The Jewish newcomers had much to learn from their more experienced Yankee competitors, particularly in the matter of dealing with rustic customers."[17]

Abraham Kohn's diary gives a lively account of his experience peddling in Massachusetts in 1842:

> We were forced to stop because of the heavy snow. We sought to spend the night with a cooper . . . but his wife did not wish to take us in. She was afraid of strangers, she might not sleep well; we should go our way. And outside there raged the worst blizzard I have ever seen. O God, I thought, is this the land of liberty and hospitality and tolerance? Why have I been led here? After we had talked to the woman for half an hour, after repeatedly pointing out that to turn us forth into the blizzard would be sinful, we were allowed to stay. She became friendlier, indeed, after a few hours and at night she even joined us in singing. . . . On Friday and Saturday business was very poor, and we did not take in two dollars during the two days. . . . It was extremely cold this week and there was more snow than we had ever seen in our lives. At some places the snow was three to four feet deep, and we could hardly get through with the sleigh. How often we thanked the good God that we did not have to carry our wares on our backs in this cold. To tramp with a heavy pack from house to house in this weather would be terrible.[18]

Actually, Kohn was lucky to be in possession of a sleigh. Most peddlers started by carrying their wares on their backs, and the purchase of any kind of transport was the first sign of success. Isaac Mayer Wise recounted an early visit to Syracuse, shortly after his arrival in New York in 1846:

> I found there several people of culture, notably a Mr. Stein, a most intelligent man. We grew acquainted rapidly, and felt a mutual respect for one another. . . . One afternoon I met on the street a man with a large, old straw hat drawn over his face. He was clad in a perspired linen coat, and carried two large tin boxes on his shoulders. He had a large clay pipe in his mouth, a pair of golden spectacles on his nose, and dragged himself along with a painful effort. I looked at him closely, and recognized my friend Stein. Upon noticing my astonishment he said smilingly: "Most of the German and Polish Jews in America look like this, and the rest of them did till a very short time ago."

Later Mr. Stein explained to Wise "the misery and the drudgery of the peddler's life":

> Our people in this country may be divided into the following classes: (1) the basket peddler, he is as yet altogether dumb and homeless; (2) the trunk-carrier, who stammers some little English, and hopes for better times; (3) the pack-carrier, who carries from 100 to 150 pounds upon his back, and indulges the thought that he will become a businessman some day. In addition to these, there is the aristocracy, which may be divided into three classes: (1) The wagon-baron, who peddles through the country with a one- or two-horse team; (2) the jewelry-count, who carries a stock of watches and jewelry in a small trunk, and is considered a rich man even now; (3) the store-prince, who has a shop and sells goods in it. At first one is the slave of the basket or the pack; then the lackey of the horse, in order to become, finally, the servant of the shop.[19]

Jacob R. Marcus, who reprinted these reminiscences in his collection of memoirs, added some skeptical remarks:

> Some historians of the American scene maintain that the Jewish peddler was a cultural force. This contention is not sustained by the evidence. . . . Some individual peddlers were intelligent men; some of them had even enjoyed a relatively good training in the schools of their native lands. But most of them were humble men of modest attainments. They were foreigners who spoke little or no English; they were frequently miserably unhappy. What cultural values could they bring to the Mississippi planter or to the successful Massachusetts farmer who subscribed to three or four American newspapers and magazines? . . . He was essentially a bird of passage, both geographically and chronologically. . . . A handful ascended to the top rung of the ladder. . . . Thousands of others reached up, lost their grip, and perished at the bottom.[20]

Most of the immigrants probably did not "perish at the bottom," even if they achieved only modest economic success. It was they who constituted, after some time, the more or less well-to-do middle class that was to become the backbone of Jewish communities throughout the country. One of these was Henry Seessel from Speyer-on-the-Rhine, whom we have already met. He arrived in New Orleans in 1843 went on to Natchez, Mississippi, to join his brother. "My brother was also peddling at that time. There were a great many young men peddling, all of them making their home at Natchez. . . . Some of them have become large merchants, while some others never did much good for themselves." He continues:

> After I had remained in Natchez about one week my brother and myself started on our first trip together. We had a horse loaded down with three large packages of dry goods and clothing. Both of us walked, and I had to lead the horse. This was an entirely new business to me. I had to learn a good deal. I knew nothing whatever about handling goods, nor did I know how to handle a horse. . . . I did not relish the work of peddling at all. Every time we stopped at a farm to sell goods I had to pack the heavy packages in and out of the houses, and while my brother was selling goods, I stood and watched on the outside, so no one would steal anything. . . . The eating did not suit me, as I was not used to eating American dishes, such as hot bread, turnip greens, and pork. The walking of from ten to twenty miles per day I did not relish either.

That pork was not kosher by Jewish law is not mentioned as the reason for his dislike.

Seessel was obviously one of those younger relatives who were brought over by earlier immigrants not solely out of brotherly love. As it turned out, he was soon sent out alone for "half the profit . . . but I would have to pay board when at home." For the first three trips he made together with his brother, "during which time I had to do work like a slave, I received no pay. My brother said I had to work to pay him back the money he sent [to] me [in] Paris and for the clothing he had to buy for me on my arrival."[21] The pattern is found repeated time and again, and must not necessarily imply unfair exploitation. For the inexperienced young immigrant, beginning work together with an earlier and more seasoned arrival was a suitable starting point, until he had learned some English and more of American business and way of life. The first-comer, in his place, profited by the help of a trusted relative, which enabled him to expand his market.

The Jewish concentration in commerce drew equivocal comments by some contemporary observers. A prominent German traveler alluded to it as an

undeniable proof that trading is the life-principle of the Israelites. [In America] no barriers are set that limit their movements; by no prejudice or laws are they bound to any occupation. . . . But whatever craft or trade they may have performed at home, in America, where they are allowed to choose, they become merchants, or if that proves impossible, shop-keepers and peddlers. . . . On arrival at one of the ports they mostly have only a few dollars left with which they proceed immediately to "start a business." First they acquire a narrow basket to be slung over the neck, and next a small inventory of dry goods, some yarn, combs and toothbrushes, . . . and they are already on their way to fortunes. The future merchant does yet not know a single word of the language. . . . "Yes" "no" and some more essential words like "very cheap" or "very good" and with likeable boldness he starts visiting preferably the American households (the Germans themselves are bad customers), starting a conversation with the help of these few barbaric words and a lively gesticulation till the people, if they have not thrown the intruder outdoors at his first entry, often buy some small item for which they will never have any use.

These "witty" diatribes went on describing the dubious practices by which many of these "German Israelites in only a few years succeeded to scratch together quite formidable riches."[22]

Why a Jewish publication should reprint this kind of reportage without any comment can only be that its editor agreed at heart with the writer's opinion. In Germany, disdain of the "unproductive" commercial occupations and degrading "wheeling and dealing" was the fashion of the day. The arguments against the immediate emancipation of the Jews were implicitly accepted by Jewish benevolent organizations for the "promotion of the handicrafts and agriculture among the Jews" that sprang to life throughout the nineteenth century. In the end the practical results of these endeavors were negligible, mainly because they ran counter to the general trend of economic development.[23]

That most of the youngsters who had learned some craft in Germany abandoned it upon arrival in America and returned to the traditional commercial activities of their fathers was seen as cause for concern by some American Jews. This was expressed in a reaction to the host of slurs and caricatures—in the American press, fiction, and juvenile reading material—that disseminated the old stereotypes, which had crossed the ocean, of the usurious, conniving, cheating Jew, "Shylock," and the "eternal alien." As in Europe, prosperous Jewish merchants, professionals, and influential publicists tried to convince those who arrived later of the benefits of agricultural colonization and manual labor as a means of uplifting the morale of the individual and, at the same time, enhancing the image of Jews as a group. "Ancient prejudices against the Jews are too deeply rooted to be foregone," wrote Isaac Leeser in 1855,

and this will continue while the business which we follow is so uniform. . . . We know well enough that it is not easy to get into a new line of business; but we would respectfully call the attention of persons anxious to commence life in a reputable manner, whether mechanical, agricultural or other industrial callings do not offer them equal advantages with the stereotyped dealing in ready-made articles for immediate wearing. . . . If too many should follow it, fancying it an inexhaustible mine of wealth, they will discover to their sorrow that they will become, many of them, bankrupt in means and reputation, notwithstanding their utmost endeavor to maintain an honest character and to give every one his own.[24]

The intent of furthering "productivization" was not confined to oral or written propaganda. Mordecai M. Noah's failure in the early 1820s to found a Jewish agricultural settlement on the 2,550 acres he had acquired on Grand Islands did not discourage later attempts. In 1837 a cooperative was founded in New York: it called itself "Zeire Hazon" ("The Tender Sheep" in Hebrew) and had as its goal to settle on the western prairies. Addressing "their brethren throughout the United States," the leaders of the group, mostly earlier immigrants already well-known in New York's Jewish community, explained its objectives:

Every year a greater or less number of Jewish immigrants arrive in the different ports of this country. . . . Many of them, particularly those from Germany, are mechanics and agriculturists; and would do well, could they locate themselves, together, in some part of this country suitable for their purposes: but this, situated as they are, without the means necessary for such an undertaking, they are unable to do; . . . they are compelled to remain in the cities, where in consequence of their being unable to compete with the native workmen, on account of the Sabbaths, and Holidays, and their ignorance of the language of the country, they are, from necessity, forced to engage in occupations of a triffling [sic] character, which tends to lessen their own respectability, and that of the society of which they are members.[25]

This project of colonization that originated in the German congregations of New York did not materialize, but one year later a group from the same milieu organized to found a Jewish settlement in Ulster County, New York, under the name *Sholem* (peace). Some members of Congregation Anshe Chesed seem to have settled there, but the experiment was apparently abandoned a few years later for lack of funds to pay for the land, and for lack of settlers. More attempts were undertaken from New York in the 1850s, and these started an interesting argument in the *Asmo-*

nean, for and against the pursuit of commerce; but, again, this had no practical results whatsoever.[26]

The romantic ideal of reversing the "abnormal" occupational structure of Jewish life with organized agricultural settlements in America found some enthusiastic support in Germany. In December 1832 Bernhard Behrend, a prosperous merchant in Rodenberg, a small town in Hesse, addressed a letter to Baron M. A. Rothschild in Frankfurt; after having profoundly contemplated the "continued unjust, and in some countries utterly unhuman repression of our coreligionists" he called upon the financier "in all solemnity to acquire a piece of land in North America, to establish a colony for our unfortunate coreligionists, and to lead those across, who are nearest to us, from Germany, Poland and Italy."

Rothschild replied curtly that he did not agree with the writer's opinion in that matter, but for many years Behrend kept on trying. In February 1844 he approached Gabriel Riesser, at the time the most prominent Jewish advocate of political emancipation, who in turn politely refused to "request of others what I myself can not be part of." In 1845 Behrend visited Rothschild in Frankfurt. The baron received him in his office, only to declare bluntly that he considered the whole project to be *"Stooss"* ("nonsense" in Hebrew), with which he refused to have anything to do. The unfaltering Behrend then composed a pathetic summons, "To my coreligionists, near and far," to join him in his endeavors. They were to establish a worldwide organization under the name "Ora et Labora" and start immediate preparations for immigration to America by studying agriculture and English. Ludwig Philippson refused to publish the appeal in his paper because of his "being too long acquainted with the conditions of the Israelites, to hope for any results from your summons."[27]

Apart from these abortive ventures, the preoccupation with Jewish "productivity" generated no apparent results. With the advance of industrialization and the expanding market economy, the concentration of German Jews in the commercial sector of the economy became ever more conspicuous. And in the United States German Jews continued to seek success and adaptation by trying to climb the steps of the economic ladder that had been so eloquently described by the formidable Mr. Stein of Syracuse. In both cases the "normalizers" had the realities of economic development working against them. Most significant among these were the expanding needs for retail outlets, in addition to the absence of comparable opportunities in industrial endeavors.

> In general, the structure of American industry was discouraging to newcomers. In manufacturing, only two roles were possible: that of the laborer from which there was no opportunity of advancement; and that of the capi-

talist, which called for a surplus of investment. On neither count were the Jews attracted. Wherever possible they avoided the dead end of the proletarian's status; and their small stores of capital could more advantageously be invested in trade.

Somewhat similar reasons explained their absence from agriculture. . . . [The Jew] lacked the training and the skill to become a frontiersman; the axe, the gun, and the ability to live off the soil were alike strange to him. Yet, to settle down in an area already developed, to buy land already cleared, required capital which he did not have. Sometimes such a man labored and saved, intending some day to be lord of his own plot. Usually, when the balance became large enough, he found it more profitable and more consistent with his own skills to invest in trade.[28]

On the other hand, it was indeed just those "traditional Jewish" traits of commercial interest that helped the immigrants to adapt themselves in a relatively short time to their new environment. In Germany the Jews adapted to, and took advantage of, the demographic growth and structural economic changes in their environment on the eve of the industrialization: they demonstrated a high degree of mobility, thrift, and enterprise. These characteristics served them equally well in America, in the expanding frontier regions of the Midwest as well as in California. In the South, "in the midst of a stratified society in which the highest ideal was the gregarious planter attached to his land," they showed the same inclinations. "Jews used their mobility to change locations and change storefronts at a rate unknown to the local population, and they saved money among people for whom conspicuous consumption was a social plus."[29] Both traits, combined with mutual trust and a common background, promoted the economic success of many Jews by creating a close web of partnerships and intragroup economic connections, one of the outstanding characteristics of this period.

"Peddling" embraces a quite diverse range of economic activities. The merchandise in demand and the ways of its distribution were quite different in New York and the other big cities from those in the shantytowns of Colorado and California, or on the agricultural Western plains. It is therefore appropriate to glance at these various conditions as they represented themselves in the main areas of the United States in which the German-Jewish immigrants made their first steps. Their choice of these locations was sometimes purely accidental. In many cases they followed earlier immigrants, family members, friends, and acquaintances known in the old home. The concentration of people from the same village or area in Germany, which has been observed in many American centers of settlement, indicates that there was at least some previous planning at home in the selection of where to start out. But the decision to stay on or to try one's luck elsewhere depended, of course, in every individual case on the economic success, as well as on the social and family bonds, in which they did or did not become entangled during this period of "Americanization."

New York and the East Coast

Approximately 65,000 of the 150,000 American Jews estimated for 1860 were concentrated in three main communities: 40,000 in New York City, 8,000 in Philadelphia, and 8,000 in Baltimore; Boston seems to have lagged behind, with only some 2,300. In 1877, before the start of the Eastern European mass immigration, more than half of all Jews were living in the main East Coast states: there were over 80,000 in New York, 18,000 in Pennsylvania, 10,500 in Maryland, 8,500 in Massachusetts, and 5,600 in New Jersey.[30] In previous years many more had come through these ports of entry before they went on to disperse throughout the country. But, judging from the census numbers alone, the greater part either remained in these states or returned there after more or less adventurous, and more or less economically successful, expeditions.

Despite this concentration, New York's Jewish community of the "German period" in American Jewish history was, until recently, the least researched. Hyman B. Grinstein's 1945 monograph ends with 1860 and concentrates mainly on cultural and religious institutions and developments. A modern social and economic history of this most important Jewish community is, to my knowledge, still to be written. From the scanty available evidence we may only gain an impression of the first experiences of immigrants in the great metropolis.

Striking at first sight is the poverty of most immigrants who decided to stay. The more active and daring evidently soon decided to search for more promising fields. An 1843 report from a "Committee of the Society for the Education of Poor Children and Relief of Indigent Persons of the Jewish Persuasion" provides some description of prevailing conditions:

> Vast numbers of Jews are compelled to crowd into very small and unwholesome tenements, occupying but one or two small and uncomfortable rooms . . . where the family consists of many individuals; for these rooms they are obliged to pay an enormous rent. . . . Being unable to pay these rents, they are thrust into the street. . . . To those who are of the opinion that charitable institutions increase pauperism, we would say, come with us and visit the abode of the poor—see them with their baskets but poorly furnished with a few articles, whereby they can realize a few paltry cents. Follow them a day, through all kinds of weather, and watch their return at night, exhausted by their protracted journey through the city and country,

with the proceeds of their work—look at their rooms, bare and unfurnished, without fuel, their children without clothing, and then ask if a few dollars given to them can increase their poverty or be ill bestowed.[31]

Before this destitute situation was registered by Jewish philanthropists, it had been discovered by Christian missionaries, who then tried to exploit it to further their own aims. One of them was James Forrester, who submitted his findings in a report of 1842:

> The number of Jews now in this city has been ascertained to be nearly ten thousand. A large proportion of them consists of emigrants from Europe, mostly from Germany, and many very recently. These are generally poor, some extremely so. . . . Sick and destitute females have been found in lonely garrets, without fire, in the coldest season, struggling to subsist themselves and their shivering infants upon a few crusts. Families on the verge of being driven by their landlords from their scarcely habitable lodgings into the streets have implored the missionary for aid in their time of need.

Jewish philanthropy was probably first alerted by the missionary's successes.[32]

German-Jewish immigrants arriving in New York would, of course, not depend for long on philanthropy, and they searched for some kind of gainful employment. As elsewhere, peddling would appear to have been the first and most easily accessible profession. But, rather surprisingly, around 1845 only a negligible part of New York's gainfully employed Jews seem to have been peddlers. And of them, many left their families in New York and went to do their business in distant towns and villages, to return only for the holidays.[33] The initial investment capital for what was soon to become the most outstanding, and most contemptuously disparaged, Jewish trade in New York City, the secondhand clothing shops of Chatham Street, was apparently accumulated in other occupations.

> Jews from Bavaria and Baden took to the needle in New York during the latter thirties, and a decade later were joined by Jews from Prussia, Silesia, and Poland. . . . Those Jews who came with no or little tailoring experience began as helpers, learned the necessary processes, and advanced to become full-fledged artisans. Others saved enough money to open small "old clo" shops on Chatham Street.[34]

In addition to this, many immigrants found employment as bakers and butchers, and in other trades.

At the start of the mass immigration, Philadelphia was a well-established Jewish community. Some of the best-known German-Jewish families had achieved social and economic prominence. For many new immigrants, Philadelphia served, like New York City, as their first station. The growth of its Jewish population from about 500 in 1820 to 4,000 in 1848, and to about 8,000 in 1860, indicates that many of them preferred to stay.[35] The existence of organized Jewish philanthropic institutions and educational facilities encouraged mainly the married immigrants to remain. One of them was Meyer Guggenheim, the founder of one of the wealthiest Jewish dynasties in America, who arrived in 1848 at the age of eighteen and started peddling shoelaces on the streets.[36]

Baltimore's Jewish community counted only about 1,000 in 1840, so that its growth to 8,000 by 1860 was even more impressive.[37] On the other hand, the Jewish community of Boston, at mid-century one of the major American industrial cities, with a population that had tripled between 1825 and 1860, numbered only around 2,000 to 2,500 souls in 1864, and by some recent estimates even less.[38] Why the Jewish population of Boston and the rest of New England started to grow so relatively late is still a matter of speculation. Some authors have tried to explain this fact by referring to the bigotry of New England's Calvinist Puritans.[39] Jewish immigrants of the 1820s were probably reluctant to try their first steps there, and so an important "pull" factor for later immigrants was absent. In any case, Boston proves how much the directions taken by the immigrants depended on a variety of both rational and incidental reasons.

The West

In 1843 Julius Stern of Philadelphia proposed the organized settlement of 70,000 Jews in a territory lying west of the Mississippi; these Jews would then be entitled, under federal law, to request admission into the Union as a state. Isaac Leeser published the proposal in his *Occident and American Jewish Advocate*, with the comment that the settlement of Jews in the expanding West might be attained gradually, and without the promotion of Jewish statehood. Eventually, he was proven to be right.[40] Already in 1808 individual Jewish settlers had opened general stores in St. Louis and other places on the western frontier, and in 1836 an attempt was made to found the first Jewish congregation west of the Mississippi. The United Hebrew congregation of St. Louis was established in 1841 by newly arrived immigrants. Its existence was somewhat unstable because many of its members remained in St. Louis only for short periods before moving further west or south.[41]

Emanuel Rosenwald was the fourth of eight children of a family from Dittenhofen, Bavaria, all of whom eventually emigrated to America. The first-born son, Joseph, "as was customary in those days, was given the benefit of all educational advantages as our parents could afford. . . . In 1851 (being 18 years old) he left Germany, going to the United States." Two years later, Emanuel, at the age of fifteen, followed him and joined him in business in Staunton, Virginia, where, as he wrote:

> I helped Joe to the best of my ability and during the winter I was sent to school to learn the language. The firm name was Goodman & Co., carrying a line of men's clothing manufactured by H. Goodman & Bros. in Baltimore [these were relatives on his mother's side, formerly Gutman of Dittenhofen]. . . . Some months after my arrival in Staunton in 1853 . . . the firm Goodman & Co. opened a second store of which Joe took charge, while I was put in charge of the first store. . . . Shortly thereafter we concluded that the business did not pay and therefore moved our stock to Richmond . . ., where we remained for about a year, but did not meet with success. We then decided to go West.

The ventures of the brothers took them to Burlington, Fort Des Moines, and Sioux City, Iowa, until they arrived in Wyandotte, Kansas:

> We were in Wyandotte some length of time doing fairly well, trading with the Indians. . . . Thereafter we removed to Lawrence, Kansas. There Jacob Goldsmith, who had married my sister Helene, joined us. . . . From Lawrence I went to New York to buy a general line of men's furnishing goods on credit. . . .
> Joe formed a partnership with Philip Strauss and Henry Rosenfield. They bought a trainload of spirits on credit and started for Camp Floyd, Utah, by bull team from Leavenworth. They were on the road three months, undergoing the most severe hardships. . . . There the firm manufactured Whisky from the spirits they had transported, bottling the goods at night and selling the entire production each day. . . . At this point the firm also had a cargo soldier trade. Joe narrowly escaped being killed by these soldiers at various times.
> They finally sold out and Joe went to Denver. . . . In Denver we bought two ox wagons fully equipped and one mule wagon, sufficient groceries and liquors and started down the Arkansas river where Ft. Wise was building at the time . . . , camped there till part of our stock was sold and we received orders from commanding officers to move on. We took the remainder of our stock herefrom to Pike's Peak. On our way up we were followed by a band of Indians, they being on the opposite of the river. We, however, escaped them. Traded our entire remaining stock for potatoes—took them to Denver, peddled them out and after finishing with their sale we sold our oxen wagons and started in our mule wagon for Wyandotte, Kansas.[42]

We leave Emanuel Rosenwald at this point of his adventurous career. What makes his story worth quoting at such length is what makes it typical: German-Jewish peddlers were very young, worked with their brothers, and conducted business inside the family, marketing the wares of relatives settled in the East. Partnerships were almost exclusively with other German Jews, preferably with later-arriving relatives or friends from their former, German homes. Their mobility was perhaps the most outstanding feature of their lives, and they changed, in short succession, not only locations and means of transport but also the merchandise that they sold or sometimes partly produced on the spot, like the whisky in Rosenwald's narrative.

Henry Frank, whom we have already accompanied on his way to America to the unkind welcome of his uncle in New York, did some peddling in New England before settling in 1854 in Cincinnati, where a friend of the family had offered him a position in his clothing business:

During that period there was a large exodus of young men further West, for "Westward is the Eldorado, the Gold Mine" became the slogan. . . . I too felt restless, for my position did not afford me much income, and I was easily persuaded to join a party of young men. . . . I had been in correspondence with Mr. Gerson Friedenheim, who was living in St. Joseph, Missouri, and was from my native village, Obbach. He offered me a position in his retail clothing business which I accepted.

In 1857 gold was found in the hills and valleys near Pike's Peak. . . . St. Joseph became the outfitting post, being the most convenient and best market for the emigrants to buy their supplies for the trip across the plains. . . . The gold fever became epidemic and our little social circle did not escape, for ten of us concluded to give up our positions and brave the danger of being killed by the Indians or buffaloes to satisfy our desires and ambitions and find gold. The preparations for the journey were soon made. We joined a party of nearly two hundred people, all armed with Navy revolvers and Bowie knives. . . . Our party bought a team of mules, wagons, tents, camping outfits, mining tools, cooking utensils, provisions to last until we should reach Denver and water for men and beast to satisfy our needs until we struck camp every evening.

Our trip was mapped out according to the General Fremont and Kit Carson Indian Trail, through the Kansas Reserve along the North Platte River to Fort Kearny. It took us twenty-eight days to reach our destination but we were young and it did not matter. I never felt better in my life. . . . We observed the rules of army life, our camp was guarded all night. . . . We were in constant danger of being entrapped and cut off from our trains. Many a night I stood guard alone after midnight and heard nothing but wolves and bears. . . .

When we reached Denver our party of emigrants separated. . . . We wandered all over that territory for nearly six months without making any discovery of gold. We could not blame ourselves for not buying any counterfeit claims which were offered at very low prices, for we had no means at our command, and were not willing to risk our luck as pioneers for an indefinite time, and yet some few remained and engaged in business. . . . The city of Denver proved a brilliant bonanza for those who had the courage to remain there. . . .

In those days Denver didn't look very promising for it had only been laid out there the year before we came. . . . The inhabitants were the roughest kind of people—miners, cowboys, gamblers—they would cut each other's throat for a trifle. . . . There were no other trades except dealing with such people. I was glad to get away. I had lost all taste for gold hunting—no romance for me. Nearly all of our immediate colony of prospectors returned to St. Joseph, being well satisfied with our experience of roughing it and glad to get back to civilization.[43]

The Jewish reluctance to get too deeply involved in the mining business, their preference for making the best of the new economic opportunities by selling the miners hard-to-get merchandise at high prices, was characteristic of the California gold rush as well. The central city of German-Jewish settlement and expansion throughout the Far West was San Francisco, whose Jewish population grew to about 4,000 by the mid-1850s, and to over 5,000 by the end of the decade. Following the usual pattern, most Jews established themselves in business, often representing family concerns in the East. Jewish peddlers followed the prospectors into the mining towns to set up general stores. In towns such as Sacramento and Stockton, small communities and congregations were founded and maintained close ties with the Jewish community in San Francisco.[44]

Jewish business practices occasionally evoked some anti-Semitic comments in contemporary publications. Some later historians have tried to "defend" these clothing-merchants, arguing that although they were not actively involved in gold mining, Jewish businessmen helped promote the industry as partners or underwriters of the prospectors, or by granting them credit and loans. In this way they too helped in the economic development of the West.[45] But if one resists this compulsion to prove time and again that Jews made an economic "contribution," it becomes clear that their activity here was quite natural. Wherever German Jews moved, striving to gain a secure foothold and to adapt to their new environment, they did so, like everybody else, by making use of the trades and occupations for which they had the most experience and talents.

On the Ohio River, Cincinnati, the "Queen City of the West," was the main channel of westward expansion during these years and therefore also an important center of German-Jewish settlement. In their own, and in their contemporaries', eyes the city was regarded for many years as "the center of American Jewish life."[46] In 1850, with a population of 115,000, it was the sixth largest city in the United States. Its Jewish community grew from about 1,000 in 1840 to 7,600 in 1860. Most of this growth was initiated by the influx of peddlers who expanded their activities to the West, while some of the more successful merchants set up wholesale supply stores for those who continued their itinerant business.

The complex system of distribution in this vast and sparsely populated region gave rise to a layered commercial network. Importers and manufacturers in the East supplied merchants and manufacturers in western cities such as Cincinnati. Wholesalers in Cincinnati in turn supplied peddlers, local retail dealers, and merchants in the smaller towns of the city's trading hinterland. These small-town merchants in turn sold goods to peddlers, who went out into the countryside. "In the case of German Jews this network of commercial relations was an almost exclusively Jewish one, and as such, constituted an economic and status hierarchy within the Jewish world."[47]

With all its lasting importance as a main center of Jewish settlememt, Cincinnati served for many German Jews as only a transitional station on their move further west, and quite a few eventually returned to the Atlantic coast after they had made some capital. One of those was Louis Stix. Born in 1821 in Demmelsdorf, Bavaria, Stix arrived in Cincinnati in 1841 to join an elder brother, who had been there since 1830. After peddling for two years in Ohio and eastern Indiana, Stix and his partners opened a chain of general stores, and in 1864 Louis Stix "found it imperative to settle in New York as the firm's resident buyer." The Cincinnati firm remained "one of the best-known dry-goods houses in the Middle West."[48]

A similar career was that of the Seligman brothers, which is inevitably used as the German-Jewish Horatio Alger story in every saccharine description of this period in the history of American Jewry. The eight sons and three daughters of David Seligman of Baiersdorf, Bavaria, arrived in America during the 1840s, following their eldest brother, Joseph, who had immigrated in 1837. Most of the brothers were peddlers and followed the common pattern. Later they ventured into clothing manufacturing, and finally they became bankers. The Civil War proved to be their great opportunity, as it was for many American merchants, Jews or Gentiles. In 1862 the United States government owed the firm $1 million for supplies to the armed forces.

Jesse Seligman later recounted his and his family's early days. Arriving in New York in 1841, he found out after two days

> that my supply of cash was diminishing very rapidly, and that I had just sufficient money left to take me to Lancaster, Pa., where three older brothers, Joseph, William and James, were then in a small business. I remained in Lancaster a few weeks, during which time I learned the English language to some extent, and, at the same time, mastered the science of smoking penny cigars.

After spending some years in Alabama, where he became "at the age of fifteen the possessor of my own store and had clerks in my employ," Jesse arrived in New York in 1848. His brothers had already established an important business there. Two years later he was again on his way west, following the California gold rush. "I determined to leave the store in the hands of my brother Henry, so that I might venture out there to ascertain whether we could not still futher improve our condition."

And improve it did. Jesse Seligman arrived in San Francisco in the fall of 1850 and was lucky enough to rent the only brick building of the city for his store. Having escaped the damages of fire and shipwreck and the temptations of politics, he returned east in 1857.

> I attended to my California business, which was continued for some years after my departure from San Francisco. We found that our capital could not be invested to advantage in dealing in merchandise, and, therefore, my senior brother, the late Joseph Seligman, . . . went to Europe for the purpose of establishing a banking house there, and also with the object of placing the United States bonds on the Frankfurt stock exchange. . . . Since then we have been identified with every syndicate that has placed the United States bonds.

In 1864 other houses were established in London, Paris, and Frankfurt, and later also in Berlin, Amsterdam, New Orleans, and San Francisco.[49]

This outstanding success story was, of course, not typical of all or even most German-Jewish immigrants. What was typical, however, was the high mobility of domiciles and places of business from one part of the vast country to another, from East to West and back again, and also from the South, which had been the second important area of Jewish settlement since colonial times.

The South

Charleston, South Carolina, was one of the first Jewish congregations of America, closely following those of New Amsterdam and Newport. Shortly after the city's foundation around 1670, a few Sephardic Jews settled there as shopkeepers, traders, and merchants, and as early as 1749 the first congregation, Kahal Kadosh Beth Elohim, was founded. Around 1800 Charleston had a Jewish population of some five hundred souls. "Culturally, religiously and possibly in other directions as well, the center of gravity in American Jewish life during the first quarter of the nineteenth century was located in Charleston, S.C."[50]

Savannah, Georgia, had the third oldest Jewish congregation in North America. On July 11, 1733, a ship chartered by the Sephardic congregation of London brought a group of forty-one Jews to be settled there. Most of them were of Sephardic origin, but some were Ashkenazi, among them Benjamin Sheftall, who served as interpreter for the Protestant settlers, who came to America after being banned from Salzburg. The community prospered during the 1740s and 1750s, when it reached over one hundred souls, Sephardic Jews and German immigrants mixing easily in religious and social organizations. Economic failure and the Revolutionary War caused its almost total dispersion, but it recovered with the new wave of immigration.

After the start of the German-Jewish mass immigration, New Orleans became the main port of entry in the South. Around 1815 only fifteen Sephardic Jews are recorded to have lived there, among them the famous and wealthy Judah Touro. But as early as 1827 the first Jewish congregation of Louisiana was founded. From New Orleans many new immigrants fanned out to take their first steps in the South.

The arrival of Jewish immigrants in Louisiana after 1830, and especially after 1840, marked a change in the composition of the community. The new immigrants, in contrast to their more urbane and sophisticated Sephardic predecessors, came from small towns and villages that had an agrarian economy similar to that of Louisiana. They seem to have been attracted from other parts of the United States, as well, by the economic opportunities in this state. For French-speaking Jews from Alsace and Lorraine, Louisiana was especially attractive. For both French and German Jews, the agricultural society of the antebellum South was similar to that of the Europe they had left. Many were able here to take up their former occupations supplying farmers and landowners. Jews traded in everything, mostly in dry goods and clothing. Some wholesalers concentrated on supplying literally hundreds of small Jewish country retailers. Throughout Louisiana and its neighboring states, Jewish traders developed their own supply system and credit mechanisms.[51]

Herman Heyman, twenty-eight years old and from Essen on the Ruhr, and Louis Merz, twenty years old and from Durkheim, Bavaria, were strangers to each other until they arrived in Philadelphia in 1852. By 1853 they were friends, and together they moved to La Grange, Georgia. In 1854, when the rail line was opened to West Point, Georgia, Heyman and Merz moved there and established the merchandising firm of Heyman and Merz:

Herman Heyman had more than a dozen years of business experience, probably for the most part in Luxembourg, before coming to America. Louis Merz had little business experience, but is said to have made an "enviable record" at college. They apparently started their business with little capital but with high ideals and strong determination. In addition to the store location in West Point they also owned a two-horse wagon, from which one partner would peddle for many miles around while the other tended store in West Point. The business seems to have gotten off to a good start.

After these promising first steps, business and family relations developed in the quite usual pattern of the times: Herman married Louis Merz's younger sister when she arrived from Bavaria in 1858, with a ceremony taking place in Cincinnati with Rabbi Isaac M. Wise officiating. In later years most younger members of both families arrived in America, and some of them joined the firm. The founding partners and later scions of the growing clan, expanding their economic activities, repeatedly changed places of residence and business between the South and the East, mainly Philadelphia; but the center remained in West Point, Georgia, until 1943.[52]

Another southern peddler was Julius Weis, whom we have already met. After he arrived penniless, in Natchez, Mississippi, in November 1845, he was installed as a peddler by his cousin.

> We selected a small assortment of goods, amounting to $125 . . . a horse, saddle and bridle for $25, and I was fully equipped; but as I was only nineteen years of age, and knew very little English, Mr. David prevailed upon another young man (also a cousin of mine) . . . to make a trip with me into the country and give me a start. . . . We accordingly left Natchez, going to Fayette, Miss. After a week he had sold about fifty dollars' worth of goods, while I had sold only about ten dollars' worth. . . . We parted company, and I started off alone.
>
> The first plantation at which I stopped belonged to an old lady. She owned about forty slaves, and had a nice little plantation situated in Jefferson County. She took a fancy to me, bought a few dollars' worth of goods, invited me to stay all night at her house, and treated me very kindly. In the evening she sent word to the negroes at the quarters, that if any of them wanted to buy anything, to come to the house. Many of them came up. I opened my goods on the gallery, and she stayed to watch them, so that they would not steal anything. I did very well, and felt happy at the result.

Weis continued his peddling trips with varying success until 1853, when he opened a store in Fayette in partnership with another German-Jewish peddler. Later he settled in Natchez, joining a former neighbor "from the village from which I came, and who had known me all my life . . . , and took charge of the business of Mayer, Deutsch & Co., wholesale and retail dry-goods and clothing." In 1865 Weis finally settled in New Orleans, where he became a banker and cotton commission agent, and one of the most distinguished Jews of the city.[53]

Lazarus Straus of Otterberg in the Bavarian Palatinate landed in Philadelphia in 1852. He had been active in the revolution of 1848, but had not been prosecuted. However, "made aware of the suspicions of the authorities and subjected to petty annoyances and discriminations," he decided to emigrate, even though his family was well-off. In America he followed the suggestions of former acquaintances to go south and started peddling with two brothers Kaufman, who "owned a peddler's wagon [from] which they dispensed, through the several counties of the state, an assortment of dry goods and what was known as 'Yankee notions.'"

There were often more "people of color" on the large plantations than there were whites in the nearby villages. The itinerant merchant, therefore, filled a real need, and his vocation was looked upon as quite dignified. The existence of slavery drew a distinctive line that gave the white visitor a status of equality that otherwise he would probably not have enjoyed.

> Provided only, that the peddler proved himself an honorable, upright man . . . he was treated as an honored guest by the plantation owners. The peddler usually stayed one night at the house of his customer and took his meals with the family, permitted no pay for board and lodging, and only a small charge for food for the horses. The peddler in turn usually made a gift to either the lady or the daughter.[54]

Successfully installed as a "dry goods and domestics" storekeeper in Talbotton, Georgia, Straus brought his family over from Bavaria and expanded his business.[54] After the Civil War they moved to New York City. His sons Nathan and Isidor became partners of Macy & Co., which had started from the crockery business, and was soon to become a well-known empire of department stores.[55]

Family biographies and memoirs make fascinating and sometimes amusing reading, but they should be handled with care as historical sources. Competition in the peddling trade was tough, and the cunning business practices ascribed to the notorious Yankee peddlers had to be met with adequate strategies. The contemporary opinion of the southern peddlers was far less flattering than retrospective descriptions tend to suggest. To return to glib Mr. Gerstäcker, who was so obligingly quoted in the Jewish press in Germany:

> In Louisiana the greatest benefit of the peddlers evolves from their dealings with the negroes, and especially with the negresses. As they are not allowed to leave the plantations, these depend solely on the itinerant traders for everything they may need. The young mestizas and mulattoes never lack money, especially if they are pretty, and know of no better way to spend their "love-pay" than to buy the finery and clothes offered to them by the smart Germans. . . . The profits from this merchandise, bought dirt-cheap at New Orleans' auctions, are immense. But the greatest benefit made by these people is made from illegal trade. Like every merchant in the slave states, they are forbidden to sell whisky to the negroes, risking heavy penalties in case of breaking this law. But the peddler knows very well how to

escape detection. There is no fear of being betrayed by the negroes, and so a double partition in the wagon holds the secret treasure from which they fill the bottles of the thirsty slaves.[56]

The prejudice of the writer, who showed little sympathy for both the Blacks and the Jews, is obvious. Still, there is probably some grain of truth in his report.

However scrupulous their individual commercial honesty may actually have been, there is no doubt that on the whole the German-Jewish peddlers in all parts of the expanding country were hardworking, frugal people who quickly adapted to the prevailing mores of economic achievement as the main avenue to social recognition. According to Oscar Handlin,

> We will never know how many of these itinerant peddlers barely scraped by without ever advancing in wealth, grew old without security; and how many more were failures, forced back upon charity, men who joined the ranks of the *schnorrers,* the beggars, the tramps, the hoboes, who wandered from town to town, living by gifts of the local synagogues anxious to be rid of them. Generally we hear only from the more fortunate.

Eventually it was these more fortunate ones who settled throughout the country. Before long "the land was dotted with general stores and groceries, dry-goods stores and some not so dry, shoe, clothing, hardware, and every other kind of establishment."[57]

In all these locations, however tiny their Jewish community, congregations and benevolent societies soon emerged, prepared the grounds for later immigrants, and laid the foundations for the growth and economic and cultural development of American Jewry.

3

Putting Down Roots

The Spread of Settlement

Starting in the mid-1840s the Jewish press in America and Germany published regular reports on the development of Jewish settlements and the foundation of new congregations throughout the United States. Many itinerant immigrants, after exploring all parts of the country, finally found a permanent place of residence. Here they brought or started their families, settled down to more stable economic pursuits, and created the social and religious framework of a versatile Jewish community life.

A reliable statistical survey of this development is still not available, and probably never will be. Starting with the seventh population census in 1850, data on religious bodies, including Jewish congregations, do appear in the official records, but obviously only a part of the already existing Jewish congregations were at that time registered.[1] However, in the absence of better sources, and assuming that omissions were more or less proportional in all parts of the country, the figures of table 3.1 provide us with an at least approximate picture of this development.

Between 1840 and 1860 the total Jewish population of the United States is estimated to have grown tenfold, from 15,000 to 150,000.[2] This dramatic increase is only partly reflected in table 3.1, but something of the essential process of demogaphic reshuffling is already evident. Although New York and the East Coast communities remained predominant, the westward drive of American Jewry had already begun. New congregations of importance had sprung up in Baltimore, New Orleans, and Boston, but the most impressive growth occurred in Ohio, and in the Midwest generally, while California was on its way to become second, after New York State, in the concentration of America's Jewish population before the start of the Eastern European immigration.

Table 3.1
Synagogues, Congregations, and Seats, 1850–1860

States	1850		1860	
	Synagogues	Seats	Congregations	Seats
U.S. total	37	19,572*	77	34,412
Connecticut	2	—	1	800
District of Columbia	—	—	1	400
Maryland	—	—	3	4,300
Massachusetts	1	200	2	660
New Jersey	—	—	1	228
New York	14	9,700	20	10,440
Pennsylvania	8	3,425	12	3,295
Rhode Island	1	300	2	279
East, Total				
No.	26	13,625	42	20,402
Percent	70.3	69.6	54.5	59.3
Alabama	—	—	2	950
Georgia	—	—	1	150
Louisiana	1	600	5	1,250
S. Carolina	3	2,400	3	850
Virginia	1	600	3	700
South, Total				
No.	5	3,600	14	3,900
Percent	13.5	18.4	18.2	11.3
Illinois	—	—	3	1,500
Indiana	—	—	2	450
Kentucky	1	600	—	—
Missouri	1	400	2	1,000
Ohio	3	1,301	8	5,300
Wisconsin	1	46	1	400
Midwest Total				
No.	6	2,347	16	8,650
Percent	16.2	12.0	20.8	25.1
California (West, Total)	—	—	5	1,460
No. Percent	—	—	6.5	4.3

*Erroneous calculation in source adjusted.
SOURCE: H. S. Linfield, *Statistics of Jews and Jewish Organizations: Historical Review of Ten Censuses, 1850–1937* (New York, 1939), pp. 29ff.

Synagogues and their various institutions are a clear sign of permanent settlement, although some of them may have stagnated in later years. Others, which like the one in Los Angeles were not even yet founded in 1860, later attained major importance. Rabbi Max Lilienthal's November 1846 report from New York recorded the most important existing congregations of the time, their institutions, and their activities. He also gave a detailed and vivid description of the ongoing process of expansion and the way in which new congregations were propagated all over the country:

> Some years ago a Jew moved to some little town and lives there now, removed from everything Jewish. Nobody knows him to be a Jew; no Jewish prayer, ritual or ceremony are performed. Some time later another Jew joins him, then a third. Approaches the time of our New-Year and Jom-Kippur holidays. People start remembering God, and from their state of well-being they conceive how much they owe Him, consider their irreligious way of life and are ashamed. Wishing to return to God they count their numbers, and there are already ten to create a "Minyan" for worship. So one of them proposes to establish a congregation. . . Some funds are thrown together, and soon a letter arrives in New York. . . . Money is sent to buy a Torah-scroll etc. . . . Arriving at such a place after five years one is overwhelmed to find such a well and freely-organized congregation, a nice synagogue, a cemetery. . . . This is the picture all-around and in a few decades we will find Jewish communities wherever civilization's blessings reach and the colonists clear the jungles.[3]

An unsigned, more prosaic description is given in a later issue of the same paper, the *Allgemeine Zeitung des Judenthums*:

> Up to now the immigrants settled in the big cities, preferably in New York. . . . As most arrived without any money they were, with the exception of the artisans, unable to establish a business, and so they took the pack. . . . For whole half-year periods they lived far from the family and half the income had to be spent on useless travel expenses. The remaining half diminished during the opulent holiday meals on return, and then everything began anew. As they did this out of their wish to visit synagogues and feast the holy days inside a Jewish community, the question arises why some of them don't move out into the country and set up communities there? Instead . . . masses of poor families crowd the cities, a heavy burden for the young congregations and charitable societies. . . .
>
> Now, thank God, matters are changing. . . . It is immensely interesting to observe how these small communities develop. Sometimes Jews are living for years at some small town, seemingly without any need to meet in religious service. . . . Suddenly one of them dies, and now the question arises where to bury him? The need to assure him a Jewish burial causes miracles. And so a plot is hurriedly bought to consecrate a cemetery. As soon as this is done they found a congregation. For a small salary some person is engaged to function as Shohet, Hazzan and teacher, a small room is rented for services and the rest is left to God.

Most new congregations started in this way, with a place not for worship in life but for burying the dead. Day-to-day religious observance, keeping the laws of Sabbath or kosher food, would be almost impossible under the conditions of the itinerant country peddler. Most of the immigrants seem not to have been overly concerned about this, the more so as in Germany, from which most of them had come, religious laxity and indifference were gaining ground. Still, the wish "to be brought to *Kever Israel*," to be buried in a consecrated Jewish cemetery, remained a deeply felt sentiment. The correspondent remarked on "another curious phenomenon here, that many Jews who had converted and been baptized in Germany return here to their Jewish faith, readily accepting the heaviest penance. . . . At the moment we have four of them under psychiatric treatment, suffering from painful remorse."[4]

During the years 1859–62 Israel Joseph Benjamin—or "Benjamin the Second," as he preferred to call himself after the famous traveler Benjamin from Tudela of the twelfth century—a half-educated wandering *schnorrer* from Rumania, toured the United States to explore American Judaism. Having somehow obtained impressive letters of introduction from Alexander von Humboldt and other German scholars, he traveled all over the country, financing his trip by the contributions he was able to collect on his way from Jewish communities or individuals. His two-volume travelogue[5] discloses an imaginative, restless mind and attentive skills of observation, and conveys a plethora of valuable information.

Benjamin spent the greater part of his time in California and the Midwest, searching for Jewish congregations and benevolent associations to keep him on his way. Where he was unable to find them he founded them. According to his own accounts, he assembled the Jewish inhabitants in remote little places and convinced them to consecrate cemeteries and to establish congregations and charitable institutions for the praise of God and for the more earthly benefit of transient Jews like himself. The Jewish communities he came across in his travels are graded as "prospering," "wealthy," and "benevolent," or "greedy" and "stingy," for quite obvious reasons. Nevertheless, his two volumes remain a valuable source of information.

In New York City Benjamin reported twenty-three congregations, three more than counted in the whole state in the census of 1860, and no less than forty-four "Jewish charitable and educational Societies."[6] In Buffalo he discovered four congregations and estimated a Jewish population of five hundred, whom he regarded as "the poorest community I have come across in America." At the same time he recorded ninety members of the Jewish congregation of Rochester, New York, and two congregations, one German and one Polish, in Syracuse, New York.

The earliest and most populous Jewish community in New York State, after New York City, seems to have been established in Albany. Already in 1833–34 quite a number of Jewish names and firms are recorded in the city directory. Most of these Jews were poor. In the early 1840s one of them went on to a collection campaign in other Jewish communities, to obtain the $500 needed to build a synagogue. In 1846 Isaac M. Wise arrived in Albany to serve as minister. His endeavors to promote some first, rather modest reforms in his services stirred some heated exchanges in the community and resulted in the foundation of a new congregation.[7]

Philadelphia had played a central role in the spiritual and organizational constitution of American Jewry since 1737, when the first Jews settled there permanently. Some of the most prominent Jewish families of the colonial and revolutionary period, the Gratzes, Franks, and Levys, as well as the legendary Haym Salomon, resided and prospered there. Early in the nineteenth century Philadelphia was overtaken by New York, but it remained a major port of entry for German-Jewish immigrants, and many of them remained there, taking advantage of the well-organized communal structure and the economic and educational opportunities.[8]

Notwithstanding its Sephardic roots, at the start of the century the majority of Philadelphia's Jews were already Ashkenazis. Barnard Gratz, born in Langendorf in Upper Silesia, had come to settle in Philadelphia in 1754, and from this time his family had held one of the first places in the congregation, upholding a conservative traditionalism with remarkable tenacity. Isaac Leeser arrived there in 1829 to serve for many years as the head of Mikveh Israel. In 1843 he founded the *Occident and Jewish Advocate,* the most important mouthpiece of traditionalist American Judaism, of lasting formative influence for the whole of American Jewry.[9]

With German-Jewish mass immigration, Philadelphia's Jewish population increased from 1,000 souls or somewhat less in 1830 to around 4,000 in 1848 and 8,000 in 1860. When Benjamin visited he reported the existence of seven congregations and no less than twenty-three different charitable and educational associations, among them five lodges of B'nai B'rith. Before the start of the mass immigration some Philadelphia Jews had already attained important economic and social positions, but the majority were small shopkeepers, tradesmen, and some artisans. For some of these immigrants Philadelphia was only a temporary place of residence, but, as the figures show, many of them preferred to stay and to join the older or newly established congregations.[10]

Perhaps the most impressive growth on the East Coast was that of Baltimore's Jewish community—from an estimated 1,000 in 1840 to around 8,000 in 1860. In 1825 no more than 125 to 150 Jews are known to have resided there. In 1830 the first congregation, Nidhei Israel, also known as Baltimore Hebrew Congregation, received its charter from Maryland's state legislature. Full civil rights had been granted Maryland's Jews only in 1826. Twenty years later Baltimore was praised in Germany "as an example of how unbelievably fast Jewish communities are here established. . . . [T]he exact number of Jewish families cannot be estimated, because more than half of them do not belong to any Jewish association or congregation, while the smaller half are divided between three local congregations."[11]

This growth was primarily the result of the expanding economic opportunities in this prospering port on the deep-water estuaries of the Chesapeake Bay. In addition to its access to important iron and copper mining industries, Baltimore had been since 1827 also the outlet of the Baltimore-Ohio railroad, which was probably what connected its Jewish community with their westward-bound coreligionists in Cincinnati. The origin and social composition of these two communities suggests, at least, some connection: both are recorded to have been established by lower-middle-class Bavarian immigrants.

In July 1846 the *New York Herald* reported the departure from Baltimore of a volunteer corps of men of the Jewish faith to fight in the Mexican War. Most of them were new immigrants. They elected a non-Jewish commander, but all other officers, and the army surgeon, were from their own ranks.[12] When Benjamin visited Baltimore in 1860 he already found six congregations there. One of them adhered to Polish ritual, while another was headed by Rabbi David Einhorn, soon to become the leader of America's radical Reform movement. Although most Jews were peddlers and small shopkeepers, some had already become quite prosperous. In 1864 the Hebrew Benevolent Society collected $5,000 at its anniversary supper, and the community started plans for building a Jewish hospital.[13]

Boston, as already noted, lagged behind, with a smaller Jewish population, mostly of people who had settled there since 1850, when only 360 Jews are estimated to have lived in the city.[14] The place of origin of Bostonian Jews is of special interest: at least half of them had arrived from northeast Germany with more than a sprinkle of Polish and Russian Jews among them. No more than a third came from Bavaria, Baden, Württemberg, and Hesse: Jewish immigrants from these regions dominated most of the Jewish communities of the East and Midwest. This obviously reflects the eastward expansion of Jewish emigration from Germany around mid-century.

Boston demonstrates the important role of chain-migration and the immigrants' preference for settling in clusters with other immigrants from the same old-country locales. This feature has been observed in many local studies of American-Jewish history.[15] When "Benjamin the Second" visited Boston in 1860 he recorded the existence of four different congregations, only one of them "German." In addition to it he described one mixed "English-Polish" and two "Polish-Lithuanian" congregations that apparently were unable to reach agreement on questions of ritual. Only in 1852 was the first synagogue of the German congregation inaugurated, but a Jewish cemetery was recorded in the city as early as 1844.[16]

No other large Jewish communities seem to have developed in the East before the Civil War. Around 1860, Pittsburgh, Pennsylvania, had no more than fifty to sixty Jewish families, mostly peddlers in the countryside who came home only for the Sabbath to get some rest and kosher food.[17] Washington, D.C., had even fewer, according to Benjamin—little more than a hundred souls, a single congregation, and one teacher providing "English and German" instruction.[18] In terms of congregations and the establishment of permanent communities, although not in strictly quantitative terms, the expansion of America's Jewish population was for a time dominated by the westward drive to the developing territories of the western frontier.

Fanning Out into the West

Cincinnati unquestionably played the leading role of starting point and supporting station for the westward movement. The first Jew is recorded as arriving there in 1817, to be joined during the early 1820s by immigrants from Holland and Alsace. This was Joseph Jonas from Plymouth, who, according to his own testimony, had read much about America. Strongly impressed with the descriptions of the Ohio River, he decided to settle in Cincinnati, disregarding the arguments of his family in Philadelphia that "in the wilds of America, and entirely among Gentiles, you will forget your religion and your God." After his arrival in March 1817, Jonas had to wait three years to attend the High Holiday services with the prescribed *minyan* of ten adult males and a Torah scroll.[19] Characteristically, the services of Cincinnati's first congregation followed the Polish ritual as did most synagogues attended by immigrants from England, who were mostly transients from East and Central Europe.

But the really impressive growth of the Jewish community occurred between 1830 and 1860 in the wake of the German-Jewish mass emigration. In 1850 some 3,000 Jews already resided in Cincinnati, and their numbers doubled in the following decade. Most of them came from Franconia and the Rhine Palatinate, repeating the already familiar pattern of group migration. Twelve neighboring villages of Upper Franconia together sent at least eighty Jews to Cincinnati between 1830 and 1865. Twenty-seven of them—virtually every young Jewish man living there—came from Demmelsdorf, where no more than 136 Jewish residents had been registered in 1811.[20] They constituted almost half of the village's population at the start of the century, and the absolute number of its Jewish population decreased to only fifty-two, or close to 19 percent, in 1875.[21]

The result was an impressive relative growth of the city's Jewish population, from only 0.5 percent in 1830 to about 5 percent in 1860. In 1844 some eighty families departed from the Polish congregation to found the German one.[22] When Benjamin arrived there in 1860 or 1861, he reported that six congregations and eighteen different Jewish associations were in existence, among them three lodges of B'nai B'rith.[23]

The Ohio and Mississippi valleys were an area of massive German settlement, and Jews were certainly a part of it. But if, according to some estimates, over half of all German immigrants settled there, Jewish settlers constituted no more than about one-fifth of all German-Jewish immigrants.[24] In the 1830s and early 1840s many new Jewish communities sprang up in this region, fanning out from the greater cities to small new settlements farther west.

Cleveland's first congregation was founded in 1840 by a clan of Bavarian Jews from Unsleben: forty-eight of the village's 225 Jews left for America between 1834 and 1853. Many of them belonged to the Thorman and Alsbacher families, who became the pillars of Cleveland's early Jewish community. Later they were joined by "Prussian" and Bohemian immigrants, who also tended to settle in clusters of relatives and former neighbors. Until 1860 the community grew to some 200 families, or 1,200 souls, an estimated 3.5 percent of the city's population.[25] Benjamin's recount of 15,000 Jews among 70,000 inhabitants of Cleveland in 1860 was wild fantasy, but he was closer to the truth when he estimated the Jewish population of Columbus, Ohio, to be 40 families.[26] Here again we find the characteristic nucleus of 3 community-founding families, 2 of whom, the Nussbaums and Gundersheimers, had arrived from the small Bavarian village of Mittelsinn.[27]

Louisville, Kentucky, had an early reputation as one of the first Jewish inland communities. A Jewish cemetery is recorded there as early as 1830. Over twenty Jewish names appear in the city directory for 1832, and in 1836 the first synagogue was consecrated. When Benjamin visited Louisville around 1860, he reported two congregations and about 2,000 Jewish inhabitants, which, again, must have been a highly exaggerated number. Between 1840 and 1860 only small groups of German and Bohemian Jews settled in the city, but many more seem to have passed through during the mid-century gold rush.[28]

In St. Louis some individual Jews are known to have done business already at the turn of the century, and the first members of the Bloch family from Bohemia arrived in 1816. Many of the early Jewish settlers seem to have intermarried with Gentiles but were later buried in the Jewish cemetery. When Isaac M. Wise visited St. Louis in 1855, he estimated that there were 600 to 700 Jews living in the city, but complained that their greater part, including the better-educated people, were not members of any of the four existing congregations.[29]

Chicago was at the time already the home of some 1,500 Jews, a suspiciously high percentage of the city's 11,000 to 12,000 inhabitants, if these estimates are correct. Jews are reported there as early as 1832, even before Chicago became a city with more than 5,000 people. Between 1840 and 1844 about twenty families from Bavaria and the Rhine Palatinate settled there, and the establishment of a Jewish burial ground society, as well as first High Holy Day services, is recorded in 1845. The first synagogue of Congregation Anshe Maariv was inaugurated in 1851 and was duly reported in the *Chicago Democrat* as a remarkable achievement of the small but wealthy and deservedly esteemed Jewish community.[30]

Milwaukee's Jewish community originates from about the same time. Its first Jewish settlers arrived in 1844 from Bavaria, Bohemia, and Austria. By 1856 the community had some two hundred families, most of them living in the second ward's "German Town." Benjamin recorded the existence of two congregations, one German and one Polish, which had merged in 1859 to accept the reformed rites.[31] Detroit at the same time counted only some 150 to 200 Jews, its first congregation and cemetery having been established in 1850–51 by no more than twelve families.[32]

The first congregation in Indianapolis was founded in 1856 by immigrants from England, when the Jewish population of Indianapolis counted about thirty adults. But quite a number of new communities sprang up in other remote spots of the frontier area, like Terre Haute, Vincennes, and Fort Wayne in 1850. The first Jews are recorded in Kansas City as early as the 1830s, but a permanent community was established there only in 1856.[33]

The data of the government censuses of 1850 and 1860, summarized in table 3.1 (see p. 000), present an incomplete picture. The classifications of "churches" were still vague, and many newly established communities did not adhere to the prescribed standards. Lacking more reliable information, the census figures nevertheless indicate the general trend of German-Jewish settlement of these years. Although sixteen of the recorded forty new congregations were established in the old settlement area of the East Coast, and only ten in the Midwest, the number of additional synagogue seats during this decade was almost equal: 6,777 in the East and 6,303 in the frontier area. Taking into account the fluctuations of settlement, the frequent moves of individual Jews, and the prevailing religious indifference, we may rightly assume that the number of Jewish settlers in the West was much greater than can be concluded from the numbers of new congregations. The newly founded congregations in the East were at least in part a result of the secession from older institutions that had been caused by the ongoing dispute on questions of ritual and religious Reform, while the newly founded congregations of the West reflect a real, new settlement of Jews along the expanding frontiers.

Another tendency that becomes evident from these data is that the South experienced a relative decline in importance. Although nine new congregations are recorded to have been established between 1850 and 1860, the number of synagogue accommodations remained almost stable. There were also important shifts of settlement in the South itself. The Jewish population of Charleston, South Carolina, the informal capital of the Old South, where the first reformed American congregation was founded in 1824, apparently numbered around seven hundred souls in 1860, the same number it had had a decade before.[34] New Orleans, an important gateway for German-Jewish immigration, now held uncontested first place. In 1841 no less than 245 business firms, half of them dry-goods and clothing stores, can be identified as Jewish-owned. Most immigrants after 1835 came from Alsace, the Rhineland, and France, and most of them resided along the river bank and in the French Quarter. In addition to the economic opportunities of this important commercial center, these immigrants' knowledge of French obviously played an important role in their decision to settle in the city. New Orleans's Jewish population of 1860 is now estimated to have been 4,000 to 5,000.[35]

In the pre-Civil War South only a limited number of new communities seem to have been founded or to have grown significantly. Atlanta, Georgia, had a small Jewish population from the early 1840s on, but the first *minyan* and cemetery did not materialize before 1860. The actual growth of the community started only after the war, and the first synagogue was consecrated in 1867.[36]

In Virginia, individual Jews, including early immigrants from Germany like the Gratz family, had been living or trading since 1767. The first Sephardic congregation was established in Richmond in 1789. Among the prominent citizens of the state capital were some German-Jewish names such as Benjamin Wolfe or Joseph Darmstadt, and we know that occasional services took place from the 1790s on not only in Richmond but also in Petersburg and Lyncher. It was only in 1841 that the first

German congregation was established in Richmond; this was followed by a Polish one in 1856. The indefatigable Benjamin visited Richmond in 1860 and reported four different benevolent societies organized along lines of place of origin in Europe.[37] Table 3.1 indicates, however, that Virginia, like all of the Old South, held little attraction for German Jews, and even in 1877 the state's Jewish population counted no more than 2,500.[38]

Some individual Jews are known to have lived in Alabama under British rule, but the first permanent Jewish community started in Mobile around 1820. A Jewish cemetery was consecrated in 1841 and the first Sephardic congregation was founded in 1844, to be followed in 1855 by a German one. In Montgomery, Alabama, 12 German Jews established a mutual aid society in 1846.[39] At about the same time, the first permanent Jewish community settled in Houston, Texas. Before 1848 an estimated 200 Jews were living and doing business in the Gulf region around Galveston, but no continuous religious or social connection between them and later immigrants has been established. The 1877 census counted 1,000 Jews in Galveston, compared with 461 in Houston. Galveston's first congregation was founded only in 1868, but a Jewish cemetery was already in existence there in 1860.[40]

New Mexico, a state with no significant Jewish population at any time, is of some interest in our present context as another example of Jewish group-, or rather family-, migration and settlement. In 1846 a Bavarian Jew named Jacob Spiegelberg who had arrived there with the American troops during the Mexican War brought his five brothers over from Germany. For quite some time the Jewish settlement in New Mexico seems to have remained a Spiegelberg business enterprise. Relatives and former neighbors arrived in trickles, and although many of them moved on, some of them remained. One employee of the Spiegelbergs brought a whole group of two hundred German-Jewish immigrants who joined the nuclei of Jewish communities in Albuquerque, Las Vegas, and Roswell.

In the 1880s individual Jews are known to have lived on the Indian reservations, like "Navajo Sam" Dittenhoefer, or Solomon Bibo, who attained the rank of an Indian chief by his marriage into the tribe. In Las Vegas a congregation of fifty members is recorded in 1890, and another one in Albuquerque in 1900. But the first directory of Nevada in 1862 contained at least two hundred unquestionable Jewish names, and Nevada's first Jewish school was established in 1861 by Herrman Bien in Virginia City.[41]

Similar communities sprang up and then disappeared in Colorado during the "Pike's Peak or Bust" gold rush that started in 1859–60. Their only remnant was the small Jewish community in Denver. In 1859, when the city was beginning to expand, a dozen Jewish merchants from Central Europe donated a plot of land to build a synagogue; the twenty-five Jews who are known to have lived there in the 1860s founded only a cemetery association. The first congregation was established in Denver only in 1871–72.[42] In Wyandotte, Missouri, which later became Kansas City, Missouri, some Jews were on record as early as 1839, but only in 1864 did they establish a burial society and in 1870 a congregation. In 1859 Congregation B'nai Jeshurun of Leavenworth, Kansas, was founded by German immigrants.[43]

Most significant for the expansion of German-Jewish immigrants all over America was, of course, the settlement in California. Thousands of Jews came there during the years of the gold rush, and many of them arrived directly from Europe and disembarked on the Pacific coast. In 1877 California's Jewish population counted close to 18,600 souls, that is, 8.2 percent of all American Jews—second only to the 80,600 Jews of New York State.[44] Reaching California in those days, overland or even by boat, was no easy task, and many perished on the way. Moses Bruml, who finally settled in Lockeford, California, arrived in 1849 from Bohemia. After three years of hard work in New York, Buffalo, and St. Louis, he decided in 1852 to buy a ticket for California:

> From New York I sailed to Nicaragua on the "Northern Light." The steamer landed us at Greytown or San Juan Del Norte, promising us that another steamer would come in soon and take us on our journey. The natives took us on small boats from the shore up the Nicaragua River, where we were left to care for ourselves. We waited here three days, but no steamer came, so the natives took us up the Nicaragua rapids and from there we footed it to the lake. We then crossed the Isthmus on mules, some twelve miles to the San Juan Del South, on the Pacific side, where we waited for the coming steamer. We waited there one month. . . . Some of our passengers got tired of waiting and exchanged their steamer tickets for a passage on board a trader steamer that landed on shore. They got to San Francisco two weeks after we did and their tales of hardships and privation were terrible. Some did not live through it. They had to live on crackers and syrup part of the time.

After many more adventures, and after some died of Panama fever, the party finally arrived in San Francisco.[45]

Bruml's trials were shared by many new arrivals who were not discouraged by the strains of voyage. When Benjamin visited California in the early 1860s he encountered quite a number of communities scattered around San Francisco, Sacramento, and the mining towns of the Sierras. As we know today, many of them later faded away with the gold fever, leaving only remnants of Jewish cemeteries. But those who remained paved the way for flourishing Jewish communities. San Francisco's Jewish population reached impressive numbers between 1855 and 1860, with estimates varying from 5,000 to 8,000, and even 10,000 souls.[46]

However, these early California congregations attracted only a small segment of the many Jewish young and single males, a tendency that was at the time typical of the region's general population. In San Francisco first services are recorded to have taken place in 1849 in a Polish congregation; services are reported one year later in a German congregation. Around 1860 Benjamin reported a third, Orthodox "Shomrei-Shaboss" founded by English, Polish, and Russian Jews. But according to a February 1856 report of Rabbi Eckmann, of the 7,000 Jews he estimated to be living in the city, only some two hundred members belonged to any of the three congregations.[47]

Up to the early 1860s Jewish communities sprang up and disappeared in many California locations, reflecting the ups and downs of Jewish business activities in this region. San Francisco's early immigrants established prospering wholesale and retail firms, taking advantage of the rapid population growth and the general scarcity of utilities. Branches of these firms sprang up in every mining place and shanty-town; they were managed by relatives sometimes brought over from Europe just for this purpose. Of the more permanent communities, Sacramento was one of the first. Its first congregation, orthodox B'nai Israel, dated from 1851. Germans and "Polishers," that is, immigrants from Posen, participated at first, but split some years later over the issue of Reform. Benjamin's account of the community, which he estimated at some 500 souls, was not favorable: in his opinion the local Jews demonstrated little religion and little charity.[48]

In San Diego, first High Holy Day services are reported from 1853; these were attended by only three Jews. The first organized congregation was officially established only in 1888, and the first synagogue was founded one year later. Other Jewish communities are known to have existed around 1860 in Marysville, Neap City, Grass Valley, Sonora, Placerville, and Stockton in the San Joaquin Valley.[49] In Los Angeles, which at the time was still in its first stages of development, some services probably were held as early as 1851. The census of 1850 counted only eight people with unquestionable Jewish names, all of them single males. A Hebrew Benevolent Society, concerned mainly with the burial of its members, was founded in 1854 with no more than thirty members. Only in 1862 was Los Angeles's first congregation founded. Benjamin had little praise for these, mostly young, men of the Los Angeles Jewish community, who showed little interest in religion.[50]

Fifty-four Jewish "male heads of households and unattached males" have been painstakingly traced for 1860 in Portland, Oregon, most of them immigrants from South Germany and only six American-born. This confirms Benjamin's report of about one hundred Jewish inhabitants who were keeping up a cemetery but had no *hazzan* or other official, all of whom were well-situated but extremely stingy.[51] Benjamin also discovered a Jewish community of some one hundred souls in Victoria, British Columbia, "representing the German element there."[52]

Stabilization: Demographic and Economic Trends

In the early 1860s the German-Jewish immigrants to the United States seemed to have come to rest. Although quite a few of them were still scouting out the country and wandering around, their greater part had already settled more or less permanently. They had started families, built houses and business stores, and established religious, social, and cultural organizations. In so doing they had laid the foundations of the future economic, social, and communal framework of American Jewry.

Permanent settlement and economic security resulted sooner or later in a more normalized demographic structure of Jewish communities. Even without sound statistical evidence we may safely assume that most of them, especially those recently established, still showed a remarkable preponderance of younger age groups. Age of marriage, at least of the male partners, was at first relatively high. Many families made up for the lost time by having many children at rather short intervals, as borne out by the demographically oriented local studies of recent years. In the case of Columbus, Ohio, only ten of the thirty-seven Jewish families identified in 1880 had less than five children. Fifteen families had five or six, and twelve from seven to ten.[53] This tendency is corroborated by the remarkable rise in the numbers of American-born Jews. In Cincinnati this percentage, according to the centennial U.S. census data, rose from 20 percent of the Jewish population in 1820 to one-third in 1850 and almost one-half in 1860; some 35 percent were still German-born. Many of the family histories of California Jews collected by Dr. Norton B. Stern demonstrate the same tendency.[54] This trend is summarized in table 3.2.

At first sight the change in the proportion of American-born Jews between 1850 and 1860 may not appear to be very significant. In some places—for example, Charleston or Philadelphia—their percentage even declined slightly. But we have to keep the massive immigration of this period in mind. The total increase of the Jewish population, from 15,000 in 1840 to 150,000 in 1860, was, of course, mainly caused by immigration. We would therefore expect a very significant *decline* in the relative number of American-born Jews. This did not occur. Even in Cincinnati, where

Table 3.2
The Jewish Population, 1850–1860: Place of Birth in Four Cities

Country	Boston No.	Percentage	Charleston No.	Percentage	Cincinnati No.	Percentage	Philadelphia No.	Percentage
United States								
1850	121	36.5	476	75.5	448	35.7	1,638	55.1
1860	474	40.9	468	73.8	2,295	48.9	3,684	53.9
Germany								
1850	123	37.0	84	13.3	645	51.4	1,042	35.0
1860	132	11.4	44	6.9	1,679	35.7	2,118	31.0
Poland and Prussia								
1850	35	10.6	34	5.4	46	3.7	69	2.3
1860	319	27.5	76	12.0	354	7.5	446	6.5
England								
1850	8	2.4	26	4.1	57	4.5	115	3.9
1860	76	6.6	12	1.9	124	2.6	198	2.9
Holland								
1850	22	6.6	1	0.1	—	—	24	0.8
1860	115	9.9	—	—	22	0.5	147	2.1
Other								
1850	23	6.9	9	1.6	58	4.7	87	2.9
1860	43	3.7	34	5.4	224	4.9	243	3.6
Total								
1850	332	100.0	630	100.0	1,254	100.0	2,975	100.0
1860	1,159	100.0	634	100.0	4,698	100.0	6,836	100.0

SOURCE: Kenneth Roseman, "The Jewish Population of America, 1850–1860: A Demographic Study of Four Cities," Ph.D. dissertation (Hebrew Union College—Jewish Institute of Religion, 1971), pp. 163–64.

the Jewish population of 1860 was more than five times larger than it had been ten years earlier, 1,507 of the additional 1,723 Jews are recorded to have been born in the state of Ohio. We may assume that most of them were small children born during these ten years in Cincinnati itself, in the established families or in those that arrived during these ten years.

Another piece of information one can glean from table 3.2 is the immigrants' settlement by country of origin. In 1850 Germany ranked first as the place of birth for foreign-born Jewish residents in all four cities. The data for 1860 are significantly different. In Cincinnati, the German-born, or—more accurately—the Bavarians, were still in first place but in Boston the immigrants from Prussia and Poland were now the majority of all foreign-born Jews. In all recorded cities they had gained ground at the expense of the southern German immigrants. (In this context I have seen fit to combine the immigrants from "Poland" and "Prussia," that is, mainly Posen and Silesia, because they did indeed belong together in their ethnic, religious, and cultural characteristics. As we shall see later, Jews from Posen were indeed regarded as "Polacks" by their contemporary Bavarian coreligionists.)

The changing pattern of the residential distribution of the Jewish population is also of interest. Generally, the first arrivals lived in modest rented homes, mostly over or near their place of business. First Jewish residential clusters were located in the poorer wards or quarters of the cities. Here rents were cheaper, and most of the customers of the retail clothing stores, which at the time was a typical Jewish business, lived in the neighborhood. As their economic conditions improved, the better-off Jewish families moved to more affluent quarters. There again they tended to reside together, and the places they had left were taken by the later-arriving Jewish immigrants of more modest means. This pattern was later repeated, when the sources of Jewish immigration moved eastward, first to Posen and West Prussia, and then to Poland and Russia.

New York City is one example of this development. With approximately 40,000 Jewish inhabitants, mostly from Germany or "Prussian Poland," in the late 1850s it was, as Benjamin observed, a city "crowded with poor Jews, and a burden for the community."[55] The residential distribution, the "semi-spontaneous formation of Jewish districts . . . [was] an attempt to retain cohesiveness in the midst of a disruptive environment."[56]

After 1850 the old ghetto was breaking up and others were being developed. As a result, two distinct residential sections of Jews evolved quite early on. By 1860 the poorer and unacculturated elements were housed in the old Jewish quarter bounded by Canal, Elm, Mott, and Bayard streets; it had become a rundown section although, some decades earlier, it had been the home of the most affluent German Jews. This section remained a predominantly Jewish quarter for later generations, forming a part of the western boundary of the later Russian-Polish immigrant ghetto. The richer, native-born or Americanized elements of the Jewish society in the 1860s sought homes in ethnically mixed midtown neighborhoods above Grand Street on the East Side. Prior to 1865, few Jews ventured north of 42nd Street.[57]

Economic and social ascent was at the time predominantly a function of the period of sojourn and the stage of "acculturation" or "Americanization." Under conditions of rapid demographic and economic expansion, almost everybody who had arrived early enough could take advantage of abundant opportunities. Some were more successful than the rest, but on the whole German-Jewish immigrants of the 1820s and 1830s were mostly better off than those who arrived later.

This development has been overstated all too often, although the generalizing enraptured admiration of the German-Jewish economic accomplishments has recently given way to a more subtle evaluation. Quite a few of the early immigrants, however, did gain prominence in the financial and general business world, and in public life. Seen in its real proportions, the Jewish role in perpetuating the American legend of unlimited opportunities deserves some attention.[58]

Prominent among the bankers rank the eight already-mentioned Seligman brothers. Another well-known financial tycoon was Salomon Loeb. He arrived from Worms in 1849, and after making some money in the dry-goods business in Cincinnati established an investment bank in New York. His partner was Abraham Kuhn, another Cincinnatian, who had retired from his clothing business. Kuhn, Loeb & Co. was headed, in the next generation, by Loeb's son-in-law Jacob H. Schiff, a scion of a well-to-do Frankfurt family, who became one of the central figures in American Jewish public life and charity. Henry Lehman arrived from Bavaria in 1844, followed by his brother in 1847, and both ran a general store in Montgomery, Alabama. The firm Lehman Brothers established its New York offices in 1858, after the arrival of two more younger brothers, to become one of the leading commodity and investment houses of the city. Herbert H. Lehman, governor of New York and a U.S. senator, champion of many Jewish causes, was the American-born son of one of the brothers.

Not all these bankers had arrived in America as poor steerage passengers and not all started their careers as peddlers. Quite a few, like August Belmont, came from established German-Jewish wealth. The brothers Philip and Gustav Speyer also descended from an old Frankfurt banking family; their banking house opened in New York in 1845 and soon became important in selling American Civil War loans to the public through their family and business connections in Frankfurt and London. A number of other financial enterprises with family connections in the old country were founded at a later stage as branches of the German houses, among others that of the brothers Paul and Felix Warburg from Hamburg, which was closely connected with Kuhn, Loeb & Co. Among the other names prominent in the financial circles of both countries were Arnhold, Bleichroeder, Hallgarten, Ickelheimer, and Ladenburg.

German Jews had a lasting impact as successful entrepreneurs in other fields as well. Abraham Gimbel came to New Orleans in 1835 from Bavaria and, after making his money as a peddler and dry-goods merchant in Indiana, became the founder of the Gimbel Brothers, Inc., department store chain. A similar career was that of Benjamin Bloomingdale, also from Bavaria, who arrived in New York in 1837. He peddled in Kansas and other Western states, and eventually opened a dry-goods store in New York that his American-born sons successfully took on. Julius Ochs of Fuerth arrived in 1845 to join siblings in Louisville, Kentucky. He served in the Mexican War and later in the Union army, and did business in Natchez, Mississippi, and Cincinnati. His eldest son became the son-in-law of Isaac M. Wise, and the publisher of the *New York Times*.

Simon Guggenheim, a tailor born in Lengnau, Switzerland, arrived in Philadelphia with his family in 1848. His son Meyer started peddling laces and ribbons in Pennsylvania until he stumbled into a chance investment in Colorado's ore mining and founded one of the wealthiest and best-known families of the American-Jewish aristocracy. Outside of New York we may mention the somewhat less-known "grain-king" Isaac Friedlander from San Francisco, who made a fortune as a rancher and grain exporter in the San Joaquin Valley.[59]

This parade of the successful elite could easily continue several more pages, but we may as well stop here. In our present context the important question remains that of relevance. How representative for the economic fate of the whole immigrant group were these, without doubt impressive, achievements of a few dozen enterprising individuals? And what was their real importance for the further development of Jewish immigrant society as a whole?

Here I tend to agree with the opinion of the late Simon Kuznets that

exceptional individual cases among a minority hardly matter. That Mr. X, a Jew by some definition, is a wealthy individual with an imposing stock of financial claims . . . has little significance in the economic life of the Jewish minority as a cohesive social group. For it is the functioning of the group as a whole that is decisive; whereas the attachment and the functioning of an individual or a small group is subject to the caprices of fortune and can never be strong enough to have much weight in the life of the minority—unless it enlists the latter through successful leadership. . . . If this argument is at all valid, the burden of emphasis in the economic structure of the Jews must be on the patterns of life and work of the larger masses, and not on such peripheral matters as their behavior as investors, or on the conspicuous successes of some small group of individuals who may have attained high positions in the world of wealth.[60]

It must be admitted that the American Jewish experience demonstrates an important deviation in the role of the wealthy elite, as compared with their parallel group in Germany. There many of the most successful wealthy Jews converted or severed all ties with the Jewish community. Those of the highest echelons tried hard to be admitted into the ranks of the ruling aristocracy, and they sometimes succeeded. In America many of the highest German-Jewish elite did play an important role in the life of American Jewry and were prominent in public leadership and philanthropy. At a later stage German-Jewish entrepreneurs became the employers of many Eastern European Jews, mainly in the clothing industry. But beside this, and in purely economic terms, their success was of little consequence for the whole group of German-Jewish immigrants, whose achievements, independent from the elite, were much more modest.

Nevertheless, almost everywhere the progress was impressive enough. Although almost no adequate quantitative studies of incomes and property are available to substantiate this impression, there can be no doubt about the process. In one of the more reliable recent studies, Stephen Mostov provides us with a well-founded picture of the income developments of Cincinnati's Jews between 1850 and 1860. His figures show that the average capital, inventory, and sales of Jewish-owned business firms in his sample doubled or more during the decade. The distribution of wealth within the Jewish community in 1860 shows an unquestionable positive relation between the amount of capital and date of arrival, and—probably owing to the same phenomenon—the place of birth.

All this stands to reason, of course, and would have been expected by sheer common sense, but some statistical evidence, partial as it is, is always welcome. Also interesting, and maybe less expected, is the fact that, taken together, the three hundred individuals in Mostov's sample were by no means a very rich group. Close to 60 percent owned up to $10,000, 10 percent less than $1,000, and nineteen people, or 6 percent of the sample, owned over $50,000—quite a lot of capital at that time. The emerging picture is one of a steadily rising middle-class group of quite notable achievements.[61]

An earlier study by the same author of Boston's Jewish immigrants reveals a similar picture. Assessments of personal and real income based on tax records indicate the close positive correlation of wealth to time of arrival, although on a remarkably lower level than in Cincinnati, probably due to the later start of Jewish settlement in Boston. As in Cincinnati, the distribution of wealth became more differentiated with the time of settlement of the Jewish community. In 1850 and 1855 nearly all Jewish taxpayers were assessed as owning between $200 and $1,000 worth of property. By 1860, 51 percent of the sample owned less than $200, and 33 percent possessed between $1,000 and $10,000. No Jew was found in the category of "$10,000 and more," in which 13 percent of all taxpayers belonged in 1860.

The main explanation for these intragroup differences is time of arrival. Many of those who had come to the United States in the late 1840s or early 1850s had gained some property, whereas those just arriving had virtually no property or money. The poorer Jews had lived in Boston an average of only two years, compared with the average of seven years for the more prosperous. The same pattern is repeated in the other local analyses that are available.[62]

This trend of development is, of course, typical for the economic adaptation of any immigrant group in expanding economies and in areas of new settlement. In the case of the German Jews it was mostly the commercial opportunities that were seized as the main route of rapid advance. Concentration in the commercial sector had for a long time been the most outstanding feature of Jewish economic pursuits in the old country; it became even more strikingly onesided in the new one. As we have seen, many young artisans took to peddling after their arrival in America, either because they could not find employment in the crafts they had learned or because they considered commercial ventures to be more promising. After a few years some diversification of the occupational structure did take place, but, again, mainly inside the commercial sector.

Boston is representative because of the large number of artisans among its first-generation Jewish settlers.

> Those who began as artisans such as tailors and cutters, opticians and watchmakers, or cigarmakers would become merchants of these products, establishing clothing, jewelry, and tobacco stores. Petty merchants succeeded through gradually accruing greater inventories, while peddlers often, though not always, established small stores after they had lived in the community for a few years.[63]

Social and occupational readjustments certainly proceeded apace as the time of immigration receded into the past, mainly for the second or third generation. But the distribution never approached "normalcy"—if we consider the occupational structure of the majority of the population to be "normal." This rigidity of occupational distribution has been observed in relevant scholarly studies whose principal results are summarized in tables 3.3 and 3.4. Some earlier studies corroborate these findings and show only minor deviations in other areas.[64]

Although these data are of only limited value for a more detailed in-depth analysis of Jewish occupational preferences and their change over time, some general conclusions can nevertheless be drawn. The concentration in the commercial sector is only the most basic and well-known in American-Jewish historiography. Also evident is the preference for

Table 3.3
The Proportion of Jews in Mercantile Trades in
Selected American Citites c. 1860

Community	Peddlers (%)	Merchants (%)	Clerks (%)	Total (%)	(No.)
Boston (1845–61)	32	9	10	51	(208)
Cincinnati (1860)	8	60	17	85	(642)
San Francisco (1860s)	10	52	16	78	(1,167)
Detroit (1870s)	20	50	9	79	(245)
Syracuse, N.Y. (1860)	53	22	9	84	(230)
Easton, Pa.	56	19	0	85	(43)

SOURCE: Stephen G. Mostov, "A 'Jerusalem' on the Ohio: The Social and Economic History of Cincinnati's Jewish Community, 1840–1875," Ph.D. dissertation (Brandeis University, 1981), p. 107.

Table 3.4
Occupational Distribution, 1850–1860

Category	Charleston		Philadelphia	
	1850	1860	1850	1860
No.	185	167	741	1,892
I. Retail Trade (%)	69.9	49.7	45.5	36.6
II. Clothing Trade (%)	7.5	13.8	23.6	24.5
III. Manufacturing (%)	3.2	5.4	13.4	14.5
V. Services (%)	5.9	15.6	6.1	13.5
Other (%)	13.5	15.5	11.4	10.1
Total (%)	100.0	100.0	100.0	100.0

SOURCE: Kenneth Roseman, "The Jewish Population of America,1850–1860: A Demographic Study of Four Cities," Ph.D. dissertation (Hebrew Union College—Jewish Institute of Religion, 1971), p. 165.

independent self-employment, which was, however, easier to achieve in the newly emerging cities of the West than in the older established communities. Peddling, for most Jewish merchants the first step to independent economic life, was pursued in smaller communities by more people and for a longer period of time.

In the larger cities Jewish immigrants could find employment in commerce or practice their skilled crafts with Jewish firms. New York had the largest percentage of workers and commercial employees. It has been estimated that between 1840 and 1860 half of New York's economically active Jews were workers, most of them tailors or shoemakers. Some 25 percent of new immigrants arriving in the early 1850s had learned these crafts in the old country.[65] Similar percentages in Boston are probably explained by the place of origin of its Jewish immigrants: Posen and West Prussia. An unpublished study of Boston's "Jewish Brahmins" identifies a Jewish working population of 932 adults in 1860, including sixty-five women. No less than 44.2 percent are classified as "skilled blue-collar workers," mostly tailors, capmakers, and shoemakers. Another 23 percent were peddlers, petty proprietors, clerks, and other "low white-collar" operators.[66]

The Jewish concentration in clothing included peddlers, independent merchants, and industrial entrepreneurs, as well as hired workers, subcontractors working in their homes, and white-collar employees. By 1860 the manufacture, wholesale distribution, and sale of ready-made clothing and other apparel made a considerable part of the livelihood of Cincinnati's Jews, who virtually dominated the industry. And what was true in Cincinnati was evidently true everywhere in the United States: on the East Coast, in the South, in the Midwest, and in the far West.

The similarity between occupational patterns of Jews in America and those of Jews in Germany, and in other European countries, raises interesting questions about a continuity of group-specific patterns that prevails under changing geographical, economic, and political conditions. In the case of the German-Jewish immigrants it was decisive that their previous skills were at just that time in demand by an emerging, and rapidly expanding, industry. The production of cheap ready-made men's clothing started first of all in New York, Philadelphia, and Boston. Historians credit the Germans of these cities, along with native-born Americans and Irish tailors, with the pioneering entrepreneurship responsible for the industry's fast development. There is reason to believe that a good part of these entrepreneurs, as well as of the employed tailors, were German Jews.[67]

The massive entry of Jewish businessmen into the various clothing branches was on the other hand a quite natural consequence of their earlier pursuits as peddlers and storekeepers selling secondhand clothing. Before mid-century rich Americans wore tailor-made garments; ordinary people sewed their own. Only the very poor bought the discarded wear of the rich in secondhand stores owned mainly by Jews. Evidence for this continuous chain of economic pursuit is the often repeated career of the Jewish peddler who somewhat later advanced to own a secondhand clothing shop on Chatham Street.

Newly arrived German-Jewish immigrants peddled on the New York streets and fanned out into the neighboring area. After saving some small capital they would invest it in a modest inventory and rent a small shop in the densely populated downtown New York, where most of their prospective customers dwelled. Caricatures and humorous verse tinged with unveiled anti-Jewish ridicule entrenched the stereotype of the "Chatham Street Clo Jew" in American folklore. The Jewish tradesman was described in spiteful terms as glibly manipulating the prospective customer, until he emerged from his store "in garments of the strangest make, dimensions and fitness. . . . This street, reader, was in the old times of this island, a warpath of Manhattan Indians to the West. . . . The old red men scalped their enemies, the Chatham Clo'men skin theirs."[68] In Buffalo, Commercial Street and Main Street played the same role as Chatham Street in New York City. The term "Commercial Street Jew," which associated Jewish merchants with this slum neighborhood, was found among the credit ratings of the Dun and Bradstreet Co., where it obviously needed no more elaboration.[69]

The fact that Jewish textile manufacturers later became almost exclusive employers of the industry's non-Jewish workers, who would toil under abominable conditions, became an inevitable source of friction. In 1853 a demand for higher wages for Cincinnati's seamstresses found

> unexpected support from the city's leading businessmen and clergy—an element of the population not previously noted for its support of working-class aspirations. The resentment of the non-Jewish elite towards Jewish manufacturers was evidenced in the tone of the debate, filled as it was with references to a certain "class of the community," and "usurers," and "Jew shops."[70]

The anti-Jewish bias was further enhanced by—but also widely responsible for—the intragroup cooperation of Jewish enterprise on almost all levels. In more than one sense, German-Jewish immigrants indeed constituted an economic subcommunity. A network of business and family relationships, within the place of residence and with other parts of the country, proved to be an equal, or even more effective, cohesive factor of Jewish solidarity as religious or social contacts. Mutual economic dependency, constantly kept alive by the anti-Jewish bias in the environment, was a feature observed in almost every local case study. Jewish preference for independent economic status, and specialization in certain economic fields, fostered and preserved these tendencies.

As business and inventories expanded, credit became a central necessity. Jewish merchants had severe difficulties in obtaining credit from non-Jewish bankers or suppliers. In mid-century America, credit was granted very cautiously, after collecting much information on the trust-worthiness of prospective clients. Special investigation agencies were employed for the purpose by wholesalers and banking firms. The full collection of the Dun and Bradstreet records, deposited and indexed at the Baker Library of the Harvard Business School, are a valuable source of information on the economic standing and contemporary image of Jewish businessmen.

The most important reason for non-Jewish bankers and merchants to refuse credit to Jews was ingrained prejudice and mistrust. Although recognized to be hardworking and competent businessmen, Jews were distrusted for their supposed dishonesty. In many cases the company's correspondents dispensed with investigating the individual Jew, his character, or his business, basing their negative verdict solely on the general prejudice against all Jews. In this situation Jewish businessmen were indeed forced to seek credit inside the Jewish merchant community itself, and sometimes even to fall back on family and business connections in their old homeland.[71]

In the first thirty or forty years after the start of the immigration, German Jews in America came a long way. They settled all over the country, founded families, and raised many children. Those who despaired and returned to Germany, or were drawn into Gentile society, disappeared from the vision of America's emerging Jewish society. Of them we have little information, and even their relative numbers remain a matter of conjecture. Most of those who remained in the fold of the Jewish communities attained modest economic security and comfort. Some had amassed fortunes and become prominent businessmen.

Having been successful as individuals, German Jews sought to assert themselves as a group. The "substitute-emancipation" found in the New World, and the tensions of a rapidly modernizing secular society, had put their Jewish identity to the test. To preserve this identity both individually and collectively, despite the religious laxity prevailing among most of them, redefinition was the order of the day. By leaving their old homes they had not only severed family ties, but they had also left the long-established legal, social, and religious framework of the largely autonomous, self-governing Jewish *"Kehillah."* Trying to build new communities in an entirely different environment was no easy task. Voluntary affiliation was the only way to achieve it, but this was by no means a matter of course. The way in which these Jews overcame difficulties and finally succeeded in this endeavor was to decide the future character of the German-Jewish immigrant society as a distinct subgroup of American Jewry.

4

The Social Structure of an Emerging Community

The "Sunlight of Freedom" and Some Shadows

Providence has opened for us this big house, this golden homeland. . . . Under the sunlight of freedom [American-German Jewry] magnificently prospers, by far more vigorously than where its progress is forced upon it, or even hampered by spiritual or secular authority.[1]

The author of this enthusiastic statement, written in 1847, was Isaac Mayer Wise. Born in Bohemia in 1819, he had arrived in America only some months earlier in 1847, to serve at the pulpit of Congregation Beth El in Albany, New York. Wise was initially more of a pragmatist than a radical ideologue of religious Reform. But in Albany even his modest attempts to modify ritual to achieve a more decorous service and the installation of a mixed choir met with ardent opposition. After being fired he established a new congregation, which he headed until his appointment as rabbi of Cincinnati's prestigious B'nai Yeshurun in 1854. There he emerged as one of the most important leaders of American Judaism. Through his newspapers, the English *The Israelite* (founded 1854, renamed *American Israelite* in 1874) and the German *Die Deborah* (founded 1855), and through his organizational zeal, Wise exerted over almost half a century, till his death in 1900, an immense influence on the pivotal religious and institutional issues of American Jewish life.

Jews had been granted full legal equality with all other religious denominations by the Constitution and the Bill of Rights. State constitutions were somewhat slower to apply these high-minded principles and lagged in granting their "non-Christians" full civil rights such as the right to be elected to office. But when Wise arrived in America, only North Carolina and New Hampshire still lagged behind in their relevant legislation.

Still, as the immigrants were soon to learn, this "Golden Homeland" was not flawless. Republican liberalism and political pluralism ruled the political and public sphere, but bigotry and anti-Jewish prejudice did not disappear from the minds of European Gentiles just because they had crossed the ocean. And although the Jews constituted a very small and dispersed minority during most of the nineteenth century—only about 0.5 percent or less of the population even in 1877—entrenched hostility was of remarkable longevity. Puritan piety could admire the "mythical Jews" as the progenitors of Christianity, but this did not necessarily apply to one's Jewish neighbor. Vicious ridicule and derogatory labels and images were not unusual. In the press, in literature and on the stage, and in daily social contacts, stereotypes like the tenacious Shylock-image often reappeared. Jews were depicted as the incarnations of greed, materialism, commercial double-dealing, and anti-Christian vengeance.[2]

We have already come across some expressions of these sentiments in American folklore and in the discreet credit ratings of the business world. Indications of more violent actions against individual Jews can also be found in the contemporary and memoir literature. In 1850 a report of a pogromlike assault that had presumably occurred on the eve of Yom Kippur in New York was reprinted in Germany, to be later vigorously denied by Isaac M. Wise.[3] Openly demonstrated hostility and social ostracism became increasingly the case toward the end of the century; this was probably triggered by attempts of the Jewish *nouveaux riches* to penetrate the closed circle of the Protestant elite. But in the 1840s and 1850s discrimination appeared only at the margins of the public scene and was couched in such indirect forms as the observance of Sunday laws, the refusal to admit non-Christian military chaplains, or the Christian wording of Thanksgiving proclamations.

In some instances Protestant zeal and competing business interests combined to promote legislative acts to force Jewish storekeepers to close on Sunday, instead of or in addition to keeping closed on Saturday. When the issue was brought to the test in Cincinnati in 1846, the court ruled in favor of the Jewish claimant that the Sunday Law was "un-constitutional and incompatible with the spirit of free tolerance."[4] But this seems to have been an exception. Similar decisions in other locations went against the Jewish communities, declaring the Sunday laws legal.

Sometimes one or the other of the legislators gave vent to openly anti-Semitic arguments. In 1855 the delegate of Santa Cruz County in California proposed a "Jew tax" that would hamper all Jewish business. He would have preferred to have all Jews banned not only from his county but also from the state, because they "were a class of people who only came here to make money and leave as soon as they had effected their object. They did not invest their money in the country or cities. They all intended or hoped to settle in their 'New Jerusalem.'"[5] The speech evoked angry reactions in the local press and may have been an exceptional outburst, but the fact that it was widely published and rebutted in the California and nationwide Jewish press, and even reprinted in Germany,[6] indicates Jewish concern about the implications of Sunday-law legislation. It is questionable that most Jewish storekeepers were at the time indeed so orthodox as to insist on closing their shops on Saturday, but the Jewish leadership obviously perceived the issue as a symptom "of the wider movement to gain official recognition of Christianity in American law. Antebellum Jewry feared the potency of the 'entering wedge.'"[7]

The affair had a wider political context because delegate Stowe was at the time seeking nomination as candidate of the nativist "American Party" for governor. This movement, better known also as the "Know-Nothing" movement, was an extreme expression of Protestant fanaticism against Catholics and immigrants. Anti-Semitism appeared only in veiled terms in its public utterances, and some Jewish politicians were even deluded enough to support the movement, be it for its anti-Catholicism or to prove their unalloyed Americanism. But most Jewish leaders recognized the imminent double danger of the movement's zeal for the principles of a Christian state, as well as its anti-immigrant demagogy.

This explains the vivid interest with which the Jewish press in Germany followed every success and failure of their American kin in the public and political arena. Isaac M. Wise, in his 1847 report quoted earlier, went out of his way to praise the civic and religious freedom of the German Jews:

> There was a time when the Israelite was ashamed and denied his religion, but now he is proud to delare "I am a German Jew.". . . He is actively participating in religious, as well as in political life. He is a patriot, because he has reason to be one. . . . In the army you can find Jewish volunteers serving the fatherland; Where state officers are chosen you will surely find the Jew voting for the best candidate; an enormous number of Jews is to be found in every voluntary service, like the fire-brigade or the citizen-guard.[8]

Some years later another correspondent, Dr. Mayer, "preacher" at the Portuguese Reform congregation of Charleston, castigated the American Jewish public leaders and politicians for their indifference toward the Know-Nothings:

> Surprisingly even some Jews have joined this party in their mistaken belief that their coreligionists are being suppressed only in Catholic countries, and

forgetting that some Protestant countries are not better in their treatment of Jews. . . . Alas, most of the politically high-positioned Jews in our Republic bear only the name, but lack any interest or sentiment for Jews or Judaism. . . . Still, all should be on guard, because also in this free country the most hideous prejudice against our people . . . is suppressed only by our constitution, but surfaces where- and whenever possible.[9]

A famous test case of the administration's willingness to defend the constitutional rights of the Jewish minority was the conclusion and ratification of a trade agreement with Switzerland in the early 1850s. The Swiss had demanded the inclusion of an explicit proviso limiting the agreed-upon privileges to American "Christians alone." After the draft was accepted by the American negotiators, Jewish reactions and the elusive responses of the administration were exchanged over several years. But this did not prevent the formal ratification of the treaty in 1855, with a somewhat watered-down version of the discriminatory clause.

One activist in the public campaign against this clause was Dr. Sigismund Waterman, who had come from Bavaria in 1841 and had in 1848, as the first Jew recorded, received a degree in medicine from Yale Medical School. Besides his many articles in the English-language Jewish press, Waterman also saw fit to inform the Jews in Germany of this matter, which he considered to be

of major importance for us, as well as for our German coreligionists. . . . It was mainly the German Israelites [in America] who paid any attention at all to this matter. They wrote and signed petitions, while our English Jews apparently did nothing. It is impossible to decide whether this was caused by their conviction that the purpose of our efforts was unachievable, or out of indifference and timidity.[10]

Sephardim, "Bayers," and "Polacks"

By "our English Jews" Waterman obviously alluded in a somewhat generalizing way to all non-German Jews in America. It is questionable if such a group really existed outside the ephemeral sphere of some mixed religious or philanthropic organizations. Some years later, reviewing the different trends in American Judaism, I. M. Wise lumped them again together: "Of all classes of American Jewry none is as neglected and demoralized as the American-English. This includes the native Americans, the English, the anglicized Poles and Germans, as well as the immigrants from the West Indies and Italy." By "native Americans" Wise obviously meant the remnants of the old Sephardic families. To the congregations of the "Poles," which had mostly been established by immigrants from Posen and West Prussia who were probably no less "German" than the Bohemia-born Wise, he was at least ready to concede some Judaistic knowledge and tradition, along with his criticism of their ritual and religious education. But "the American-English Jews have nothing left, beside their Minhag [i.e., ritual], be it Portuguese or Polish."[11]

The first German-Jewish immigrants of the colonial and revolutionary period, and even those who arrived around the turn of the century and who cared to preserve their religious identity, had been welcomed into the old Portuguese congregations. Some of them had married into the old Sephardic families and been well-integrated into Sephardic society. They behaved, or posed, as original "Sephardic Grandees," despite their Bavarian origin.

This does not necessarily describe the whole range of mutual group relations, which were probably not always harmonious. But it certainly applies to quite a number of the more prominent early German-Jewish immigrants. Once accepted, they seem to have shared not only the religious conservatism but also the prejudice and condescension of the old established Portuguese Jewish aristocrats toward the later-arriving German Jews. Naomi Cohen finds for the "aristocratic pretensions of the Sephardim, who would not permit the 'boorish' Germans to ride on their coat-tails" a precedent in the European experience of the seventeenth and eighteenth centuries, but she also emphasizes the integration of the German-Jewish immigrants of the earlier period. "Despite their snobbishness and peculiarities, the Sephardim were still Jews who provided an anchor in an alien society which preferred men to affiliate with any church rather than with none. In the minds of some Germans 'Sephardization' also symbolized a way of achieving social status."[12]

The Sephardic attitude changed with the influx of more German Jews into the country, a change duly recognized by contemporaries: "Time which brings with it many changes in the condition of men," wrote the *Asmonean* in 1850,

> increased the nominal force of the German Jews and rapidly advanced them in education and enterprise. . . . It must be conceded that there has been . . . more enterprise, energy, and resolution, more ambition and more decision of character displayed by the German Jews than among the Portuguese, although we are bound to admit that the Portuguese Jews have ever been orthodox and strict in the observance of their religion. . . . So fierce and vindictive were the prejudices entertained by the Portuguese toward the German Jews, that they mourned a son or a daughter as dead, who intermarried with them.[13]

Even if this last statement was exaggerated, in view of the quite frequent intermarriage of Sephardim with German Jews (as, in fact, also of Sephardim with non-Jews), the paragraph certainly reflected the spirit of its time. A conservative Jewish periodical in Breslau praised the religious orthodoxy of the Sephardim, even showing some understanding for their attitude:

> The first arrivals from Germany and Poland were received in the most brotherly fashion, but as the stream began to flow stronger and many an unworthy individual came here, the newcomers began to be looked upon with hostile eyes. . . . These peddlers and common laborers could hardly expect to be treated by the English-speaking aristocratic bankers and great merchants as equals even in respect to religion. When they visited their synagogue they were, if at all admitted, given permission to occupy only the seats nearest the door, since only a small place was reserved for strangers.[14]

The "Bavarian grandees" identified with the Sephardic elite, and sometimes they replaced them. The Sephardic congregation of Charleston, founded in 1749, had for over a century adhered to its traditional rites, to what Nathan Glazer called a "dignified Orthodoxy . . . a living museum of the Sephardic practice."[15] Around 1850 the orthodoxy of the founders had been preserved, but the leadership of many congregations had been taken over by Germans. But "even though the elitist Sephardim had disappeared, their Ashkenazi successors continued to pretend to the aristocracy and high status ascribed their predecessors."[16] How and whereto these predecessors "disappeared" remains a matter of conjecture.

In some locations, such as Baltimore, no early Sephardic congregation existed. In the mid-eighteenth century, individual Jewish families are known to have arrived there from Germany, sometimes via New York or Philadelphia. After they became part of the city's merchant elite they demonstrated the same pattern: although they did not renounce their religion, and took the lead in the constitutional fight to grant full civil rights to Maryland's Jews, they painstakingly kept aloof from later Jewish arrivals. They contributed to Sephardic congregations of New York and kept up their membership and seats in Philadelphia's Sephardic Mikveh Israel, but took no part in the establishment of Baltimore's own congregations. In 1857 one prominent community leader related that when he arrived in Baltimore "there were about a dozen of native Jews. . . . Although of German origin, they kept to themselves, strictly apart from the newcomers, considering it rather below their dignity to have any social relations with them."[17]

As could be expected, the immigrants' reaction was ambiguous. At first awed by the wealth and stature of the established Sephardic and Bavarian "grandees," they soon discovered the advantages of sheer numbers. Already in 1825 the first German congregation seceded from New York's Sephardic Shearith Israel, and it was soon followed by many others. Some of these congregations were able to engage the services of the first ordained rabbis in the United States. Consequently, standing at "the receiving end of Sephardic snobbishness," they criticized the religious laxity and communal indifference of the older families, boasting the superiority of their own, university-trained rabbis. On the other hand, the earlier German immigrants "looked down upon those Jews who had come from Prussia-dominated Poland and places farther east. Farther east, as in the Sephardic-German case, presupposed a less cultured stratum."[18]

Conceit was, however, no monopoly of the Sephardic-Bavarian "grandees." In 1846 a member of New York's most prestigious German congregation, Emanu-El, describes a meticulously ranked social order:

All congregations here are far behind the great German communities in their educational level, a quite natural situation, considering the fact that most of the local Jews belong to the lower classes. . . . If South-Germans are so different from the North-Germans, the differences between entirely foreign nationals must be tremendous. The Portuguese regards himself to be the aristocrat among the Jews and his bearing is in complete accordance with his conceitedness. He is a gentleman. Some individual English Jews can be found here, but the majority are Dutch and Polish Jews who have come here after living for a long time in England, where they adopted English customs and manners. He belongs to the genteel class.

The local Pole is the dirtiest creature of all classes, and he is responsible for the disparagement of the name "Jew" even here. The Dutch Jew is by far better, an honest fellow despite his coarse clumsiness. The German, the majority among the Jews here, is industrious and adapts soon enough to the American way of life. Men of substance can be found among them, businessmen and manufacturers as well as landowners. The German is haughty toward the Pole, who in turn hates him. The Dutch competes with the German, and though the English deems himself superior to the German he associates with him on quite friendly terms.[19]

Rudolf Glanz has tried to explain the antagonism with reference to the social, cultural, and religious differences between Bavarian and Prussian-Polish Jews at home, and to the various times of emigration. In his opinion, once in America the "Polack"'s adjustment was further handicapped by the fact that, in contrast to the "Bayer," who arrived together with Gentile German immigrants, the "Polack" had no non-Jewish fellow immigrants from his own country. Compared with the Bavarian-Jewish peddler of the West, whose customers were German-speaking settlers, the "Polack, because of his ignorance of the German language and customs, was at a definite disadvantage."[20]

Glanz's assessments suffer from a somewhat simplistic overrating of alleged economic factors. The subject of the economic and cultural relations of Jewish and Gentile Germans will be dealt with later, but its importance appears to be highly exaggerated. The fact that massive Jewish emigration from Posen, West Prussia, and Silesia started some decades later than the Bavarian exodus provides a far more plausible explanation of their lesser economic achievements in America.

Although we lack exact statistical evidence, it is quite possible that by 1860 the "Poles" may well have balanced the numbers of West and South German Jewish immigrants. The Jews of Prussian-dominated Poland were at the time the main source of the immigration of "Polacks." In their cultural and religious outlook these Jews were admittedly closer to their Eastern Jewish neighbors than to the Bavarians, but they were by no means ignorant of the German language. In Posen many Jews regarded themselves, and were manipulated by the Prussian authorities, as the standard-bearers of German culture in the newly annexed territories.

According to some estimates, close to 47,000 Jews emigrated from the Grand Duchy of Posen between 1824 and 1871, many of them to the United States. Up to 12,000 of them crossed the ocean between 1835 and 1852.[21] Adding the unknown number of West Prussian and Silesian Jews, in addition to those from Galicia and Russian Poland, the numbers of the "Polacks" at mid-century must have been quite considerable. Also, their places of settlement cannot have been far from those of the "Bayers." Otherwise the quite early establishment in all parts of the country of so many congregations adhering to Polish ritual would be unexplainable.

Toward 1860 the part of the "Polacks" among the new immigrants increased, as evidenced in Syracuse, New York, where the number of Polish-Jewish immigrants between 1855 and 1860 is recorded to have been almost the same as of German Jews from all regions.[22] In New York as well, many new Polish-ritual congregations were established after 1840. As Grinstein states,

> Many of these Polish Jews came from the province of Posen . . . but were always called Polish, and had little in common with the German Jews of New York; . . . On their arrival in America they either clung to the English and Dutch Jews or created their own synagogues and institutions. The Polish Jews, particularly those from Posen, set up distinctions between themselves and the Russian Jews.[23]

The same was true of San Francisco as well. In 1856 Dr. Julius Eckmann complained that

> the people [who] even in this land of freedom [have] still to fight outside prejudice, fritter away [their] power by internal strife. All over the United

States the Bavarian and Alsatian immigrants are so opposed to the Poles that even marriages between them are extremely rare. This antipathy is here demonstrated by the fact that we have a duplicate of each of the few creations we were at all able to accomplish—two synagogues, two Benevolent Societies of the men, and again two of the women . . . one for German, and the other for Poles (including Russians, Prussians, Bohemians, etc.).[24]

Two years later Eckmann returned to the subject in a (this time unsigned) report. Although he had meanwhile founded an English-language paper, *The Gleaner,* he explained that "its editor" was unable to print his opinion on the true conditions of the Jewish community, fearing the reaction of the "blind power of the people, whose vanity may be offended." What he had to report, among others, was apparently his own story: Three years earlier he had been engaged as rabbi of the reformed German congregation, and had established a religious school. "Unfortunately, it was discovered that, born in Posen, he was a 'Polack.' This alone would have been enough to rouse the hatred of the Germans." To make things worse he had refused to admit a *Shohet* [ritual slaughterer] who was known to do work on the Sabbath and to eat non-kosher food. Consequently the rabbi was fired, to be replaced after a vacancy of two years by a candidate from Landau, "who as their landsman will probably be more successful." It is, however, noteworthy that this particular "Polack" had been ordained in Berlin after studying there for nine long years.[25]

In religious observance the Poles undoubtedly outdid the Germans, and their congregations therefore gained the membership of many English and Dutch Jews, who tended to be more conservative in religious practice. As for their secular culture and education, they may have been somewhat behind the "Bayers," but certainly not so much as to justify the latter's contempt. On the other hand, their economic accomplishments were indeed far less impressive. An investigation of residential patterns of the early Jewish population in Syracuse, New York, has shown that Bavarian Jews, who were the first to settle in the city and to succeed in their economic endeavors, moved together to better neighborhoods, whereas the later-arriving Polish and Russian Jews took the places left vacant downtown.[26] Similar developments have been established for Cincinnati by comparing the respective properties recorded in 1860 for the members of German and Polish congregations.[27]

There may be some substance to the argument of Rudolf Glanz ascribing the economic success of the Bavarians first and foremost to their close family and "old country" connections in the sphere of business. We have already noted the importance of these relations inside the closeknit Jewish community. There is, however, no evidence that Jews of "Polish" origin were excluded from this community, or, alternatively, did not develop a similar system of their own. In my opinion the single most important factor of economic and social success remains to be found in the date of arrival of the various groups of immigrants. Especially in the developing West, before and until the many new settlements were connected by railroads, being first on the spot could make all the difference. Many of the luckier Bavarians made use of these opportunities by simply being there before the "Polacks."

Social stratification according to the date of arrival is, of course, a typical trait of every immigrant society, as was the case at all times, and in other ethnic groups, in America. Still, these different economic and social accomplishments did not necessarily cause intragroup barriers or even the hostile antagonisms that have been observed in the case of German Jews. It is therefore doubtful that they constituted the main, or even a major, cause for these tensions.

The reasons must be sought elsewhere. The "Bayers" had evidently brought their prejudiced attitude toward the "Polacks" from the old country, where it had its own manifestations among the autochthonous "Germans" of Jewish communities. Additional factors were the family-oriented chain-migration and settlement of the first immigrated German Jews, and their remarkably persistent group cohesion. But the core of the problem seems to lie in the tenacity of an isolationist self-confidence, or even arrogance, generally ascribed to the German Jews. According to Marshall Sklare, writing in 1971, these "differences and antagonisms persist and can [still] be readily observed, even when Germans and East Europeans are no longer separated by wide class and cultural gulfs."[28]

Whether or not in fact these attitudes persist today to any significant degree, the clash of mentalities was certainly disturbing at the time. However, between 1840 and 1880, it was still far from attaining the critical dimensions of the intragroup conflict of later years, after the start of the Eastern European mass immigration. Up to that time Gentile Americans generally regarded the Jews as members of one of the many nationality groups and identified them by language. "Neither natives nor immigrants had ears sensitive enough to discriminate among all the shades of German dialect; furthermore, the spoken German of Bavarian Jews in these years was not much closer to the language of Goethe than was the spoken Yiddish of Posener Jews."[29]

The two decades before the Civil War were the formative years for the institutional and religious framework of American Jewry, and important elements of this structure have been preserved to this very day. The process of creating new congregations, charitable associations, and cultural or recreational establishments went on all over the United States, as more and more immigrants arrived. Mobility and change were the main characteristics of this period, but even present-day institutions of Jewish communal life bear the signature of the different shades and peculiarities of the immigrant society and its internal strife.

Congregations, Lodges, and Jewish Identity

"Judaism here is still young but awaiting a fortunate development," wrote Rabbi Max Lilienthal in one of his first reports from New York.

> But it would be wrong to view it with German eyes and evaluate it according to German perspectives. It would indeed be a grave error to expect the local communities to accomplish what [European] German communities can do. We lack here the rich class, as so far only poor people have immigrated, who have still to work hard; also we lack the great educated class of city-dwellers, as most of the immigrants came from rural regions; on the other hand, we also lack the disgusting class of the indifferent: America's Jews are attached to their faith by heart and will.[30]

We may be skeptical about the assumed religious fervor of the American Jews, and Lilienthal himself may have been less optimistic after a few more years. Yet he was unquestionably right about what could be expected of Jewish communities in the United States, for the simple reason that no communities resembling in any sense the European type of Jewish communal organization existed.

America's congregations lacked the legal status of European Jewish communities, which were granted the rights of taxation and internal jurisdiction. Nevertheless the synagogues exerted some disciplinary power over Jews through the social pressure and the monopoly of certain religious rites.

> In particular, they controlled the cemeteries, and almost all Jews wished to be buried in hallowed ground. But more important . . . was the fact that . . . the individual Jew could not yet conceive of himself as totally separated from the group. And so the heads of the Jewish community could in turn make certain demands on Jews. They could insist that their members obey the dietary laws, be married by the "minister" of the congregation, attend services, and so on. And they actually secured some measure of obedience.[31]

As long as congregations were few, small, and relatively homogeneous they could, uncontested, perform these functions. Their members had gained economic and social positions in colonial times, and many of them participated in the revolutionary struggle for independence. With growing affluence and integration in the non-Jewish environment, synagogues became more ostentatious and services more decorous, imitating the example of the predominant Protestant churches. The leaders of the Sephardic congregations aspired to a situation in which, through the "dignified orthodoxy" of their worship, Judaism would have enhanced respectability and equal standing as one of the many religious denominations in American society. At the same time continuous and deepening contacts with non-Jewish neighbors and friends, and frequent intermarriage, entailed the diminishing observance of strict religious laws and rituals. The first stirring of reformed ritual and ceremony, such as requests for a weekly sermon and some prayers in English, had appeared in the 1820s in the Sephardic congregations of Charleston and New Orleans.[32] These early tendencies were a part of the Jewish communal and religious situation with which the new immigrants were confronted upon their arrival in the New World.

The early immigrants had adapted to the ritual and religious standard of the existing congregations. After some time and with growing numbers the immigrants, accustomed to the German or Polish ritual of their home synagogues, established their own new congregations. In 1840 there were only eighteen officially recognized Jewish congregations in the United States. In addition to them we may assume a greater number of rudimentary congregations that assembled more or less regularly in private homes on Sabbaths and holidays. A decade later the number of established congregations had risen to 76, to reach a full 277 in 1877.[33]

Whether or not "immigration stirred signs of life in the near moribund American Jewish community,"[34] there can be little doubt about the religious and communal Jewish renaissance in its wake. The native Sephardic Jews, and the earlier Central European immigrants that had integrated with them, constituted a progressively acculturated group inside which trends of assimilation were already far advanced. Even if they preserved the Orthodox ritual in their synagogues, this was mainly a matter of form. In their everyday life religion did not play a major role. As early as 1777 a German officer who fought in the Revolutionary War observed in his diary: "The Jews cannot . . . be told, like those in our country, by their beards and costumes, but are dressed like all other citizens, shave regularly and also eat pork. . . . Moreover they do not hesitate to intermarry. The Jewish women have their hair dressed and wear French finery like the women of other faiths."[35]

Fifty years later the picture had certainly not changed, and assimilation had become even more visible. In 1783 Haym Salomon had complained in a letter from Philadelphia about how *venik Yidishkayt* (little Jewishness) there was in America. Almost sixty years later Rabbi Max

Wiener still lamented the poor state of religious observance in both Portuguese and Polish congregations. In contrast to these voices, Rabbi Hochheimer, after his arrival in Baltimore in 1849, was full of praise of the religious attachment of American Jews:

> Naturally everyone here decides independently to join any communal organization. As this is a costly matter, the remarkable number of adherents may prove to you, that the religious spirit has not disappeared in America. . . . Many who in Germany did pay little attention to religion discover here, being far from the fatherland, the kind of sentiment which I would name religious homesickness, which they try to overcome by joining a community.[36]

Hochheimer was, of course, alluding to recently established Ashkenazi congregations.

Religious dissatisfaction played a certain role in the establishment of new congregations intended to preserve a more conservative Judaism. One of Chicago's early settlers recalled in his memoirs how "the families had all brought with them their old country piety. . . . On holidays it was customary to close all places of business. . . . The ritual [*Minhag Ashkenaz*] was transplanted in its entirety from the old country. . . . The traditional Sabbath was scrupulously kept by the members."[37] Yet in the establishment of separate congregations religious considerations were mostly secondary to feelings of homesickness and the desire for ethnic homogeneousness. The immigrants wished to re-create their accustomed ways of worship. If the initial congregation followed the German rite, newcomers organized a Polish congregation, and vice versa. But after only a few years almost all of these congregations were involved in the heated argument concerning religious reforms, whatever *minhag* (ritual) they had initially embraced.

The growing number of new congregations was therefore due not only to the rapid growth of America's Jewish population and its dispersion, but also to the new immigrants' insistence on the rituals of their old home. Furthermore, the congregations were more than religious institutions. They were centers of communal organization, embracing mutual aid, philanthropy, and education, and conveying sentiments of security and group identity. The freedom of religious organization and faith enabled the unrestricted establishment of as many congregations as desired by whatever small number of interested patrons. The same constitutional conditions could at the same time also promote tendencies of religious and ethnic dissociation, but in the immediate aftermath of immigration the practical and emotional need for assistance and social contact prevailed. Additionally, the American social environment fostered organization in independent and self-governing "churches." In adhering to their own ways of worship the immigrants "were becoming a part of the American mainstream even as they preserved their links to their Jewish identity. . . . The institution that had been intended to serve as a link with the Old World soon emerged as a bridge to the New."[38]

At first sight this last statement seems paradoxical. One would have thought that the fragmentation caused by the abundance of congregations and rituals, in addition to the devout attachment to old traditions, language, and loyalties, would delay rather than promote integration. As it turned out, "Americanization" took place "en group," as well as being a process of individual adjustment. Congregational secession and diversity seem to have been part of this process.

The first stirring of the Reform movement, which only after the Civil War would become the dominant faction in American Judaism, reflected the contradictory tendencies in the American social and political structure. Individual dissociation from the Jewish community was an easy, almost unperceived gradual act of estrangement, especially in the scattered frontier communities. Isolated individuals simply lost contact and disappeared from the Jewish scene. Conversions to Christianity were apparently no major phenomenon, but intermarriage was quite frequent. This informal "leakage" aroused a concern in the emerging Jewish communal leadership about the future of Judaism in America. Even Jews who were lax in religious observation feared a split between the generations and attempted to keep their children within the fold of their faith. "Americanizing" the synagogue was perceived to serve that purpose. "If the synagogue does not adjust to the spirit of the age," said the *Israelite* in 1854, "we will have no Jews in this country in less than half a century."[39]

At this stage questions of formal ceremony, not of theology, were the main subject of virulent arguments about religious reform. What was required was more decorum and respectability, in line with, and unquestionably influenced by, the modes of worship of other, mainly Protestant, American denominations. The somewhat tumultuous and undisciplined prayer of the homely traditional *Shul* should be replaced by a more orderly service. The *hazzan* became a garbed "reverend," who exercised most religious functions. Some ordained and university-educated rabbis arrived around mid-century, yet the employment of learned officials brought over from Germany was not yet financially feasible for most communities. Gradually, more extreme revisions were proposed, heatedly disputed, and sometimes even brought to court: English prayers and sermons, organs and mixed choirs, family pews to replace the veiled women's galleries, and finally uncovered heads during services. These changes, together with the more ideologically inspired abolition of certain prayers, fasts, and holidays, had, however, still to wait for several decades. In the 1840s and 1850s the proposed, and only partially initiated, reforms were of a mainly practical kind, seeking more dignified service inside the synagogue, and more respected acceptance from without.[40]

Along with the maintenance of synagogues, at first mostly in modest rented locals, and the election of officials to perform and oversee the services, other communal functions soon became part of congregational activities. Religious and general instruction of the young was regarded as one of the congregation's major tasks. Up to the late 1850s, most immigrant congregations maintained Jewish day-schools. Here English and German, and in at least one instance Yiddish, were taught. The public school system was not yet well-established, and Jewish parents feared the potential Christian indoctrination of their offspring. Congregations therefore fought to maintain educational facilities, despite the financial burden and the generally poor performance of underpaid, semi-educated teachers.

In 1851 seven congregational day-schools with over 850 pupils, and several Jewish private and boarding schools, still existed in New York. However, most of these were to be short-lived. As the principle of nonsectarian instruction in public schools gained ground and as, on the other hand, the concern for rapid Americanization became more urgent among Jewish parents, most day-schools were found to be unsatisfactory and were eventually closed down. Instead, American Jews "embarked on their passionate love affair with public schooling," which they regarded as the great equalizer that hastened Americanization and fostered good citizenship. On the public scene Jewish spokesmen fought to ensure nonsectarian religious neutrality in the public schools. As the matter remained in the domain of state legislatures and local school boards, this fight went on with variable success far into the twentieth century.[41]

Religious instruction was left to Jewish Sunday schools, which started in Philadelphia and imitated the Protestant movement for religious education. The first steps were initiated in 1838 by Rebecca Gratz, one of the leading ladies of Philadelphia's Jewish society, and were supported by Isaac Leeser. Some German congregations at first considered the institution an un-Jewish, distasteful imitation of Protestantism. However, by 1860 the failure to establish a full-time Jewish school system for all or at least a great part of Jewish children convinced most congregations to settle for the Sunday school as an acceptable surrogate. How many children actually attended them is not known.[42]

Any combined communal action on the local or national level was generally a sporadic affair, and would occur mainly in response to anti-Semitic outbursts in America or Europe. The attempt to organize an

American-Jewish Board of Delegates, patterned on the British Board of Deputies, was induced by the Mortara Affair of 1858, the case of a Jewish child of Bologna, Italy, who had been secretly baptized and then forcibly abducted from his parents by papal authorities. Jewish petitioners tried in vain to mobilize the American administration's intervention. Assuming that unity instead of scattered and duplicate efforts would have brought about a different result, a small number of mainly Orthodox congregations founded the Board, as a first attempt of American Jewry to establish a defense agency. Yet most Jewish congregational leaders demurred and remained absent. "The very idea that they might need a defense agency in a free land could be interpreted to mean that their faith in the United States was imperfect."[43]

In the philanthropic sphere no such apprehensions came to the fore. The second institutions molded on existing American models were the benevolent societies, the first organizations active on a community-oriented supra-congregational level. True, Jewish solidarity had always been created in part by outside pressures. Ever since 1655, when Peter Stuyvesant and the Dutch West India Company reluctantly admitted Jewish settlers to New York under the explicit condition that "the poor among them shall not become a burden to the company or to the community, but be supported by their own nation," American Jews had tacitly accepted this principle. The system of self-reliant communal charity in the European-Jewish tradition of *Tsedakah* (charity) found itself transplanted to America, where it met with the prevailing attitudes of privately organized and financed philanthropy. In this way the rapidly expanding network of benevolent societies effectively connected old-country customs to the new, American way of life. The self-esteem that demanded that one take care of one's own immigrants and poor, and the insecurity of the outsider always on the alert to reactions from non-Jews, combined to mobilize financial support and volunteers for these organizations.

Up to the 1820s, charity had been taken care of by the congregations, occasionally by special voluntary associations in their fold. The first breakthrough occurred in 1822 when a group of Ashkenazi members of New York's Sephardic Shearith Israel formed the first Hebrew Benevolent Society to assist the growing number of new immigrants. The organizers attempted to link the society with their congregation by requesting permission to have offerings for its purpose made in the synagogue. But they were prepared to bypass the old establishment and create a new instrument outside the congregation to cope with unmet needs. Thus "without ideological formulation or revolutionary intent, the foundation for a new communal pattern was laid."[44] In 1843, after the arrival in New York of many thousands of new immigrants, the German Hebrew Benevolent

Society was able to expand across congregational lines. And after another two decades a report on the foundation-stone laying of New York's Jewish orphanage in 1863 exalted the combined, supra-congregational endeavor as a sign that "here at least differences of nationality will disappear from the ranks of Israel. Origin and religion will unite Englishmen, Frenchmen, Germans, Poles, etc., as Jews."[45]

Other older and newly established Jewish communities followed suit, and although separate German and Polish organizations continued to co-exist, cooperation in fund-raising and the distribution of relief evolved in most communities. Philadelphia's six congregations united their philanthropic work in the Hebrew Relief Association, dividing the city into seven districts administered by separate, supra-congregational committees. The Depression of 1857–58, which made unusual funds necessary for the assistance of its many Jewish victims, especially fostered these cooperative efforts. In times of special disasters, like the yellow fever epidemic in New Orleans in 1858, appeals for help from sister communities in the North were met with sympathy and apparently only meager amounts of money.[46] This was another appeal to practice nationwide Jewish solidarity, which had its roots and precedents already in colonial America.

The attempts of associations outside the congregations did not remain confined to the practical needs of philanthropy. After the first few years in America, and having gained some economic foothold and a growing sense of security and permanence, immigrants began to seek social and cultural contacts with each other for secular, leisure-time recreation. Associations of varying kinds, dedicated to a variety of declared purposes, sprang up in every substantial immigrant community. Nonsectarian German clubs like literary circles, theater groups, or *Sänger-* or *Turnvereine* (singing and gymnastics clubs), served to satisfy some of these needs, but evidently did not fill the void. In many cases Jewish members did not feel at ease, or were not welcome, in some of these associations. In some instances Jewish applicants who wanted to join established American fraternal lodges like the Freemasons or Odd Fellows were blackballed and refused admission. Be it for this reason, or because they preferred and felt more at ease among their own, many secular, supra-congregational Jewish associations were founded during the 1840s and 1850s.

The most prominent and lasting of these organizations was B'nai B'rith, which was founded in New York in 1843 and soon became the most important nation- and worldwide association of Jewish lodges. By 1851 it had over 700 members in New York alone, with membership and foundations of new lodges rapidly growing in all major Jewish settlements.

The first English-speaking lodge was established in Cincinnati in 1850. Its aims, as stated by the founders, were to "unite Israelites in the work of promoting their highest interests and those of humanity; of developing the mental and moral character of the people of our faith; of inculcating the purest principles of philanthropy, honor and patriotism; of supporting science and art . . . [and] coming to the rescue of victims of persecution . . . on the broadest principles of humanity."

The foundation of B'nai B'rith was an expression of Jewish group consciousness inside the immigrant society under the new American conditions. This was underlined by the Hebrew name of the order, which had been proposed by Rabbi Leo Merzbacher, as well as by the Hebrew terms used as titles of its officers and in its rites. The German language at first prevailed, but with growing acculturation English took its place. In addition to the imitation of practices developed by American fraternal orders, this indicates the character of the organization—a vehicle of Americanization. And although some of the lodges did at first not accept Eastern European Jews as members, the order, like other supra-congregational organizations, soon became a major "homogenizer" within the American-Jewish community.[47]

The rapid development of the lodges—by 1860 three other orders existed in addition to B'nai B'rith—proves that they filled a void. Synagogues, congregations, and even the first benevolent societies could take care of their members at best in cases of acute necessity. Many immigrants were not affiliated with any congregation, but found support and company in these secular organizations. Lodges maintained funds for their members in case of sickness, and for widows and orphans. Special committees visited the ailing; funerals were attended *en masse*. The ceremonial rites and secrecy were later abandoned, and soon gave way to more sophisticated cultural and philanthropic activities. Already in 1855 English was declared the official language of the order. B'nai B'rith also became active in the cultural sphere by establishing libraries and organizing German and English lectures and musical entertainment.[48]

Jewish intellectuals in America and the old country lamented the poor cultural level of the first waves of the immigrants. In 1852 an unsigned reader took offense at a report that had appeared earlier in the *Allgemeine Zeitung des Judenthums:*

> People who come to a foreign country, mostly without any means, ignorant of the language and of how to conduct business, have so much to fight these awkward conditions, that little time is left for reading anything. First the German in America has to learn English; then he wants to learn something about politics, which he can obtain from English newspapers only; and so the more literate part becomes anglicized after a very short time.

The writer then launched a violent attack against "our scholars" who complain about the people's neglect of literature but do not produce anything worth reading in English. "In Germany people read much because much has been written; here they read little because nothing has been written." Ludwig Philippson could not refrain from adding his own footnote: "If the gentlemen admit that they themselves have produced nothing, why don't they translate good German [Jewish] works?"[49] This unconcealed dig at the recently emigrated intellectuals indicates the complicated relationship between the immigrant society and the Jewish establishment in the old country.

Attempts to improve the cultural content of Jewish community life, which met at first with moderate success, were closely observed, as in a report from Cincinnati praising the efforts of Isaac M. Wise:

> One of the most meritorious initiatives of our worthy Rabbi . . . is a series of lectures in German and in English in the local *Allemania* during this winter. . . . Unfortunately till now these lectures attracted only a small, spiritually inclined audience. The masses do not attend them. Even if no entrance fee is demanded they prefer to remain at home or behind their beer and cards, be it because they believe to have already learnt enough . . . or because they find a greater spiritual enjoyment in those.

The list of the topics of these lectures included popular surveys ranging from the works of Shakespeare and Schiller to "the influence of natural sciences on our times" or "jurisprudence of the United States" by I. M. Wise himself, "who proved to be versed even in this area."[50]

The activities of Isaac Mayer Wise, one of the most ardent "Americanizers" of the German-Jewish immigration, reflect the complexity of cultural adjustment. True, the general level of early immigrants' education and cultural interests was not high, but most immigrants were not illiterate. It was therefore only natural that Wise, like Isaac Leeser before him, should try to disseminate his religious and educational ideas in print by founding a weekly. And just as he preached before his congregation, or delivered his lectures and sermons alternating between German and English, his paper, *The Israelite,* largely a one-man enterprise, appeared in English with a German-language supplement, *Die Deborah,* which soon became an independent newspaper and appeared until 1903. If indeed, as Oscar Handlin contended, "the German Jews who emigrated to the United States had not habitually read newspapers at home for lack of interest and high cost," they very much did so in America. By 1860 seven English- and four German-language Jewish monthlies or weeklies appeared more or less regularly, from New York City to San Francisco. Moreover, nearly one hundred German-language papers are known to have been started, many of them not outliving their first and only issue. This abundance proves how much the immigrants had already adjusted to the political and cultural ways of expression in their new environment.[51]

All these attempts at cultural and journalistic communication have to be regarded in the context of the immigrant society's overall effort to come to grips with their Jewish group identity under extremely new conditions. Having left behind the old bonds and fetters of communal and familial structures, and after their first years of individual adjustment, those immigrants who had not become totally estranged in the process attempted to find new ways to express their Jewish identity. Chain-migration and group-settlement with former neighbors and friends facilitated the formation of a new kind of totally voluntary Jewish community life. Religious affiliation alone soon proved to be insufficient to fill all requirements. Charitable and mutual aid associations, fraternal lodges, and cultural and recreational clubs were therefore established wherever a greater number of German-Jewish immigrants settled together. As a result, American-Jewish identity emerged as a complex and diversified entity, in which the distinction between the religious and the secular spheres of life became increasingly blurred.[52]

What part of the German Jews who had come to America were actually taking part in this "new entity" we do not know. The "land of unlimited opportunities" enabled those who for one reason or other wished to shed their former identity and alliances to do so at will. Still, judging by the impressive numbers of emerging congregations and fraternal organizations, we may assume that complete dissociation from the Jewish community was, at least at this period, not overwhelming. Mutual dependence and the social and cultural needs of the immigrants, combined with an environment where anti-Jewish sentiments were, although limited, not totally absent, seem to have effectively countered such tendencies. Unlike the old country, however, here the immigrants were not tempted to convert to Christianity in order to gain promising economic, political, or social positions. In both countries the religious, cultural, and psychological heritage of German Jewry was still alive, and not so very different. What *was* different was the environment of their individual and group existence. These differences had a decisive influence on the development of communal life and the respective patterns of modern Jewish identity in both countries. A process of rapidly advancing assimilation and disaffiliation was staged against one of acculturation and group-conscious integration in a pluralistic society.

5

Loyalties and Assertion: The Civil War Years

The Immigrants and the Civil War

In more than one sense the most crucial years in American history were also a turning point in the course of the German-Jewish immigration. During the years of the Civil War (1861–65), immigration from Central Europe, including that of German Jews, declined sharply. But, contrary to what is still widely assumed, this was by no means the end of German-Jewish immigration. After the dust of war had settled, it started again, to achieve new momentum in the 1870s. But by then conditions had changed on both sides of the ocean, and with them the character and composition of immigration and the immigrants' ways of adjusting to life in America. Before we deal with these differences, a short survey of the implications of the war for immigrant society, and that society's reaction to these events, is in order.

Prior to the war, rabbis or Jewish communal or nationwide organizations had refrained from taking any official stand on general political issues, and the question of slavery in particular. As a still insecure immigrant group, Jews usually went out of their way to demonstrate a strict political neutrality, leaving such allegiances to individual decisions. The time of Jewish political pressure groups and lobbies had still to come; American Jewry did not yet constitute a self-conscious, integrated ethnic group. Both Isaac Leeser's traditionalist *Occident* and the Reform-oriented *Israelite* of Isaac Mayer Wise stated that Jewish religious bodies should best keep aloof of political involvement. This apprehension was rather exceptional in a country whose population was composed mainly of recent immigrant groups. Some of these, like the Irish or Germans, became involved in American politics soon after their arrival as identified

109

ethnic voting- and pressure-groups. But until the end of the century, Jewish voters were too few to attract the consideration of ambitious politicians. On the other hand, Jewish political attitudes were still influenced by their European experience. The fear of anti-Semitic reaction to the involvement of even individual Jews in the heated political conflicts of the 1850s and 1860s was always present and was occasionally brought to attention in the press or from the pulpit.[1]

The absence of a nationwide Jewish "church" relieved religious or congregational leaders of the necessity to take sides officially on the political issues of the day. Contrary to other denominations organized in national bodies, organized Judaism was not called upon to commit itself. Christians—like the Baptists or Methodists—were divided on sectional lines and had split on the issue of slavery years before the Civil War. Such a split did not occur among the Jews. B'nai B'rith and other organizations generally ignored the South-North conflict in the prewar years, tolerated the enforced separation of the war years, and continued as before once the war had ended. The Board of Delegates of American Israelites discussed only Jewish subjects before and during the war. Its moderate leaders were careful not to let general political conflicts enter into its proceedings.[2]

In those single cases in which individual rabbis spoke their minds for or against the institution of slavery they were immediately called to order by their constituency or its officers. Rabbi Morris Raphall of New York's B'nai Jeshurun circulated a sermon in which he declared slavery to be sanctioned by the Bible. Bertram Korn regarded this sermon to have "aroused more comment and attention than any other sermon ever delivered by an American rabbi." The *New York Tribune* held the whole Jewish community responsible for Raphall's statement, proving that Jewish caution and aloofness was justified. Accordingly, Raphall's board of trustees "respectfully suggested to Dr. Raphall the impropriety of any intermeddling with politics, as we firmly believe such a course to be entirely inconsistent with the Jewish clerical character, calculated to be of serious injury to the Jews in general and to our congregation in particular."[3]

On the opposite pole stood David Einhorn, rabbi of Baltimore's Har Sinai congregation and editor of his own German-language periodical *Sinai*. He had been preaching against slavery soon after his nomination, true to his liberal conviction that had brought him disapproval in his earlier career in Mecklenburg and Pest. In May 1861 he was forced to escape from Baltimore during the riots between Baltimore Unionists and Confederate sympathizers. The printing press of the *Sinai* was set on fire, and friendly soldiers informed him that his name was listed among the secessionists' proscriptions. According to Einhorn's own account he resigned shortly after his escape to Philadelphia because he found it impossible to accept the congregation's request to refrain in future sermons from all political allusions.[4]

The general attitude not only of newly arrived immigrants but also of the older established Jewish communities is reflected in a comment on Einhorn's flight in the *Jewish Messenger,* one of the oldest Jewish periodicals, which was published in New York by Samuel M. Isaacs: "It seems he has been mistaking his vocation, and making the pulpit the vehicle for political invective. . . . We commend his fate to others, who feel inclined to take a similar course. A minister has enough to do, if he devotes himself to the welfare of his flock. . . . Let Dr. E's fate be a warning."[5] Baltimore was, however, a special case due to the division of Maryland's sympathies between Unionists and Confederates. Where the lines were more clearly drawn, the true tradition of conservative Jewish political conduct prevailed: individuals and communities went out of their way to demonstrate their loyalty to the cause of their home states. When the war began, American Jews were as divided as their Gentile neighbors. Most Jews who lived in the South were loyal to the Confederacy, those in the North to the Union. Both fought in the contending armies, often against their own relatives.[6]

The active participation of Jewish officers and soldiers in the fighting units of both camps, and the supporting activities of volunteer organizations behind the front line, was widely publicized in the Jewish press. As most new immigrants had settled in the old northeastern communities or the expanding Northwest, most Jews fought in the Union army. Their part was sometimes wildly exaggerated, as in a communication from New York of February 1865, where the number of Jewish fighting men in the ranks of the Union was reported to count "at least 60,000, among them 12,000 from Ohio, 5,000 from Illinois, and 3,000 from Michigan." Some months later the same paper published a more "modest" estimate of over 40,000 fighting men, quoting this time the Southern *St. Louis Democrat,* whose recognition of Jewish patriotism on both sides was apparently especially noteworthy. These exaggerations brought a somewhat caustic response from Isaac Leeser, warning "editors of European Jewish journals . . . not to trust empty affirmations as long as no comprehensive statistical data, which may never be available, confirm them." Philippson reprinted this critique with the remark that the numbers had been copied from "four or five North American, non-Jewish papers. If this was humbug, it was North American humbug which we could not avoid, though we had our doubts from the very beginning."[7]

Bertram W. Korn confirmed an earlier estimate of "at least ten thousand Jews" who served in the Union and Confederate armies. Yet at the same time he emphasized the small success of some efforts to organize Jewish patriotism on pronounced ethnic lines, by the establishment of special Jewish units or war-service organizations:

> The fact that so few Jewish companies were organized did not stem from any lack of patriotism among Jews, but from a reluctance to form Jewish enclaves in the army. . . . The majority of American Jews consciously sought to avoid clannish or restrictive actions; the [Jewish] hospital idea undoubtedly struck most of them as unnecessary segregation. Indeed it would appear that most Jews were quite willing to ignore religious observances, such as the dietary laws which tended to require separate Jewish facilities, rather than create "ghetto" institutions.[8]

Evidently, the confrontation with open and vehement anti-Semitic sentiments and actions that marked the Civil War years played some role in fostering this reluctance.

Anti-Semitic Interlude

It was probably the awareness of this confrontation that caused the exaggerated reports of the alleged Jewish patriotic fervor on both sides of the ocean. In 1861 Ludwig Philippson expressed his concern for the young Jewish communities in America, where the strife over the slavery question "obscures all social and moral attitudes. It is therefore only natural, that the position of our co-religionists is endangered . . . and the prejudice transplanted from Europe gains new ground." Following a report on anti-Semitic remarks in the Missouri state convention, he nevertheless did not hesitate fervently to take the side of the Unionists:

> Of what avail has Mr. Raphall's sacrifice been? Neither did it appease the country, nor prevent the accusation against the Jews to be gathering in Abraham's [Lincoln] fold. Should the secession be accomplished and the Declaration of Independence be thrown overboard, then before long— everything goes fast in America—the black deed of the Crucifixion will no less be held against the Jews than their black color against the Negroes. And still there are recently immigrated Jews who are deluded to enthuse over secession and the institution of slavery![9]

Philippson's sympathies for the Union and his enthusiastic support of David Einhorn indicate the close ties that at this stage still connected German Jewry with its American branch. Engaged in its fight for full

Despite the legal and social discrimination in German lands, Jewish immigrants often remembered their old home with nostalgia, as in this painting of Urspringen, Bavaria, by Sigmund Heilner, who emigrated in 1855 when he was nineteen. *(Courtesy, The Heilner Collection, Jewish Historical Society of Oregon)*

Sigmund Heilner settled in Oregon, following his older brother. Like many of the first wave of German-Jewish immigrants, he was young, single, adventurous, and quite poor. *(Courtesy, The Heilner Collection, Jewish Historical Society of Oregon)*

German-Jewish immigrants often replaced Yankee peddlers as pioneering distributors of goods in the countryside and western territories. This photo of a peddler in Pennsylvania was taken in 1867. *(Courtesy, American Jewish Archives, Cincinnati Campus, Hebrew Union College, Jewish Institute of Religion)*

Born in Westphalia, Adolph Sutro arrived in San Francisco, the main city of German-Jewish settlement in the Far West, in 1850. He was eventually elected mayor. *(Courtesy, Prints and Photographs Division, Library of Congress)*

Sutro *(third from left)* is pictured in the tunnel of his silver mine. Although most German-Jewish settlers in the Far West were not actively involved in mining, many set up businesses to provide miners with goods. *(Courtesy, American Jewish Archives, Cincinnati Campus, Hebrew Union College, Jewish Institute of Religion)*

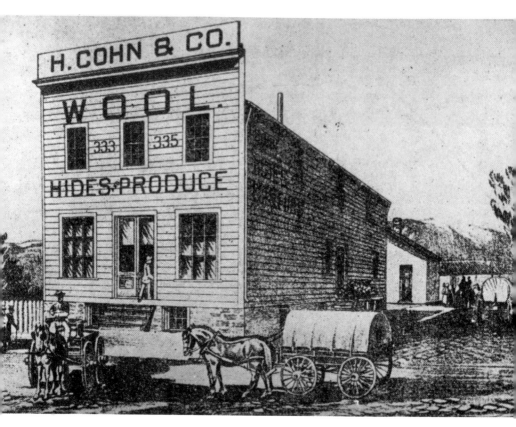

German-Jewish settlers in the West established wholesale supply stores that sold goods to itinerant peddlers and others. This is a photo of Henry Cohn's warehouse in Salt Lake City, c. 1880. *(Courtesy, American Jewish Archives, Cincinnati Campus, Hebrew Union College, Jewish Institute of Religion)*

German Jews participated actively in the Civil War as soldiers and officers in fighting units of both camps. Despite the demonstration of sectional loyalties, however, outbursts of anti-Semitism occurred on both sides, leading to the Jewish community's assertion as a distinctive group in the political arena.

Colonel Marcus M. Spiegel *(opposite page, top)* was a German-Jewish immigrant who died fighting for the Union cause. Major Adolph Proskauer *(opposite page, bottom)* was a Confederate soldier. *(Courtesy, American Jewish Archives, Cincinnati Campus, Hebrew Union College, Jewish Institute of Religion)*

Although he himself did not emigrate, Ludwig Philippson (1811–
1889), a rabbi and publisher of the influential weekly *Allgemeine
Zeitung des Judenthums,* encouraged German-Jewish immigra-
tion to America as well as the maintenance of ties to the Old
World. *(Courtesy of Leo Baeck Institute, NY, and Bild-Archiv der
Österreichischen Nationalbibliothek, Vienna)*

Isaac Leeser (1806–1868) was the most important spokesman for traditionalist American Judaism in the pre–Civil War period. Arriving in America in 1824, he served for twenty years as the *hazzan* of Mikveh Israel, the prominent synagogue in Philadelphia founded by Sephardic Jews in 1747. *(Courtesy of American Jewish Historical Society, Waltham, MA)*

Isaac Mayer Wise (1819–1900), who arrived in America in 1847, became the leading promoter of religious Reform. During the 1880s Reform Judaism became the predominant religious affiliation of American Jews of German descent. *(Courtesy, American Jewish Archives, Cincinnati Campus, Hebrew Union College, Jewish Institute of Religion)*

Congregation B'nai Yeshurun, known as Plum Street Temple, was
founded in Cincinnati, an important center of German-Jewish settlement during the nineteenth century. Isaac Mayer Wise became
its rabbi in 1856 and made the congregation a beacon of Reform
Judaism, "Americanization," and communal life. *(Courtesy,
Prints and Photographs Division, Library of Congress)*

Temple Emanu-El in New York, dedicated in 1868, became a prestigious meeting place of the German-Jewish financial and social elite. *(Courtesy, Prints and Photographs Division, Library of Congress)*

Women in German-Jewish families during the nineteenth century were held to the traditional role model of a middle-class matron, illustrated in this photograph of the Kuhn sisters of Cincinnati. A few women, however, expanded their roles outside the family, particularly in the fields of education, social work, and philanthropy. (*Courtesy, American Jewish Archives, Cincinnati Campus, Hebrew Union College, Jewish Institute of Religion*)

Lillian Wald (1867–1940) established the Visiting Nurse Service on the Lower East Side to care for the health of poor East European Jewish immigrants. Her work also led to the founding of the Henry Street Settlement. *(Courtesy, Prints and Photographs Division, Library of Congress)*

Jacob Henry Schiff (1847–1920), a wealthy financier, settled in America in 1875. He became the leading figure in the philanthropic efforts organized by the German-Jewish establishment, many of which were intended to "Americanize" the new East European immigrants. *(Courtesy, American Jewish Archives, Cincinnati Campus, Hebrew Union College, Jewish Institute of Religion)*

Rebecca Gratz (1781–1869), from Philadelphia, who supposedly served as a model for the Jewish heroine of Walter Scott's *Ivanhoe,* established the first Hebrew Benevolent Society in 1819, and Jewish foster home in 1855. *(Courtesy, American Jewish Historical Society, Waltham, MA)*

Julia Richman (1855–1912) was a social reformer dedicated to educating the East European immigrants who arrived in New York during the mass immigration of 1880–1914. As district superintendent of schools for the Lower East Side, she was the highest-ranking woman in the public school system. *(Courtesy, American Jewish Archives, Cincinnati Campus, Hebrew Union College, Jewish Institute of Religion)*

Louis Marshall (1856–1929), the American-born son of German immigrants and a founder of the American Jewish Committee, represented the legal and political interests of American Jewry. He played an important role in arbitrating the long strike against Hart, Schaffner and Marx in Chicago in 1910, and fought for the right of East European Jews to unrestricted immigration. *(Courtesy, American Jewish Archives, Cincinnati Campus, Hebrew Union College, Jewish Institute of Religion)*

emancipation at home, German Jews closely followed the fate and achievements of their friends and relatives who had chosen emigration as a substitute for emancipation. Unlike their more cautious colleagues in the United States, liberal intellectuals like Philippson had no qualms about declaring their condemnation of slavery. For them this was a matter of principle, the only possible position for members of an oppressed minority group. Therefore they were not surprised to find open anti-Semitism in the Confederate camp, tending to overlook similar symptoms among its adversaries.

Rabbi Bernhard Felsenthal of Chicago, next to Einhorn the only openly active abolitionist among the American-Jewish leadership, expressed the same ideas and parallels in a letter to the German-language *Illinois Staatszeitung* of June 1862, duly reprinted in the *Sinai* and in Philippson's paper:

> How can it be . . . that [Jews] who for thousands of years were persecuted and enslaved . . . should be defenders of the most ignominious institution of slavery and enemies of freedom? People whose brothers and relatives in many German or non-German states of the Old World even today have to agitate and petition for their own emancipation expose themselves here as fanatical apologists of Negro slavery!

But as much as he accused his fellow Jews, Felsenthal also tried to excuse their position by their lack of political education and their general ignorance: "Such people are unthinkingly drawn into the mainstream of their present environment. . . . Others are unable to rise to a higher moral viewpoint, believing that the material well-being of the country and their own precious self are endangered by 'this damned agitation . . . of the abolitionists.'"[10]

The letter was in fact a response to frequent attacks in the German-American press against Jews who supported the Confederacy. Felsenthal sought to defend his people, recognizing that the attacks were motivated more by hostility to the Jews than by anti-Confederate fervor. They were often begun by Gentile Germans, who had brought their prejudices across the ocean. Due to their concentrated settlement in Union states, the Gentile Germans were at the time a much more compactly organized group than German Jews. Their general pro-Unionist position did indeed create strong prejudice against them in the Confederate South.[11]

A later study on the Jews of Atlanta, Georgia, offers a more complex explanation of the immigrants' attitude in the South. They were, first of all, a very small minority, estimated at no more than 10 to 15 percent of American Jewry. Second, the choice of a place for permanent settlement seems to have been influenced, to at least some extent, by the issue of slavery. "Those who were squeamish about human bondage were apt to avoid the region or did not remain long." Third, those who decided to stay enjoyed the fact that here even a poor Jewish immigrant was socially accepted as a member of the master class. "While suspicion engendered by their foreign birth and alien religion may have induced some Jews to conform outwardly to regional values as a means of protective coloration, most willingly embraced Southern attitudes because they had a consuming desire to succeed in their new home."[12]

In this desire the Jewish immigrants in the South were, of course, not different from those in the Union states, who also went out of their way to prove their patriotism. The demonstration of sectional loyalty proved, however, no effective barrier to the rather unexpected outburst of Judeophobic sentiments in both camps. The recent-immigrant image was during these years prominent in many anti-Semitic utterances. Newspapers did not abstain from identifying every "Israelite," "Jew," or, worse yet, "German Jew" suspected of illegal trade, smuggling, or any kind of disloyal activities. In contrast, Jews who enlisted in the Army or who were reported in the casualty columns were never identified as such. As always and everywhere this journalistic technique was at one and the same time the product of prejudice and an agency for its dissemination.[13]

Anti-Semitism was, of course, a European import, and it would be of interest to compare its specific expressions among the different groups that comprised American society in the mid-nineteenth century. In chapter 7 I intend to examine its influence on the relations between Jewish and Gentile German immigrants in their respective routes of settlement and adjustment. The often repeated allusions to the "accursed race who crucified the Savior" or "who shed the blood of the early Christians" in the English-language press seem to indicate a strong element of fundamentalist prejudice and bigotry also among the Americans of Anglo-Saxon descent. The contemporaries were certainly aware of these symptoms, as can be seen from a communication from Philadelphia in 1864:

> The sword of Damocles of the Jewish question is now suspended also over our head. We still hope that it remains a phantom, but should the phantom ever become real, we would in fact fare much worse than a good part of European Jews. The fanaticism of many Puritan-Christian parsons has so far been suppressed by the unimpeachable Constitution. At the present disorder . . . they believe to have found the right moment to let intolerance triumph."[14]

It was at least partly the fear of the evangelical religious zeal of the abolitionists, in addition to the overt anti-Semitism of some of them, that caused rabbis like Isaac M. Wise to be cautious about committing themselves and their flock.[15]

However, as was the case in Europe, economic issues, rather than religious bigotry, came increasingly to the fore in the anti-Semitic campaigns and acts of this time. On both sides commodity shortages and inflation were a constant matter of concern. They were also a source of considerable enrichment for enterprising merchants and speculators. There is no reason to believe that Jewish businessmen, many of whom were dealing in and manufacturing some of the most needed goods, were more squeamish than their Gentile competitors and missed their chance. We may even be right to assume that because of their former concentration in the commercial and financial sector, many of the immigrants were successful in improving their economic situation during these years, and some may have amassed considerable fortunes. Nevertheless, the constant accusations against the "speculating" Jew that abounded in both camps were wildly exaggerated generalizations. By sheer numbers alone the small Jewish minority could not be responsible for all the economic disasters of the time. There is ample evidence that not only Gentile merchants, brokers, and manufacturers but also prominent politicians and soldiers took their share of war profits and grew rich during these years. The Jewish businessmen were, as everywhere and at all times, a convenient scapegoat, onto which one could divert the fire of public critique and popular rage. The fact that most of them were recent arrivals and were still regarded as aliens made the accusations plausible and all the more effective.

Prominent Jewish bankers were the preferred targets of anti-Semitic invective. One of them was August Belmont of New York—even though he had married into one of America's most distinguished non-Jewish families, was rearing his children as Christians, and maintained no Jewish affiliation. As in Germany, France, and all over Europe the Rothschild-myth cast its shadow on the Jewish community, and Belmont, as Rothschild's representative, was especially vulnerable. He was also a well-known national politician, chairman of the Democratic National Committee, reason enough to be accused as a Confederate sympathizer by the Republican press and party spokesmen. That he had recruited and equipped the first German-American regiment in New York and had offered his financial services to the Union was passed over in silence. "The Jew banker of New York" and his "knot of German-Jewish bankers" were too well-fitted as anti-Semitic stereotypes to be dismissed out of hand because of these facts. The ghost of Rothschild was mobilized in an article of the *Chicago Tribune* in the election campaign of November 1864: "How much is McClellan to get from the Rothschilds . . . if he succeeds in betraying his country and handing it over to [the Confederates'] tender mercies? . . . Will we have a dishonorable peace in order to enrich Belmont, the Rothschilds, and the whole tribe of Jews . . .?" The fact that another Jewish banking firm, Seligman Brothers, were ardent Republicans and placed millions of dollars' worth of Union bonds in Europe remained mostly unmentioned. But the same kind of service rendered to the Confederacy by the Frankfurt banking house of Erlanger, who had long before converted to Christianity, was a preferred topic of *Harper's Weekly* and the *Cincinnati Gazette.*[16]

The latter example is of special interest because of the large German-Jewish community in Cincinnati. The city was an important trading and contraband post with the South and the center of German-Jewish clothing enterprise in the West. In October 1861 the *Cincinnati Enquirer* reported that a "combination of Jewish clothing houses in this city had been organized to take advantage of the pressing necessity of our Western soldiers for blankets, etc." In this case the paper printed a retraction after being approached by some of the Jews and admitted that, to the contrary, the Jewish firms "had made contracts at an early period in the war, when prices were down, and were now uncomplainingly living up to them, since prices have materially raised."[17]

Trying to understand the reasons for the spread of anti-Semitic sentiment during the Civil War, Bertram Korn has traced essentially the same motives to have inspired what he defines as the Union and Confederate versions of American Judeophobia: "Economic tensions, personal fears and frustrations, and mass passions required an outlet and a victim in the South just as in the North." He then goes on to explain the specific condition that made anti-Semitism in the South an even more pronounced phenomenon:

> Additional social factors peculiar to life in the South tended to strengthen and heighten the reaction to the Jews: a general dislike of all aliens and foreigners which, during the War, created the legend that the Union Army was a band of German and Irish hirelings and mercenaries, while the Confederate Army was said to be exclusively native; a wide-spread suspicion of the merchant and storekeeper, typical of a society dominated by the plantation owner and farmer; a deeper commitment than existed in the North to fundamentalist "Bible" Christianity; . . . Granted an original suspicion and dislike of the Jew before the War, the four-year long travail of the Confederacy was certain to emphasize it.[18]

We have no way of knowing how many of the Southern merchants or storekeepers were Jews, but certainly most of the Jews living in the South, and especially the newly arrived German Jews, were merchants, storekeepers, or, still, itinerant peddlers. The more the war dragged on and the more unbearable conditions became, Southern Gentiles tended, even more than the resourceful Northerners, to blame the "extortionist" storekeepers for the shortages and high prices, and the Jews as the "chief extortionists." The argument reappeared constantly not only in the popular press but also in the debates of the Confederate House of Representatives. In January 1863, during a debate on the drafting of foreigners into military service, Congressman Foote of Tennessee accused the Jews of having "flooded the country and controlled at least nine-tenths of the business of the land. They were engaging in all kinds of illegal trade with the enemy without any official hindrance." All Southern commerce was being transferred "to the hands of foreign Jews."

The similarity of accusations in both camps and the familiarity of the stereotypes prove how the haunting ghost of Shylock had crossed the ocean. Sometimes the hostility took on violent forms, as in one Georgia town, where soldiers' families raided Jewish stores. The Jewish merchants were accused of speculating on the shortages and making fortunes "while the men were fighting for the life of the nation." Similarly, in August 1862, a public meeting in Thomasville, Georgia, discussed the "unpatriotic conduct" of Jewish merchants. Resolutions were passed in which German Jews were denounced, and prohibited from visiting the village, banishing "all those now resident in that place."

This was the general background for the notorious General Order No. 11 of the Union general Ulysses S. Grant, according to Bertram Korn "the most sweeping anti-Jewish regulation in all American history." It was issued in December 1862 and expelled all Jews, "a class violating every regulation of trade," within twenty-four hours from the Department of Tennessee.[19] We need not elaborate here on this well-known incident and the details of the order's eventual revocation by the presidential decision of Abraham Lincoln. What is important is that it became a signpost in the process of the Jewish immigrant community's self-assertion and in its establishment as a distinctive group on the political arena.

Coming of Age

There had already been some organized political action of Jewish individuals and communities a few months before the Grant order. At issue was the nomination of Jewish military chaplains by units whose majority of volunteers and officers were Jews. The problem did not arise in the Confederate army because no denominational qualification was attached to the relevant acts on the appointment of "clergymen" and/or because there was not a sufficient number of Jews in any one of the Confederate regiments to enable the election of a Jewish chaplain.[20]

In the Union camp the situation was different. Most American Jews were living in Northern states, and many volunteered to serve in its regiments. One of these was the 65th Regiment of the Fifth Pennsylvania Cavalry, popularly known as "Cameron's Dragoons." Its commanding officer was Colonel Max Friedman, a German Jew like many of the 1,200 soldiers of the regiment. It was therefore only natural that they elected Michael Allen, an American-born Philadelphia Jew, to serve as their regimental chaplain. In doing so they were probably unaware of a clause in the Volunteer Bill, passed by Congress on July 12, 1861, requiring that regimental chaplains "appointed by the regimental commander on the vote of the field officers and company commanders present" had to be ordained ministers of "some Christian denomination." This discriminatory clause had passed despite protests by some Democratic congressmen, who had denounced the underlying implication of a Christian United States. Excepting a short remark by Isaac M. Wise, the episode had at first attracted little notice. Only in September 1861 did a worker from the Young Men's Christian Association who had visited the training camp of the regiment start a public campaign about the fact that a Jew was serving as military chaplain in defiance of the law. Michael Allen resigned his commission on the excuse of ill health, but this was only the beginning of the story.

Friedman and his officers decided to fight back, and this time they elected an ordained rabbi, Dutch-born Arnold Fischel of New York's Shearith Israel. After being elected, Fischel, as a civilian, had to apply for commission to the secretary of war, the same Simon Cameron, paradoxically, after whom the regiment was named. Cameron's refusal was on a friendly note, reassuring the applicant that "were it not for the impediment . . . directly created by the provisions . . . the Department would have taken your application into its favorable consideration." In this way American Jewry found itself confronted with an instance of legal discrimination in a Congressional enactment. Starting with the release of the Cameron-Fischel correspondence to the press, organized Jewish groups now began a "three-pronged campaign" to effect a change in the law."[21]

The three prongs of the campaign were the usual practice of the American political process: publicity, petitioning, and lobbying. Together they succeeded before long in having the law reinterpreted in such a way as to permit the election and commissioning of Jewish military chaplains. Congress passed the amendment on July 17, 1862, by changing one single word: "Christian denomination" now read simply "religious denomination." In September 1862, Bavarian-born Jacob Frankel, minister of Rodeph Shalom of Philadelphia, was appointed by President Lincoln to serve as military chaplain in the hospitals of Philadelphia and its surroundings.

Once the issue became public it was closely followed by the Jewish and non-Jewish press in America and abroad. Isaac M. Wise, who from the beginning had shown a cautious attitude, had condemned the "Christian denomination" clause even before the affair of the "Cameron's Dragons," but Wise was suspect because of his sympathies with the Democrats. Now, in December 1861, the *Sinai* of David Einhorn, an early partisan for the abolitionist cause and unrestricted supporter of the Republican administration, called for more vigilance on the side of

> friends of the Constitution and the Union of whatever denomination [to bring about the amendment of the "chaplaincy-law"] . . . But least of all are the Jews, who are directly attacked by this illegality, allowed to remain silent. The best would be for the Jews in those cities where they are most numerous to complain in writing before the Congress . . . against this anti-Constitutional exclusion. A *centrally combined* action would take too much time. Under the prevailing conditions it may, also for other reasons, cause more damage than benefits.

Reprinting this article, Ludwig Philippson could not refrain from adding his own comment to the last statement: "We earnestly wonder why the American Jews let such laws be at all passed in Congress . . . without moving, or even taking account of them, only to be surprised by them after the fact. This only shows the very small attention paid by the leaders of the Jewish affairs."[22]

This was more than just another of the frequently exchanged pinpricks between Philippson and his American readers. It deserves some consideration because it discloses a central problem of Jewish political involvement on both sides of the ocean. The German liberal rabbi was committed to an unceasing effort to stabilize, through his paper and public activities, the staggering achievements of piecemeal emancipation in the German states. For him, united Jewish political action to further the process was always desirable, if not always a reality even in Germany. That a Jewish community that had already achieved this longed-for legal emancipation should neglect the precious tools of united political assertion was almost incomprehensible to him. On the American side, matters were much more complicated.

The chaplaincy campaign had in fact been started by a minority group: the Board of Delegates of American Israelites. The following publicity campaign was taken up by all Jewish periodicals. Most congregations took part in organizing the stream of petitions from all parts of the

Union, which were signed also by many non-Jews who were asked to lend their signature to the cause of constitutional freedom. But Fischel's mission in Washington and the costs of his lobbying activities were defrayed by the Board alone, and apparently to a considerable extent by Fischel himself. An appeal of the Board for financial support, circulated among congregations and well-off Jewish individuals, reaped the contributions of only four congregations plus a donation of five dollars by the children of the Pittsburgh Hebrew School. That this was not simply due to the stinginess or indifference of the prospective donors becomes evident in the light of a rather perplexing action by some of the most important Reform rabbis, before the sought-for amendment of the chaplaincy clause had been achieved.

Fischel's mission on behalf of the Board of Delegates had been derided from the start in editorials of Einhorn's *Sinai* and the *Israelite*. In January 1862 six prominent rabbis, all German immigrants, including—in addition to the two already mentioned—Rabbis Felsenthal, Lilienthal, Adler, and Hochheimer, issued a public "Protest" against the alleged claim of the Board "to represent all the Israelites in the United States" by petitioning Congress "in the name and on behalf of all citizens of the United States professing Judaism." Although the signatories emphasized their demand to repeal the clause objected to by the Board's petition, they

> considered it their duty in behalf of truth to protest against the assumption of titles and functions . . ., and to state that . . . neither their congregations, nor any of those presided over by regularly ordained Rabbis, have ever delegated men or powers to that body, or otherwise recognized it. Justice to the Hebrew community demands the announcement that, as a religious organization, it is represented by no particular body in this country or elsewhere.[23]

Bertram Korn has condemned this "Protest" as a "deliberate attempt to sabotage the campaign being waged in Washington by Fischel for the revision of the chaplaincy clause, published with an eye to the national lawmakers." This harsh judgment raises some doubts about the real motives of the protesting rabbis, be it only because Korn does not give any reasonable explanation for the alleged "sabotage." All existing evidence suggests that the Reform rabbis, and the rest of American Jewry, were actually no less concerned about the chaplaincy issue than were the members of the Board, whose merits in starting the campaign and mobilizing Jewish public opinion and action remain above all doubt. In the eyes of the protesting rabbis, the issues at stake were evidently an important matter of principle, outlined in German in an unsigned "private communication" dated January 1862:

> It is encouraging that many of the petitions presented to the Congress bear more signatures of Christians than of Jews—of American Christians, of course: The Germans have even here not yet advanced much in matters of tolerance. Even some of the most prominent statesmen, members of the state-legislatures, felt disposed to lend their names to the protest against any curtailment of religious freedom. To doubt the eventual success of these petitions would mean to entirely misjudge the American nation.

The writer then explained the circumstances of the initiative taken by the Board of Delegates, which in his opinion represents no more than some 1,500 citizens, but claims to be the spokesman of 200,000 American Jews:

> Had we remained silent in the face of such presumption, we would have conjured the greatest dangers upon our heads. The practical American generously grants to everyone his personal freedom and religious conviction. But he hates and fears nothing more—and rightfully so—than those closed corporate bodies who under the pretext of furthering religious purposes soon encroach upon other spheres and so create a state within the state.

Recalling the recent xenophobic outbursts of the "Know-Nothing" party aimed against the much more numerous and powerful American Catholics, the writer concludes:

> Should the handful of Israelites [in this country] succumb silently to the ambition of a few men who like so much to see themselves in the roles of a president, vice president etc.? [The vice president of the Board was Isaac Leeser—A.B.] This could not be allowed to happen, and therefore an emphatic protest . . . was published in the most important political papers of the United States, with the main purpose . . . to open the eyes of the American public and the Congress about the unauthorized machinations of this Board and to deny any involvement of themselves or their congregations in the same.[24]

If these arguments sound strange to present-day American Jews, they certainly must have sounded familiar to their fathers, up to the first half of our century. It was not just envy, or the unexplained intention of "sabotage," that motivated the American "Protest Rabbis" in 1862, but rather serious disagreement about the ways and means for Jewish political assertion and representation in America. The practical differences of opinion had an even deeper underlying ideological foundation. If, as the advocates of religious Reform claimed, Judaism was no more than one of many religious denominations, without any further bonds of belonging to the Jewish minority group in and outside the United States, any separate Jewish political organizations or actions were not only superfluous. They were considered dangerous for the very reasons expressed in the above quoted communication to the Jewish readers in Germany: the fear of "how would it look" in the eyes of American Gentiles.

On the other hand, it is important to keep in mind that the attacked Board of Delegates had come to life in the wake of the notorious Mortara case of 1858. Like many Jewish communities in Europe, American Jewish leaders had tried in vain to convince President Buchanan's administration to take diplomatic action in Rome on behalf of the forcibly abducted Jewish infant. Their failure revealed the still uncertain position of the Jewish community in America, as well as its political immaturity. Jewish leaders were not yet willing "to air Jewish interests collectively in the political marketplace."[25] This reluctance came to the fore in the chaplaincy campaign, and even more pronouncedly so in the Jewish reactions to Grant's edict and its aftermath during the presidential election campaign of 1868.

The infamous edict, implying that all "Jews, as a class" were law-violating speculators, was first attacked by a hitherto quite unknown individual: Cesar J. Kaskel of Paducah, Kentucky. It was his persistent and persuasive efforts that moved Jewish communal leaders, editors, and rabbis to action in Washington. Kaskel succeeded in preventing an obstructive clash between Isaac M. Wise and the representative of the Board of Delegates. Some prominent Jews who had been known supporters of the Democrats or Republicans had for an instant joined their voices to condemn the Grant order. Three days after the president's decree, Isaac M. Wise and Max Lilienthal arrived in Washington at the head of a delegation to thank the president, in the name of all Jews. They then ventured to lobby senators and congressmen of their respective parties in order to secure a resolution censuring the edict, but with no success. The matter soon became an issue of party politics, dominated on both sides by considerations of political convenience and opportunism. On the other hand, Jewish lobbying in its infancy was split, sporadic, and unexperienced, and the Jewish vote was of negligible importance.

The first Jewish reaction was shock, pain, and anger. Jewish soldiers had lost their lives in battle, while Jewish congregations and charitable societies were raising funds for the support of war widows and orphans. Now they felt victimized as the scapegoats for all the crimes in the war area.[26] Such, for a while, was the general tenor of the editorials and letters of the Jewish press. Even the always cautious and conservative *Jewish Messenger*, the unofficial mouthpiece of the Board of Delegates, called Grant "a marked man" and hinted that the "Jewish community will claim and receive full and complete satisfaction" after the war. It went on to "warn our coreligionists to beware of being used by designing politicians for partisan, unpatriotic ends." Instead of being deceived by those who posed as their friends, American Jews were called to prove that "Israelites are among the most valuable, useful and influential members of society."[27]

However, when the opportunity arrived to live up to these intentions American Jewry, including the *Jewish Messenger,* was back again at its fearfully guarded political neutrality. The expelling order of 1863 was taken up as a widely discussed issue in the election campaign of 1868 regarding the nomination and election of Grant. The Jewish position in the election campaign reflected the stage of American Jewry's political adjustment to American conditions. Jewish leaders found themselves confronted with one of the more serious problems of any minority group: "What influence would or should its own unique experience have on its stand in an election? Could Jews, whatever their previous political beliefs and affiliation, vote for the author of so flagrant an anti-Jewish measure?"[28] In the election of 1868 the Jewish immigrant society and its individual members faced, probably for the first time, the dilemma of the priority of minority-group interests before other political loyalties.

The outcome of the dilemma was that no united Jewish attitude evolved to leave any impression on the political scene. The same *Jewish Messenger* that some years before had predicted retaliatory actions against the author of Order No. 11 now insisted that no such thing as a Jewish vote existed: "If Jews desire to take one side or other . . . they can do so as citizens of the Republic. But as Jews they should abstain from bringing religion into politics." The *Messenger* nevertheless announced its support for Grant's Democratic opponent, supported also by Isaac M. Wise, an inveterate Democrat. In Memphis, Tennessee, the most closely affected Jewish community, speakers in a mass meeting of the community urged "that the only position Grant deserved to be elevated to was the one occupied by Haman in the last moments of his career."[29] The meeting passed a resolution that castigated Grant as "unfit for the high position to which he aspires" and urged Jewish communities everywhere to endorse their initiative. Only one community followed suit. On the other hand, numerous Jewish leaders supported the Republican ticket and established "Hebrew Grant Clubs" for this purpose.[30]

According to Bertram Korn, this result was inevitable because "the very nature of American life and growth militated against the development of an organically unified American Jewry. America offered its rewards for individual effort and initiative." The immigrating Jews had joined this American race, and "for a whole century . . . the American

Jew has been captured by the mood and modes of American life. The election of 1868 was an effective demonstration of that."[31]

One may agree or disagree with this way of justifying, at least implicitly, the lack of nationwide, coordinated Jewish political activity. Maybe such activity could not possibly have been realized under the conditions that prevailed at that time. But in any case the Civil War was unquestionably an important and irreversible stage in the history of the Jewish immigrant society. In its first stages, Jewish community leaders on either side of the conflicting camps had cautiously tried to keep aloof, or demonstrated their loyalty to the cause of their respective states of residence. Before long they were forced to realize that the general uproar of emotions did not stop at their doorstep: it evoked ingrained bigotry, which drew them into the fray. On both sides of the front line, Jews found themselves under attack, not only as fighting partisans in the conflict but as members of an abused religious minority on both sides. Willingly or reluctantly, American Jewry for the first time mobilized its forces to take organized political action as an avowed interest-group. In this way the Civil War, as in many other aspects of America's history and society, activated catalyzing forces in the ongoing process of the German-Jewish immigrant society's coming of age.

6

The Second Wave

1865–1914

More Than a Trickle

According to Rudolf Glanz, the process of German-Jewish emigration remained "incomplete." It was interrupted in the 1870s, when as a result of Germany's industrialization Jewish emigration was "reduced to a mere trickle."[1] Glanz was unquestionably one of the first and most knowledgeable historians of the subject,[2] but nevertheless this still widely shared opinion does not stand up to recent demographic research concerning German-Jewish population movements on both sides of the ocean. General estimates that are today more or less standard among scholars of American Jewish history should cause skeptical reconsideration of this claim. If indeed "the number of Jews, which stood at about 15,000 in 1840, was authoritatively estimated at 150,000 in 1860, and probably reached 280,000 in 1880,"[3] immigration must have been a major factor for this growth. From the emigrating side of the process, the cautious estimates of Professor Usiel Schmelz are highly corroborative. Calculating natural growth rates and migration balances he concludes that "if the negative [net] migration balance of the Jews between 1852 and 1895 was approximately 115,000 to 135,000, the number of actual emigrants must have been greater, because there were at the time also some Jewish immigrants." For 1872 through 1895 Schmelz calculated a migration deficit (i.e., natural growth minus migrations) of no less than 75,000 Jews from the boundaries of the German Reich alone. In another estimate, for 1890 through 1910, Schmelz arrives at an emigration of over 60,000 Jews from the same area.[4] Allowing for a cautious estimate of between 20,000 and

35,000 immigrants in the same period, the number of actual emigrants must have been around 100,000.

For the preceding period, starting in 1845, I have elsewhere independently calculated an approximate 113,000 proper emigrants, that is, not counting offspring born abroad.[5] All these figures add up to no less than 250,000 German-Jewish emigrants for the 65 years between 1846 and 1910, and of them at least 100,000 left Germany after the American Civil War. Of course, not all of these emigrants arrived eventually in the United States but we may safely assume that most of them did. The general German emigration continued throughout this time, reaching a new peak in 1881–82: in these two years alone 425,000 Germans left their homes. All available evidence indicates that the disproportionate Jewish participation in the earlier emigration waves did continue, although the Jewish part may have been somewhat lower than in the pre–Civil War period.

Estimates of German-Jewish arrivals on the American shores are even more difficult. In 1914 Joseph Jacobs commented on this state of affairs:

> Owing to the rigid separation of Church and State in the United States no attempt has been made in the census investigations to determine the distribution of population according to religion. However one may regret this as a statistician one has to acquiesce as a good citizen. But as a consequence, any attempt to ascertain the number of Jews in the United States must take the form of estimates which are notoriously untrustworthy, and as a rule overshoot the mark.[6]

Confronting various estimates and complementing them with a reasonable calculation of birth- and natural-growth rates of the Jewish immigrants and native-born Americans, Jacobs arrived at a total of 2,350,000 Jews in the year 1910, of which he counted some 315,000 as first- or second-generation German immigrants. He also estimated that "nearly 200,000 of the original quarter of a million Jews, in 1881, were probably of German descent," which is, in the light of more recent research, a conservative and cautious calculation. The additional 115,000 German Jews estimated by Jacobs were the descendants of the earlier and later immigrants between 1882 and 1910.

All these sources together clearly show that German-Jewish immigration after the Civil War and up to 1914 was certainly much more than a "mere trickle." I doubt if the real number of new immigrants proper can ever be exactly ascertained. However, I believe that I am on the conservative side when I estimate it at no less than 70,000, and probably much more. This figure represents only 2.2 percent of the 3,157,400 German immigrants to the United States during this period, which is very close to Jacob's calculations for 1900–1910, which are derived from the reports of the Commissioner General of Immigration and from Jewish sources. From all we know, the Jewish part in the earlier German emigration was much higher, between 3 and almost 4 percent of the total.[7] Compared with the total Jewish immigration of the period after 1880, the number of Jewish immigrants from Germany, or even of German-speaking Jews as compared with the Yiddish-speaking Eastern European immigrants, was, of course, not very impressive. Nevertheless this does not justify ignoring this second immigration wave of German or German-speaking Jews.

Background and Motivations

The "reactionary" 1850s and 1860s, following the revolutionary turmoil of 1848 and its anti-Jewish riots, were probably the most fortunate and optimistic years in the history of the Jews in Germany. True, political emancipation was a slow and protracted process, and full social integration remained for most German Jews an unfulfilled dream even before the unexpected outbreak of the violent new movement of political anti-Semitism in the early 1870s. But in every other aspect an unmistakable upward movement was nevertheless characteristic of this period.

Economically the lowest strata of homeless, indigent *Betteljuden,* who in the early decades of the century still constituted a considerable part of German Jewry, gradually disappeared. Peddlers were becoming shopkeepers, and shopkeepers wholesale merchants and manufacturers. Village Jews moved to nearby small and middle-size towns, some even to Berlin. Elementary education became general, for girls as well as boys, and more and more young Jews continued on to high schools and universities. Yiddish, the "Judeo-German" sponsored by Moses Mendelssohn and the Jewish educators of the Enlightenment, disappeared, to be replaced by "pure" German and the idolization of Goethe and Schiller, not to mention the much-adored Lessing. At the foundation of the German Reich in 1871 equality before the law had been established for all German lands. Even in Bavaria the loathed "Matrikel" laws were revoked in 1861.

It was therefore only natural that the immigrants who arrived in the United States after the Civil War and during the whole "Gilded Age" differed a great deal from those of the prewar period. "Modernized German Jews began to come to America only in the 1850's and then again after the Civil War."[8] Because scholars have tended to neglect this second-wave immigration, we have far fewer learned studies about their demographic and social composition than for the earlier arrivals. Scanning the archives and some local community histories produces, however, a picture of the situation. First, the skewed gender proportions of the first decades gradually leveled out, as more young girls came, or were brought over, to marry earlier immigrants or their sons. This development was particularly evident in faraway pioneer settlements like Portland, Oregon. In 1860, adult Jewish men in Portland still outnumbered women by a ratio of 3.3 to 1. In 1870 the difference was already reduced to 1.6 to 1, and it was further diminished to 1.06 to 1 in 1900.[9]

Second, although most of the immigrants were still young, their greater part arrived after an orderly voyage, mostly by steamboat. In many cases German Jews now traveled second, or even first, class. Accounts of their preparations for emigration tell of careful assembling of all necessary equipment before starting out to the New World. Most available sources, like memoirs and published or unpublished family histories, suggest that these immigrants had a reasonable income, or came from moderately well-to-do middle-class families. Only rarely is material need mentioned as the motive for emigration.

Third, chain-migration of younger siblings was naturally much more usual than in the first wave. Almost all new arrivals knew in advance where they would go after disembarking. In most cases they were expected by earlier-arriving relatives and would live with the family and join them in business, at least for their first steps in the new country. In the first half of the century, "push" motives of legal discrimination, the impossibility of settling down and marrying, and material necessity were dominant. In the second half the "pull" factors of family connections and economic enterprise, following already well-prepared paths, gained increasingly in importance. One outstanding "push" factor, now perhaps even stronger than before, was the desire to avoid military service, which induced many young men to leave home before their seventeenth birthday.

Some illustrative examples may serve to substantiate this summary. Edmond Uhry, born in 1874 in Ingweiler in Alsace (which had become German by annexation in 1871), relates in his memoirs how his elder brother went to America in 1884:

> The German laws required that male emigrants place their application to be released from the German Reich before their 17th birthday. . . . After this *"Entlassungsurkunde"* [document of release] was granted the applicant had to depart within six months. Otherwise the release was recalled, and the applicant's name remained on the conscription list, to be called to service at the age of twenty. . . . Today one may wonder how parents could bring themselves to send such young sons into the world . . . when sea traffic

was slow and dangerous and the prospects of a reunion much more uncertain than today. Still, almost every family in our town sent their sons into the far world. Greater chances and freedom in the New World were some inducement, but more important was the future conscription. In our frontier land, oppressed by Prussian militarism, the three years of military service were much dreaded. . . . If the sons could escape this, the farewell became easier. In some cases the families hoped for a later reunion in the land which the sons had yet to win as pioneers.

This indeed was the case in Uhry's family, who followed his two elder brothers in 1891, traveling second-class from Le Havre.[10]

That unwillingness to serve in the army was a main cause for emigration is evidenced by the many young Jewish men who arived in America just before their seventeenth birthday. In the American Jewish Achives some copies of "release documents" are preserved with other biographic material: Adolf Feibelmann, a cattle dealer's apprentice from Germersheim in the Bavarian Palatinate, received his *"Entlassungsurkunde"* in 1889, at the age of "16¾ years." Samual Haas, a commercial apprentice aged sixteen, of Homburg, was released from the citizenship of the Hessian Grand Duchy in 1879, under the explicit condition that he leave within six months.[11] Herman H. Goldschmidt, born 1865, left Furfeld in Rhenish Hesse "to avoid being drafted into military service. His brother Max, born in 1862 or 1863, had come to Los Angeles in 1886."[12]

Following siblings or even friends to America was as strong an inducement as the "pull" of American prosperity and the success stories of earlier immigrants. Letters and visitors from the New World spread the promising news of what could be achieved across the ocean. Herman (Weil) Wile's elder brother arrived in Buffalo, New York, in 1867. Nine years later he visited the family home in Baden and returned in the company of an eighteen-year-old sister. Herman remained at home, finished school and started as an apprentice to a Freiburg merchant, but at the age of sixteen decided to leave: "One of my most intimate childhood friends had gone to America 9 months before me and that was a great inducement to come to this country." His family was quite well-off: Herman's father paid his master the 600 marks required to release him from his three-year contract, and Herman went on his way:

I came to America on April 25, 1881. I arrived in Buffalo the next day and the following day I went into the clothing manufacturing business to work for my brother, Mayer Wile. At that time I lived with my sister, Caroline. . . . My first visit to Europe was in 1888. I visited my parents and relatives. Two of my brothers and two of my sisters [out of eight siblings; Herman was the youngest] never came to this country, but eventually all of their children did.

The fifteen-page memoir continues to dwell on the narrator's many trips to his hometown and the many relatives he helped emigrate to the United States through the late 1940s.[13]

Similar stories abound in archives and family papers. Sigmund Seligsberger, born 1863 in Bavaria as the third son of a teacher, came to America three months before reaching the age of seventeen: "An older brother had been in America for several years, writing enthusiastic letters from Terre Haute, Indiana. His praises of this country made me long for the day when I might come over. I kept after my parents until my father went with me to the proper authorities and got me a visa." Seligsberger sailed second-class from Hamburg, having "renounc[ed] all claims to German citizenship."[14]

On May 5, 1884, Jacob Behrend wrote his family in Bodenberg:

> Dear Parents and Brothers and Sisters! I have received your letters, and I am glad to note from them the well-being of all of you. As I see from your letter, dear Bertha, Bodenberg is becoming too small for you, and therefore you would like to exchange it for Philadelphia. Of course, a large city always offers more than a small place. Now should it be your wish to come here, and should our dear parents agree to it, you will be welcome to me and to my dear Sara. We shall receive you with open arms, and I shall do everything to further your welfare. . . . Where eight persons eat my dear Bertha also can eat something gratis, and I shall presumably find employment for you. Of course, it would be better if you had come here sooner. But there is always more chance for you here than there.[15]

For some still unexplained reasons, most published biographies, autobiographies, and family histories, as well as unpublished material of this kind so far unearthed in the archives, stem from Jewish immigrants from the western and southern parts of Germany or their descendants. This is probably another result of the neglected research on the second-wave immigration, which to a far larger extent than before originated from the eastern and northeastern parts of Germany. Although it is generally known that the emigration from Germany, that of both Gentiles and Jews, "moved East" in the second half of the century, this development has earned only marginal attention. The conflicts between "Bayers" and "Pollacks" during the first stages of the immigration are extensively recorded and sometimes exaggerated, but the later arrival of many thousands of immigrants from Silesia, Posen, and other East German provinces, and their specific ways of adjusting to the earlier-established and institutionalized Jewish society, has so far been for the most part neglected.

On the German side, information is also only partial. The massive exodus of the Jews from the Prussian provinces of Posen and West Prussia, and somewhat less drastically also from Silesia, are well-recorded in

German-Jewish historiography, but little is known about where these people went. The Posen Jews, derogatively termed *"Hinter-Berliners,"* who in the late nineteenth century became real Berliners, were one of the main factors of the growth of the capital's Jewish population. Therefore it is generally assumed that most of the Jews who left the eastern provinces moved to Berlin. Many indeed did, but hardly all of them. A considerable part went abroad. Many of them—although we will probably never know exactly how many—came to America. The combined result was the drastic decline of Posen's Jewish population in relative, as well as absolute, terms. From its peak number of close to 80,000 in 1843, constituting 6.2 percent of the province's total population, the number went consistently down to only 26,500, a mere 1.3 percent of the population in 1910. The main exodus occurred between 1861 and 1900, when the Jewish population declined to less than half its number: from close to 74,200 to 35,300. As these are net migration deficits, neglecting the natural growth during this time, the number of emigrants proper was naturally much higher.[16]

The development in the three Prussian provinces with a relatively large Jewish population is shown in table 6.1. Keeping in mind that many Jewish immigrants entered at the same time from across the neighboring Polish border, raising even more the relatively high Jewish birthrates of these regions as compared with the whole of Germany, the absolute net decline of the Jewish population between 1871 and 1910 must have been caused by a considerably larger number of emigrants. A part of the Posen Jews probably simply moved to Silesia; another part remained in Germany, many of them in Berlin. But many thousands emigrated to America.

Table 6.1
Total Jewish Population, 1825–1910

	1825	1871	1910
West Prussia	15,300	26,600	13,900
Posen	65,100	62,000	26,500
Silesia	19,700	46,600	45,000

SOURCE: H. Silbergleit, *Die Bevölkerung- und Berufsverhältnisse der Juden im Deutschen Reich* (Berlin, 1930), pp. 18–19.

Due to the consistent patterns of chain-migration and settlement in clusters, we are able to trace their arrival in the later-established Jewish communities. In cities like New York, Philadelphia, and even San Francisco, whose Jewish population also increased during these years, the new immigrants were absorbed into the existing communities and recorded together, if at all, as "Germans." However, some recent studies investigating, among other things, places of birth of community members suggest that in later-established Jewish communities the percentage of those born in the eastern Prussian provinces was considerably higher than in earlier settlements (see table 6.2).

Table 6.2
Boston: Places of Birth of the Jewish Population,
1860–1900 (percentage)

	1860	1880	1900
Massachusetts	1.2	45.2	59.0
Southwest Germany	33.7	9.5	8.2
Northeast Germany	45.3	35.7	18.0
Other	19.8	9.6	14.8
Total	100.0	100.0	100.0
Foreign-born (%)	98.8	54.8	34.4
Northeast Germany in percentage of foreign-born	45.9	35.7	52.4

SOURCE: Burton S. Kliman, "The Jewish Brahmins of Boston: A Study of the German Jewish Immigration Experience, 1860–1900," B.A. thesis (Brandeis University, 1978), pp. 465–67.

As is evident from these figures, the "Prussian" immigrants, coming from Posen and other eastern German parts, were the single most important group in Boston's Jewish population. That they had also arrived somewhat later than the "Bavarians" is borne out by their growing numbers among Boston's foreign-born Jews as late as 1900. Stephen Mostov has also shown that 44 percent of all German-Jewish immigrants to Boston between 1840 and 1861 were born in northeast Germany or in Poland, and the trend seems to have continued.

Although "Bayers" and "Polishers" lived in the same general neighborhood, and both groups were German-speaking, cultural and social differences very early led to communal factionalism. . . . Besides its effect on the internal cohesion of the Jewish community, the relatively large number of German Jews from the Eastern provinces undoubtedly also inhibited social and cultural interaction between Jewish and other Germans in Boston, given the very low proportion of all German emigrants coming from that region.[17]

Boston was a relatively late-established Jewish community. This was one reason for the preponderance of "Polishers," in contrast to earlier places of settlement like Cincinnati. Of the Jews who had arrived there between 1817 and 1865 only 14 percent came from "Prussia," as opposed to 82 percent from southeast Germany, mainly from Bavaria.[18] On the other hand, in Los Angeles, also a late place of settlement, close to 40 percent of the foreign-born Jews in 1880 were born in Prussia, and many of them came from the same small town, Loebau. The Polish-Prussian Jews born between 1830 and 1850 remained the single largest foreign-born Jewish group, and of the native-born many were listed in the census of 1880 as having one or both parents born in Prussia.[19]

If immigration from northeast Germany started in significant numbers thirty or forty years later than from the southwest, the "pull" of family chain-migration must have played a minor role as a motive, at least at the start. This was, however, more than compensated in these cases by the "push" of economic necessity. The Jews of Posen and West Prussia, the two provinces with the absolute and relatively largest Jewish population in Prussia, were long regarded to be the poorest German Jews. Forbidden to settle in the villages, they crowded some of the greater and middle-size towns, where they could hardly eke out a living as small peddlers and artisans. Many of the vagrant *schnorrers* or *Betteljuden* who toured all German lands set out from these parts, returning home to rest with their families after each trip. Their position improved only in the 1860s. The Poseners disappeared from the ranks of the beggars, and the German Jews ceased to call them "Poles."[20] But in economic terms, even in the 1870s, the Prussian-Polish Jews still lagged behind. In contrast to the general advance of most German Jews, their position had deteriorated from the 1830s and 1840s on. The decline in the traditional crafts compelled many to seek a living in petty trade, mainly as itinerant hawkers. Thousands of families lived in utter poverty. These were the economic and social factors for the gradual depopulation of the Jewish centers in the Grand Duchy of Posen, "centres which had become famous for their handicrafts as well as for their intellectual life."[21]

What role did the growing anti-Jewish sentiment and the rise of political anti-Semitism in Germany play at this stage of the emigration? In Posen it certainly was an important inducement, along with the economic pressure. The Jews, discriminated against by the German authorities, were no less abused by the traditionally anti-Semitic Polish population, who regarded them, not entirely without reason, as agents of Germanization. In other parts of Germany as well, despite the emancipation and acculturation of the Jews, popular Jew-hatred had not passed away. In Bavaria the abolition of discriminatory laws in 1861 caused anti-Jewish riots. In at least two Franconian villages in 1866, the situation required military intervention from the central authorities. The local population evidently took offense at Jews being admitted to the so-called *Gemeinde-nutzungen*, that is, the use of common lands for pasture and wood. Quiet was restored only after these small Jewish communities "volunteered" to give up participation in the commons, trading some of their newly won rights for peace.[22]

Contemporary Jewish spokesmen ardently repudiated any suggestion that associated emigration with the rise of political anti-Semitism, but this does not mean that they reflected the feelings and actions of Jewish "men on the street." In 1880 an anonymous letter from "a very distinguished source from one of the greater American cities" told of the "painful impression which the modern Jew-persecution in Prussia left among our coreligionists in this country." The writer asked the editor, as "the Nestor and foremost champion of Jewish emancipation," if it "would not be the time to found a general emigration society for the German, or better, the Prussian Jews?" Specifically, he proposed to settle the emigrants on newly developed territories in Tennessee and Texas, "which alone could provide a blessed and free home for our brothers."

Ludwig Philippson rejected the idea out of hand:

> First, the sole announcement of such an emigration society for the German Jews would cause us great damage. Our opponents would immediately say: Yes, this is exactly what we want, to expel all Jews from Germany! They themselves prove our assertion that they are no real German patriots, but cosmopolitans, ready to leave the *Vaterland* at the first storm. Second, there is so far no reason to emigrate. Matters are not as bad as they look by the noise made in newspapers and speeches. We go on living here quietly and unperturbed.

After adding several more practical objections Philippson concluded that

> according to their doctrine and history the Jews have to faithfully hold out in their fatherland until immediate self-preservation compels them to emigrate. Their mission is to serve as the instrument and touchstone to promote justice and humanity among the peoples, as many sacrifices as this may cost.[23]

As we have seen, not all German Jews shared Philippson's optimism, least of all the "Prussian" Jews who at the time made up the greater part of the emigrants.

Integration of the Newcomers

Arriving forty or more years after the start of the German-Jewish mass immigration, the later immigrants found an entirely different scene. Most of the earlier immigrants had already permanently settled, founded families, and established businesses and congregations all over the United States. The census of the Jews in America in 1877, based on a meticulous survey by the Board of Delegates and the Union of American Hebrew Congregations, recorded the existence of 277 congregations in 174 cities, dispersed over thirty-seven of the thirty-eight then-existing states of the Union and the District of Columbia. The geographic distribution of the German Jews had "rooted Judaism in all corners of the United States."[24]

The second wave of German-Jewish immigrants after the Civil War was for obvious reasons a far less mobile group than its predecessor. It largely consisted of the siblings, parents, or other relatives of those who had arrived earlier, who naturally found their first station with the earlier arrivals. In most cases younger men and women were welcomed to the households of their already settled relatives. Taking in a boarder, preferably a relative or at least a German Jew, seems to have played some role in household financing. In Boston the South End became known as a "boarding and tenement district." In 1860, 14.7 percent of all Jewish Bostonian families had boarders; the percentage declined to 12.0 percent in 1880 and became negligible in 1900.[25] Besides the economic and social ascent, the decline may have been caused also by the decreasing number of newly arriving relatives.

Very often the new immigrants also started their economic careers as the partners or employees of earlier-arriving relatives, a time-honored arrangement that benefited both parties. Herman Wertheim, for example, arrived in New Mexico in 1910

in the company of my cousin who had settled in Dona Ana, near Las Cruces, and who had been living there for many years. . . . I worked in his store for only about three weeks. It was indeed a very short time to stay on a job. . . . Working conditions and living conditions were not very good in Dona Ana. I stayed in my cousin's home during that extremely short period of three weeks that I worked in his store, and I could not stand the living conditions there. . . . Then my brother (who had come to the country four years earlier) got me a job in Bernalillo, New Mexico. . . . The entire personnel of the company then was composed of boys who had come over from Germany. . . . The German-Jewish boys did not stay for very long with the Bernalillo Mercantile Company. . . . After a short time they would leave the employ of the store, and would open up their own stores in the various towns of New Mexico. The Jewish folks in Bernalillo consisted of the Seligman brothers and the several Jewish boys who came to work for them. This is how the German-Jewish boys got their start in business.[26]

Settlement in New Mexico or other territories of the United States was all but typical for the second wave of immigrants. Settling in these last American pioneer areas was an exception at this stage of the German-Jewish immigration. The Jewish census of 1877 recorded 108 Jews in the whole territory of New Mexico, and 48 in Arizona.[27] Induced to leave Germany by the opportunities promised in the reports of earlier immigrants, most newcomers preferred to seek their realization in the more secure surroundings of already established Jewish communities. First among these ranged the East Coast cities: New York, Philadelphia, Baltimore, and Boston seem to have absorbed the greater part of this second immigration, judging by the recorded or estimated growth of their Jewish population between 1860 and 1880. In New York City it doubled from 40,000 to 80,000, in Philadelphia it grew from 8,000 to 12,000, in Baltimore from 8,000 to 10,000. The figures for Boston are somewhat inconclusive: in 1860 the Jewish community there counted about 2,500 persons by most estimates, but the figures for 1880 given by various sources range from 3,000 to 7,000.[28] In my opinion, the latter number is the more convincing.

The second important aim of the later immigration was California, whose Jewish population of 1877 counted over 18,500 souls, second only to New York State's 80,600. Most of these California Jews, in fact 16,000 or more, lived in San Francisco, at the time the second-largest Jewish community in the United States, after New York City. Los Angeles was still a relatively new and small place of settlement. In 1870 only some 150 Jews lived there, among the recorded total population of no more than 5,600. In 1880 their number had increased to close to 500, of which over 50 percent were native-born and under nineteen years of age. The foreign-born Jews over twenty-five were mostly of "Polish" origin in their cultural tradition, but not according to their formal "Prussian" nationality.[29] Chicago, which was also later to become a large community of Eastern European Jews, counted 1,500 Jews in 1860 and already 10,000 in 1880. By comparison, Cincinnati's Jewish population increased only moderately during these years, and only 14 percent of the city's German-born Jews originated from Prussia. Given the scarceness of comparable data, these facts nevertheless prove the family-oriented character of this later chain-migration and the tendency of settling in clusters according to the regions of origin in the old country.

This same tendency can also be traced in the choice of residential quarters inside various cities. Besides being indicative of differences in the social status of the later arrivals as compared with the older residents, residential patterns also reflect the cohesiveness of the respective groups, as well as their wish to detach themselves from the later arrivals. In Boston the formation of a new "suburban ghetto" of higher-class "German-Jewish Brahmins" has been convincingly established.[30] For New York a similar development was induced after the Civil War by a group of better-off German-Jewish merchants, who moved their homes and founded a new congregation in Harlem's Third Avenue commercial district, while their former quarters were taken up by less fortunate, later-arriving immigrants.[31]

These residential movements reflected not only the time-lag of immigration, but also, and probably even more importantly, the social stratification among the German-Jewish community. The larger the Jewish community of any given city, the less homogeneous it tended to be in economic and social terms. The time of arrival was only one, albeit important, factor of a person's place in this social structure. It is therefore not surprising to find the most outstanding evidence of social differences in New York's Jewish society long before the arrival of the East European mass immigration. Around 1880 the greater part of them still dwelled on the Lower East Side, in the German enclave called *Kleindeutschland* (little Germany). More prosperous German Jews lived in Chelsea, around Seventh Avenue and 19th Street. The community was already in a process of advanced social stratification. This was reflected in its residential expansion to "Yorkville" between 72nd and 100th streets east of Lexington Avenue, and some, as we have seen, had already ventured farther north. Class antagonism was already present within the German-Jewish community.[32]

In the end both of the two consecutive groups of immigrants merged socially, and over time no sharp distinction of respective economic or occupational structures is discernible. However, the cream of the commercial opportunities of the pioneer era had obviously already been skimmed off by the time the second wave arrived. It is almost exclusively in the few newly settled regions that the spectacular success stories of the former period are found repeated, and only some single, exceptional individuals from among the later arrivals really gained entry in the German-Jewish financial aristocracy. Even in Los Angeles and other parts of California it was generally the earlier arrivals who were the founders of the most prosperous enterprises. Herman W. Hellman, the father of a famous banking and real estate dynasty, arrived in Los Angeles in 1859, following two cousins who had been there since 1853, and started a wholesale groceries business.[33] Another example is Morris Lasker, another founder of a prosperous family business. He arrived in America in 1856 from Jarocin, Posen, and after several business attempts in Virginia, New York, and Florida came to Weatherford, Texas, in 1860. Lasker served two years in the Confederate army and later ranked "as one of the leading and representative citizens of Galveston, and one of the most successful financiers in the South."[34]

Most of the second-wave immigrants seem to have been less success-ful and remained at best well-situated middle-class entrepreneurs or higher-rank commercial employees. If this may appear as a somewhat risky generalization, it is borne out by most local or regional studies, as from the vast collection of California Jewish genealogical histories col-lected by Norton B. Stern and deposited at the American Jewish Ar-chives. Most of the families recorded as arriving in California did so in the 1870s and 1880s. At the time of the investigation, in the 1950s, most of the interviewed persons of the second and third generation were inde-pendent middle-class businessmen. Many of them had completed college, but their greater part had later returned to business, either in the old established family firm or in new enterprises. Marriages were to a great degree—although, of course, not exclusively—inside the inner circle of German-Jewish society. Large families, often with eight to ten children, were for a time characteristic, at least for the first-generation immigrants. There also was a relatively high rate of persistence in the cities and locations of the immigrants' first place of permanent settlement.[35] In this, too, the group of later arrivals in the West deviated from the practices of their successful predecessors, who in many cases returned to the eastern states after they had amassed capital in the West.

An attempt to detect and follow up the development of Boston's "Jewish Brahmins" arrived at some rather disappointing results. In 1900 only 8.3 percent of the families of the investigated sample, who had ar-rived in Boston before 1860, owned real estate, including the houses in which they lived, and 67.8 percent owned no property at all. "In 1860 Boston's German Jewish community consisted of an unorganized collec-tion of poor entrepreneurs struggling to get ahead. By 1900 the poor had, for the most part, left the city, leaving behind a middle to upper middle class of German Jewish businessmen."[36] At this time the German-Jewish group, including the later immigrants and the native-born descendants of the first-comers, already constituted a minority among American Jewry. Former social differences inside this group had not yet totally disap-peared, but they were almost negligible compared with those that divided the group from the masses of newly arrived Russian and Polish Jews. The group-specific occupational and social structure of the German immigrant group persisted for quite a long time, even in the first decade of the twentieth century, after the immigration from the German-speaking coun-tries had become indeed only a trickle.

Depending, again, on the pitifully few local studies, we may briefly outline the most characteristic traits of this group. Socially it consisted of mostly middle-class or upper-middle-class families, concentrated up to 60 or 70 percent in white-collar occupations. While most of the older heads of families were self-employed, a good part of the younger, native-born generation worked as clerks in the family business. In most cases this was a temporary stage on the way to later upward mobility and the establishment of their own independent firms. A very high percentage of these businesses were commercial and, to a lesser extent, manufacturing enterprises, and they were concentrated in the branches of "typical Jewish" economic activities, i.e., ready-made clothing and the dry-goods industry, with a sprinkling of food and liquor manufacturing and distribution.[37]

Interestingly, the native-born offspring of the group preferred to return to business after achieving an education, instead of entering the professions. In Milwaukee around the turn of the century, sons and daughters of the Eastern European Jewish immigrants are recorded to have become "doctors, dentists, lawyers, teachers, academics, accountants and civil servants," but only the grandchildren of the early immigrants tended to enter these fields.[38] This may, of course, be explained by the general economic and social development of the country: the increasing importance of the professions and the services connected with industrialization and the rising standard of living. At that time the second generation of the Russian-Jewish immigrants coincided roughly with the third generation of German Jews, which would explain the difference between "children and grandchildren."

The same tendency has, however, been observed also in other places and seems to reflect a general preference among the younger German-Jewish generation that persisted over a relatively long period of time. Marshall Sklare's study in 1967 of "Lakeville, an upper-status Midwest suburb in which both groups are represented" induced him to conclude that

> despite the fact that East Europeans . . . are highly successful and very prosperous, their incomes are noticeably smaller than that of residents of German descent. Another aspect of cleavage is in levels of education. In this case it is the East European who exceeds the Germans. Thus some 37 percent of East Europeans have studied for an advanced degree in contrast to only 9 percent of the Germans. Given their superior educational attainment, East Europeans are impelled to claim equal status with Germans despite their fiscal inferiority.[39]

One may have some doubts whether Sklare's findings at this relatively late period, over a hundred years since the start of the German immigration, and eighty years since the beginning of the Eastern European immigration, were indeed representative. For the late nineteenth century, however, the tendency of young, native-born Jews to return to the secure haven of their father's prospering enterprises after having attained academic degrees is well-documented. On the other hand, most second-generation Eastern European immigrants had nothing similar to return to. This was probably the reason why they chose academic education and the professions as their main instrument of social mobility, while for the descendants of the German Jews "commerce appeared to be the surest avenue to status and riches."[40]

Family relations and cultural traditions played their part in maintaining these group-characteristic traits. For quite a long time even third-generation German Jews married mainly among themselves and kept socially to themselves. The evolving demographic and social developments among German Jews in the United States very much resemble developments in the Jewish society of Germany of that time, but they also differ in at least one important respect: between 1850 and 1900 marriages of Jews in America of German descent were consecutively performed at a younger age, and families had on the average more children than among the Jews in Germany. Actually, these differences were two sides of the same coin. The improved economic situation of the immigrants after their settlement in the United States must have predisposed them to earlier marriages and larger families. At the same time, the massive emigration of the younger age-groups was undoubtedly one of the decisive factors for the considerable decrease in Jewish birthrates documented in Germany since the early 1860s. Toward the end of the century—that is, at least one generation later—a similar fall in the birthrate seems to have taken place also among American-born Jews of German descent.[41]

On the other hand, the similarity of occupational and social structures of the two Jewish societies is striking. Despite the evident differences in economic opportunities and, up to the late 1860s, of legal conditions as well, German and German-American Jews remained similarly concentrated in commercial pursuits, mainly in retail trade of all kinds, from the small-town general store to the department stores of big cities. In both countries they were prominent in the clothing branches of trade and manufacturing, and some of the prosperous families attained important positions in banking and investment-financing. In both countries they kept to their traditional preference of independent self-employment. If in America the massive entry of young Jews into the professions was somewhat delayed, the reason was probably that they had better opportunities in the business sector than did most of their peers in Germany. Even so, they seem to have discovered the same path after several decades and made up for the delay.

Very much like the Jews who had remained in Germany, the German-Jewish immigrant society that at the end of the century had absorbed and integrated the second wave of immigrants evolved as a middle-class society in every sense. As in Germany, despite the impressive ascent of a small group of prominent bankers, merchants, and industrialists, its economic achievements remained, on the average, modest. They may have been more successful than some of the other ethnic immigrant groups, but many of them did not "make it," and quite a few left the country disillusioned. The greater part, however, remained in the United States—and to a much greater degree than did other immigrant groups. In New York, the largest German-Jewish community during the whole nineteenth century, many Jewish immigrants or their native-born sons had achieved secure economic positions, but before the turn of the century only a few Jews were known as millionaires. "The exception, Henry Hart, a member of an older New York Jewish family, was ranked thirty-second, far below such grand proprietors of wealth as John D. Rockefeller, the Astors, the Vanderbilts and the many lesser magnates who chose to make their homes in the nation's greatest city."[42]

Assessing the social structure of American Jewry in 1941, Jacob Lestschinsky cast a glance over the development of its segment of German descent:

Already 50 or 60 years ago German Jews achieved a high social standing. Some of them at the peak even approached the ranks of the American great bourgeoisie. But in its masses this Jewry remained essentially middle class, with a very small stratum of higher elements, quite a few professionals and a broad mass of white-collar workers. While in the 1860's and '70s some groups of workers still existed even among the German Jews, especially in the clothing industries, they have long ago moved into the camp of the proprietors. . . . The similarity with the German Jewry at the start of the Hitler era is really amazing, not only in their respective occupational and social structure, but also in the level of their positions. . . . It would be one of the most fascinating subjects to investigate the parallels between the German Jewry that perished in Europe and its real heir, the German-American Jews.[43]

Before the start of the Eastern European immigration, as long as the German Jews were the dominant group, American Jewish life bore the characteristics of a modestly prosperous middle class, by its occupations and "set of values (emphasizing steady work, sobriety, saving, calculation)."[44] These values and behavioral patterns of the immigrant society show a high degree of similarity to, but also some important deviations from, those that were current among the German Jews in the old country.

An important component of these group-specific traits was family life and the position of Jewish women within the community.

Women in Family and Society

The interplay of tradition and change, characteristic for the development of the Jewish community in Germany since the Enlightenment, affected the lives of the women probably even more than those of the men. More than in church-centered Christianity, the Jewish religion was observed and performed in the home. Keeping the Sabbath, holidays, the dietary and sexual hygiene laws, and the religious education of the small children were the traditional domain of the Jewish housewife. "Judaism relegated women to a peripheral role in the synagogue, but placed them on a pedestal in the home."[45]

"It is not to be denied," preached Isaac Leeser in 1835,

> that it is almost entirely useless for the female to become learned in the strictest sense of the word; it would indeed unsex her, if she were to study the legal professions; if she were to step abroad as a physician; if she, forgetful of female decorum, would lay on the harness of war and wage a mortal combat with the enemy. . . . For the female's sphere is not the highway, not the public streets, not the embattled field, not the public halls. But her home should be the place of her actions; there her influence should be felt, to soothe, to calm, to sanctify, to render happy the rugged career of a father, a brother, a husband or a child.

From here he continued to lay out the rules of religious education for the Jewish girl, how she should be taught to behave, to dress, to speak and what to read, in order "to become qualified for this holy, for this noble task."[46]

Commenting on Leeser's sermon, Jacob R. Marcus is skeptical about how much his ideals did indeed reflect "the views of the typical Jewish papa or mamma of the 1830s." In his opinion the very serious *hazzan*, a twenty-nine-year-old bachelor, was "far over on the right." But there can be little doubt that Leeser's sermon did express the opinions and attitudes of the settled and established Jewish middle class. These were the norms that prevailed in the Jewish communities in Germany, as well as in the old Jewish settlements of the American East Coast or the South. Keeping in mind the need of a differentiated gender-specific analysis, which is still unavailable, we may nevertheless arrive at a more or less accurate, if somewhat generalized, description of women's role in Jewish middle-class families, which around 1830 already constituted a considerable part, and were soon to become the majority, of German-Jewish society.

Woman's role as a housewife, economically dependent on the male family members, had its compensatory sides. She was esteemed and cherished as the magnetic center of Jewish life. She was expected to create the atmosphere of intimate care and pious religiosity that has created the image of the humble Jewish home, in literature and memoirs, as a peaceful haven in an alien, often hostile environment. Women were responsible for the social and communal network of the broader family circle. They took care not only of their spouses and children, but also of grandparents and orphans. Single or widowed women lived in the households of their parents, siblings, or children, where they found economic security, carrying or taking part in the burdens of housekeeping, infant care, and education. Until late in the nineteenth century, employment outside the home was generally regarded as unsuitable, and "only a minority of German-Jewish women (as distinct from *Ostjüdinnen* [Eastern Jewish women]) were integrated in the work force. Those who worked outside the home were affected by sexism and by anti-Semitism."[47]

Marriages were usually arranged by the families or with the aid of a *Shadchan* (matchmaker) in line with generally accepted norms of propriety. The main concern was endogamy, social standing, and economic security for the envisaged family, but considerations of the financial advantage of parents or brothers in business often played a role. Dowries, "trousseaus," and other obligations were discussed, and often settled contractually before the couple was allowed to meet. Fathers and elder brothers were held responsible for marrying off daughters and sisters, and these were expected to heed their arrangements. Romance and individual courting were the exception, not the rule.[48]

Similar characteristics applied, although with some important deviations, to the immigrants of the first wave. Alexander Lachmann, writing from Attenmuhr in Bavaria in April 1866 and again in 1868, repeatedly expressed his thanks for the financial aid he received from his three sons in America: "You certainly can imagine, that a man of my age [he was over eighty] cannot make much money . . . [but] you make my old age as easy as possible." The old man was full of praise for his children: "God blessed me with you, that I do not have to starve at my age. My daughter Jutta goes out of her way to please me." As was very often the case, the unmarried daughter had remained at home, to take care of the old parents. Now, advancing in years herself, she also depended on the assistance of her family abroad:

I always work to make the days easier for the old father, I do what I possibly can, but now the days and years will come, when I should take care of myself. . . . You know, dear brother, that I helped all of you, I labored hard to make the money for it. Now I have nothing for myself, and what I earn now I have to give to father. So, my dear brothers, keep your promise, that in my old days I will not be naked and unprotected for my good deeds. I know you would not like that. I do not ask for anything but to have the money back, which I spent for you. Dear brother and sister-in-law, don't be angry with me. If one is old and has nothing in reserve, it is hard to live.[49]

Financial assistance was often granted to aging or needy sisters at home, but relatives who had emigrated also felt obliged to choose suitable spouses for their sisters and to bring them to America to find a husband. The sources are full of such planned or performed alliances of family members with business partners in the new homeland. The Jewish press in Germany published idyllic descriptions of the dignified position of women in America, and the Jewish husband's concern and care for her in the land of freedom and prosperity: "Thus, the reverse of the European marriage for money, the financially successful [male] emigrant became a much-sought-after subject of matrimony wherever he undertook the search for a fitting mate in the old homeland."[50]

The already mentioned records of Jewish emigrants from Jebenhausen show no less than 53 single young women, that is, close to 17 percent of the 314 known emigrants between 1825 and 1870. Forty-two of them crossed before 1860 at an average age of 21 years, ranging in age from 16 to 31.[51] Most of these women were between 20 and 23 years old, at that time an age at which unmarried women and their families already started to worry.[52] We have no way of knowing how many of these young women were already betrothed to their future husbands in America, as Jebenhausen was a very special case of the group emigration of almost a whole community. But we do know that emigration was often an attempt to avoid spinsterhood, especially in poor families.[53]

Financial considerations played a far less important role in the choice of a suitable bride than in Germany. Bridegrooms were usually much older, as young immigrants wanted to settle down and found a family only after having gained secure economic standing. Amelia Ullmann, who arrived in 1852 as a single girl from the Rhineland, met and married her husband in St. Louis a year later; and more than forty years later she reminisced:

When my husband asked me before our marriage what dowry my father would give me, I told him: "I know not how much he has; but I do know that I shall take nothing from him as he has a large family to care for. In America, though, anyone who will work and be economical can earn money for themselves. We are young and in order that we may not be in want in old age and that we honestly earn a competence, I shall go with you to the end of the world."

Standing by her promise, Amelia followed Joseph Ullmann in 1855 to the frontier post of St. Paul, Minnesota:

> Only a conscientious housewife, only a devoted mother who had lived in St. Paul in those days knows all the inconveniences and miseries I was forced to endure to do what I felt to be my duty. No servant, no house help of any kind was to be obtained. Every drop of water used had to be carried across the prairie from a well . . . , and to get this it was necessary to crowd in among drivers and rough men from the prairies. My child was ill much of the time from lack of proper nourishment; for good, wholesome food was difficult to obtain. . . . The experience taught me, as it had many another woman who has left the comforts of civilization to go into the new lands of the Great West, that many vexations and privations must be nobly borne. I thus found myself becoming more contented with the conditions as I found them.

Amelia had even more reason to be content when she wrote this, after having established, together with her husband, one of the world's great fur-and-hide companies, whose agents and branches reached as far as Shanghai.[54]

Although they were generally better-equipped, and assisted by already established relatives who had immigrated earlier, the immigrants who arrived from Germany after the Civil War still had to employ most of their resources and abilities to achieve a secure material footing in the new homeland. Many took advantage of the amenities and easier life of the coastal gateway cities like New York City and San Francisco, but for others the opportunities of the Western frontier were still an attractive challenge. One of these later Jewish pioneer women was Anna Salomon, who wrote her reminiscences between 1904 and 1909. She arrived from Posen shortly after her marriage to the son of a neighbor on visit from America. For four years the young couple lived in Towanda, Pennsylvania. In 1876, when "business was very dull," they moved with their three small children to New Mexico:

> We sold everything we possessed except our three children [aged three, and two years and the youngest daughter three months old] and started to New Mexico. We had a very hard time. Even travelling on the railroad with three babies was enough, but when we reached La Junta . . we had to travel by stage, packed in like sardines. . . . I lived in Las Cruces with the children four months, while my husband was looking around for a business location. He found a place and this is the place where we are living now, for thirty years. . . .There were only four shantys in the whole place besides our own shanty. . . . After we lived here a short time we bought the place

and an adjoining ranch. We had the place laid out in lots several years after that, and I had the house built on several of these lots.

In addition to taking care of the household and her children, Anna appears to have been an active and efficient businesswoman. "I baked bread out of cornmeal for three months in a dutch oven. I cooked meals outdoors like campers but I did not mind all that, as I could sell goods and the future commenced to look a little brighter. . . . We had a contract of delivering charcoal to the Clifton Mining Co., which belonged to my uncle J. Freudenthal and my cousins Lesinsky. This started our business and also started the valley." Eventually the family prospered in Solomonsville, today shortened to Solomon. They built a hotel and founded a newspaper, and in 1893 opened one of the first banks in the area.[55]

In the older established Jewish communities of the United States, women's position and activities were not much different from those in the homeland. But in the emerging new settlements the trials and needs of the immigrants' first steps required of women endurance and a very different kind of familial companionship than that prescribed by the "Victorian ideal of womanhood—the woman of delicate sensibility and the noblest of feelings, pillar of the family (and its prisoner as well)," accepted by the older American Jewish commuity.[56] Wives followed their husbands to remote frontier regions, sharing in their hardships and predicaments before they could afford to turn back to the rules and way of life of comfortably settled middle-class families, as eventually most of them did.

The life stories of some exceptional, untypical Jewish women will give a sense of the general picture. Anna Rich Marks married at the age of fifteen, and in the late 1860s followed her husband to Utah Territory. "When Anna's wagons loaded with goods were barred by a tollgate on the road to Eureka, she called her bodyguards, and with drawn guns moved on through." On many more occasions Anna stood her ground at gunpoint, while her husband, "a quiet, law-abiding gentleman," handed out sticks of candy to children in his store. Meanwhile, Anna became wealthy by speculating in real estate, mines, and diamonds.[57]

Josephine Sarah (or Josie Sadie) Marcus was another legendary Jewess of the Wild West. Born in 1861, she left home in San Francisco to become the common-law wife of a notorious frontier gunman named Wyatt Earp. After his death, and after almost fifty years of traveling, Sarah sat down to explain what "a strictly raised girl not yet nineteen and from a prosperous Jewish family" was doing in places called Tombstone, Hangtown, Shoot-Em-Up, and the like. Her only explanation was the musical *H.M.S. Pinafore* that had stirred the "adventure in my blood. I don't know where I got it. Certainly not from my parents, who were the soul of middle-class, solid respectability. My upbringing was all directed toward taking my place some day as a proper matron in a middle-class setting. I probably would have fulfilled this destiny if it hadn't been for Gilbert and Sullivan."[58]

Besides these colorful exceptions from the nineteenth-century ideal of midde-class matrons, some Jewish women gained celebrity as writers, or as political activists, pioneers of feminism and social reform. It may be a coincidence, but probably not, that most of them were neither German immigrants nor of German-Jewish descent. Ernestine Rose, around 1840 one of the leading feminists, social reformers, and an ardent abolitionist was "undoubtedly the most famous Jewess in the United States during mid-nineteenth century." Rose was Polish-born, educated in England, and although she never denied her Jewish origins and identity, she played no role in Jewish community life.[59] Another early feminist was Lee Cohen Harby, who came from an old Jewish family of Charleston.[60] The poet Nina Morais was the daughter of Sabato Morais, the Sephardic rabbi of Philadelphia's Mikve Israel. Also from an old Sephardic family, one that had settled in America in the eighteenth century, was Emma Lazarus, the author of the famous fourteen-line poem inscribed in bronze on the base of the Statue of Liberty.[61]

None of these outstanding women served as a model of Jewish middle-class womanhood. The best-known figure to attain this role was probably Rebecca Gratz, and she only came close to it because she remained a spinster. Gratz, a graceful and well-educated person who is supposed to have served as the model for the gentle Jewish heroine in Walter Scott's *Ivanhoe*, was of one of the oldest German-Jewish families of Philadelphia. Brilliant and charming, she had all the attributes for becoming the American counterpart of the famous Jewish salon-hostesses of early-nineteenth-century Berlin or Vienna. In contrast to these glamorous European women, who almost all married outside their faith and converted to Christianity, Rebecca Gratz was an Orthodox Jew who dedicated her life to Jewish Sunday schools and philanthropy. The reason is, of course, to be sought in the general attitude of the old established Jewish elite in America, which generally did not imitate the frantic efforts of the descendants of German court Jews to assimilate and marry into the Christian aristocracy. In addition to her public activities, Rebecca Gratz spent her life raising her deceased sister's children and caring for her unmarried brothers. "Thus, in spite of the fact that she never married, she followed the traditional woman's role throughout her long life. And when she turned to community service, it was an extension of female caretaking and nurturing roles."[62]

As soon as the families of the first wave of immigration became permanently settled and attained a more or less secure economic standing, many women expanded their routine beyond their own kitchen and child care. Jewish education and philanthropy became increasingly the domain of women's organizational efforts. More than in Germany, Jewish women in the United States participated in the establishment and maintenance of synagogues and congregational services. "American [Jewish] women," wrote I. M. Wise, "are more religious, and in many instances more intelligent than their 'lords of creation.' They are the religious teachers of their children, the priestesses of the house, and we are morally obligated to attach them close to the synagogue." Charity soon became one of the predominant, and socially legitimate, occupations of Jewish middle-class women. Again, it was Rebecca Gratz who in Philadelphia established the first Female Hebrew Benevolent Society in 1819, and a Jewish foster home in 1855. Philanthropic societies were established by women throughout the United States before the Civil War, and these were "the forerunners of the great American Jewish women's organizations of the twentieth century."[63]

A girl's education was accordingly directed so that she could "attain her perch on the Victorian pedestal . . . long on social graces and short on serious content." Isaac Leeser prompted Jewish fathers to have their daughters learn "the science of music, and to learn French" for at least ten years. Wealthier Jews sent their daughters to finishing schools that were to "equip them for their family responsibilities. As the *Israelite* intoned, 'Young wives acquire useful knowledge of household affairs first; other education can follow afterwards.'"[64] Emily Fechheimer-Seasongood, the daughter of one of the first Jewish families of Cincinnati, recalled in her memoirs the pains of attending, with her sister, early morning piano lessons and instruction in drawing, etching, and cross-stitch by private teachers at home. She enjoyed lessons in dancing and gymnastics, which she took in group with other girls, much more. In addition to these, she attended the school annexed to the synagogue, where they were taught in English and Hebrew. "The *Chumish* [Pentateuch] I could not understand, and told my beloved father I could not see why it was taught us [in Hebrew] and please to have the teachers do away with it. As he was president of the congregation then, he brought it before the board, who quite agreed with me, and I was very happy after it was removed from our studies."[65]

After the Civil War and the arrival of the second wave of German-Jewish immigrants, the perception of women's role and position underwent slight, but no essential, change. The female immigrants who came from Posen were far better-educated than the young girls who had arrived thirty or forty years before. At a time when no public schools existed, private Jewish schools for girls were already established in large communities like Lissa, Posen, or even smaller townships, and instruction was given in part by women teachers. Another difference was the relatively larger proportion of young married couples in the later immigration from the east of Germany. At the same time, girls who arrived later in the course of the ongoing chain-migration from west and southwest Germany had also been able to profit from the much more advanced Jewish schools of this later period.[66]

Prevailing perceptions had at the time somewhat changed in America as well. Generally, new occupational opportunities opened up for women in the commercial and educational sector, and some Jewish middle-class daughters took advantage of them, most of them becoming teachers, social workers, or professionals. Work in factories or domestic service remained reserved for the poorer class of Eastern European immigrants, and it was mainly to them that educators or social reformers of German-Jewish origin dedicated their work. One of them was New York-born Julia Richman, who in 1893 addressed the Jewish Women's Congress in Chicago, asserting:

> In no other country and in no other direction is progress more noticeable than in the relative position to man and the affairs of the world that woman occupies today. . . . In almost every walk of life it is my belief . . . [that] this progress is more noticeable in the position held by the Jewish women of America (notably the descendants of European emigrants driven from their homes forty or fifty years ago), than in that of any other class in our cosmopolitan community. . . .
>
> Perhaps it was due to custom and tradition, perhaps due to our oriental origin, but notwithstanding the fact that there may have always been a certain number of Deborahs, Ruths and Esthers, in general the wives and daughters of Jews were . . . regarded as man's inferiors, their chief mission in life being to marry, or rather to be given in marriage, to rear children, to perform household duties, and to serve their lords and masters.

Now, in this "age of progress," Julia Richman claimed that "thousands of women, many of them good, true, pure, womanly women, . . . have, in the face of opposition, succeeded to join the ever-increasing army of women wage-workers, striving to lead useful, if sometimes lonely lives, with the hope of making the world . . . a little better and a little brighter than they found it."[67]

Even in 1893, when she delivered this eulogy, Julia Richman was well ahead of her time. Her own descriptions of Jewish women's occupations and working conditions that follow these optimistic opening remarks prove that it was the daughters and wives of the later-arriving East European Jews, women of lower income and different background than those of the German-American Jewish middle class, to which her words applied. In her own social environment, Julia Richman, like the young Henrietta Szold, was an exception.

A few American-born Jewish women had achieved professional positions in the arts and sciences. Fanny Bloomfield-Zeisler came to Chicago as a child with her parents, and became a famous concert pianist. Sallie Strasburg of Cincinnati was a well-known dentist and an author of noteworthy publications on oral surgery. Rose Eyting of Philadelphia was an internationally recognized actress, and was careful to disguise her Jewishness. There were more Jewish women who were known as writers, actresses, or musicians, but the list is not long.[68] However, a parallel list of male scientists or artists of distinction descending from the first generation of German-Jewish immigrants is probably also not very impressive. The achievements of this generation, men and women alike, were mainly in the economic sphere.

Until late in the nineteenth century, official Jewish public opinion seems to have been quite unanimous in its perceptions of woman's role and place in both home and society. There were only slight differences between Orthodox traditionalists and religious reformers. I. M. Wise favored the family pew in the synagogue, more equality in marriage and divorce procedures, and religious education and confirmation for girls. Isaac Leeser and other Conservatives argued against most of these changes, in which they believed women would be "the actual losers in the estimation that they were formerly held at home, as wives, mothers, daughters . . . , the true characters in which women should excel . . . instead of forcing themselves into positions which our religion wisely did not open to them." But basically these opinions did not differ that much from those offered in I. M. Wise's *Israelite* of April 1860:

> You are a wife and a mother, and therewith your position is nobler and grander than that of the master mechanic, the merchant prince, the man of letters, the soldier and the statesman of the land; . . . If you are true to your husband, if you take a lively interest in his occupations . . . if you speak kindly to your children . . . , bring them up domestically; if you set them a good example with a sweet temper and good manners . . .—then you are worthy of your exalted position; then peace and harmony prevail in your house; your husband gathers strength in your loveliness, in your noble counsel and your manners . . . , he earns abundantly because he is a happy man, and a happy man is a host within himself.[69]

It is true that most public utterances on the subject were at this time presented by rabbis or other male "community leaders." Many women may have resented this attitude and the role assigned to them. Some of them are on record to have protested publicly, mainly in letters to the editors of the Jewish press. But, fundamentally, most women probably did agree that the role of wife, mother, and homemaker was certainly more desirable than holding the jobs reserved for women in mills and factories. Brought up in the German-Jewish middle-class tradition and milieu, most of them were at the time not prepared, and lacked the professional education, to enter the competitive arena and fight for appropriately middle-class vocations. The majority seems either to have consented to, or to have been unable to effectively contest, the prevailing idolization of the "sweet Jewish home girl" propagated on the pages of the *American Jewess:*

> The girls that are wanted are girls with hearts;
> They are wanted for mothers and wives;
> Wanted to cradle in loving arms
> The strongest and frailest lives.
>
> The clever, the witty, the brilliant girl
> There are few who can understand
> But Oh! for the wise, loving home girls
> There is constant and steady demand.[70]

Only after the mass immigration from Eastern Europe did radical feminism, or for that matter, any radical political or social reform movement, gain adherents inside the hitherto quite homogeneous middle-class Jewish society. Meanwhile, Jewish women who sought satisfaction beyond the family circle created their own field of activities in the many voluntary benevolent and communal associations that formed an important part of the emerging framework of Jewish community life. In the 1890s, "ladies' societies" became "women's clubs," united in the National Council of Jewish Women. The perception of a separate "women's sphere," extending the traditional norms of the "woman of valor" from the private into the public sphere, was still maintained, but some women had already started to speak publicly "in terms of female power, autonomy, and equality."[71]

7

Americanization Delayed

Since Jews started to settle in America, they had at several stages reached
a point where it seemed that the immigrant society had been integrated,
and that American Jewry had been established as a moderately but steadily growing community of distinctive character. These junctures usually
followed periods of limited or interrupted immigration, as in the years
around 1820, when "for the first time . . . the majority of American Jews
were English-speaking, many of them second- and even third-generation
(or more) Americans. . . . They were busy exploring ways of adjusting
to their environment, concerned with their identity as Jews, and anxious
to help their less fortunate Jewish brethren overseas."[1] It is estimated
that at that time only some 3,000 Jews lived in the United States. Scholars
are skeptical about the chances of these few known congregations to
withstand the already quite remarkable process of disintegration, a process marked by conversions, exogamous marriages, and religious indifference. As we have seen, the German-Jewish mass immigration that began
in the early 1830s overturned the prospects of an undisturbed, organic
growth of a homogeneously "Americanized" Jewish society. This vision
was to reappear only some forty years later, at the time of, and shortly
after, the Civil War. As before it appeared after a longer pause in the flow
of immigration, and a period of territorial dispersion and the institutional-
ization of Jewish community life. And, again, it proved to be illusory, or
at least exaggerated, due to the renewed immigration, first of Jews from
the German-speaking countries, and then Eastern European Jews, in an
explosive flood that started around 1880.

Some brief remarks on the notion of "Americanization" seem appropriate here. The dilemma of being caught between differing ethnic or
religious identities and the creation of an integrated American society
was, of course, never a specifically Jewish one. Consciously or uncon-
sciously the problem touched the core of America's immigrant society in
its formative periods in the nineteenth century. It reappears time and
again up to the present day, whenever greater groups of immigrants of a
more or less homogeneous ethnic character settle permanently in the

United States. From the days of St. John de Crèvecoeur to the time of Theodore Roosevelt, ideologies of the "melting pot," which focused around the dominant Protestant establishment, had increasingly given way to more pluralistic approaches. Progressives turned against the ideology of American uniformity, pleading the case of a vibrant, multi-ethnic heterogeneity. Immigrants should learn English, adjust to American values and norms, and be loyal to American institutions. But they should at the same time also "value the heritage and customs of their ancestral homes. Cultural pluralism undermined the argument that one could or should be loyal to only one country or culture."[2]

The German Jews in America had to grapple with a double identity problem, for they were both Germans and Jews. "Americanization" implied the conscious or unconscious loosening, if not severance, of emotional and cultural ties with the homeland. On the other hand, personal contacts with parents and siblings in Germany, who often were financially supported and occasionally were visited as well, kept the feeling of being a part of a larger and more self-conscious German-Jewish entity alive. The second-wave German-Jewish immigration of the later nineteenth century, of people more educated and more proud of their German culture than the earlier immigrants had ever been, delayed the ongoing process of "Americanization" exactly when it seemed to be approaching its goal. In addition, the complex relations with Gentile German society in America complicated the issue of identification.

Nevertheless, a commonly accepted conception of a new American-Jewish identity had begun to redefine the contents of Jewish community life in religious and social terms, and its integration in the general environment. American Jews who looked back on the time when their group was relatively small as a golden age of ascent and integration were not deluding themselves. The small communities of German Jews could feel they were on their way to coping with American social and political life. Reform Judaism seemed to be an adequate spiritual sytem to unify American Jewry. On the whole, Jews lived modestly comfortable lives, had large families, and started to enter professions. "In short, before 1880 or 1890 there were too few American Jews for them to constitute a question." When the Russian-Jewish immigration started and grew ever larger, the German Jews were dismayed and worried: "It is as if a man who had built himself a pleasant house and is leading a comfortable existence suddenly finds a horde of impecunious relatives descending on him."[3]

Later we shall deal more extensively with the ways in which the German-Jewish establishment tackled this problem. How far the more acutely felt social discrimination and anti-Semitic political expressions in America that started in the 1870s was caused or intensified by the East

European immigration is still a matter of scholarly dispute. There can, however, be no doubt of the crucial importance of the confrontation between "Eastern and Western Jews" in the formative process of American Jewry, a process in which, after several more decades, the Americanization of the Jewish community in all its social, cultural, and religious aspects was finally accomplished. The "German heritage" continued to play its part in the process, and much of it was preserved, as was the cultural tradition of the Eastern European Jews. "After 1900, it was very clear what a Jew was—and that he was neither a Russian nor a German."[4]

Family Ties and Obligations

Most of the immigrants, especially in the early stages of the immigration, had left home as very young men and women. Emigration meant the abandonment of their habitual social and cultural, as well as famiilal, milieu. Keeping in mind the traditionally close and intimate fabric of Jewish family life, the process involved in many cases not only a cultural but also a severe emotional trial. How each individual came to terms with this situation depended on his or her personal disposition and family relations. Memoirs and letters that have been preserved provide a very diversified picture. Some immigrants seem to have lost, or even deliberately severed, all contacts with their families in Germany. Others went out of their way to keep in touch, sent financial help where needed, and eventually helped siblings and relatives to join them in the United States.

Morris Lasker, who arrived as a young orphan from Posen, may serve as an outstanding example of deliberate disconnection. In a letter written in 1909, Lasker gave a lively description of his life in Texas, where he had settled in 1860: "I had had no communication with my family in Europe . . . because I was ambitious to establish myself in business before I would let them know of my movements. Then came the interval of 4 years of war, and being comparatively penniless after that, I again thought it best to get a start before writing." Some years later he somehow had a letter forwarded to his brother Eduard Lasker, a well-known leader of the Liberal Party in the German parliament. "From what I have learned since, my two brothers had set afoot all kinds of inquiries . . . but being unable to learn anything at all of my whereabouts, they had years before taken my death for granted."[5]

The inclination to contact the family at home only after "they had made it" in the United States reappears time and again in the sources. In a letter written in April 1866 to Israel (Charles) Reizenstein, a pioneer of the Pittsburgh Jewish community, his mother and brother in Germany inform him of events that must have happened many years ago: houses that had been destroyed and rebuilt, the marriage of the brother and the birth of his two children, one of whom died several months before the letter was written. They also request information about the fate of two other brothers in America, "from whom we don't hear a thing anymore. Where do they live? What do they do?"[6]

Contacts with the old country were obviously harder to keep up in the earlier period, when travel and the postal services were still so slow and erratic. During this period emigration was often regarded by the emigrants, as well as by those who stayed behind, as an act of final separation. In the spring of 1837, a party of youngsters started on their way from Unsleben, Bavaria. The local Hebrew teacher gave the emigrants

> by way of saying goodbye a list of names of all the people of your faith, with the dearest wish that you may present these names to your future heirs, yes, even to your great-grandchildren. . . . I further wish and hope that the Almighty, who reigns over the ocean as well as over dry land, to whom thunder and storms must pay heed, shall give you good angels as travel companions, so that you, my dear friends, may arrive undisturbed and healthy in the land of freedom . . . where the opportunity will be presented to live without compulsory religious education. Resist and withstand this tempting freedom and do not turn away from the religion of our fathers . . . for quickly lost earthly pleasures, because your religion brings you consolation and quiet in this life and it will bring you happiness for certain in the other life.[7]

It seems to have been characteristic of many of the early immigrants not to be too sentimental about what they had left behind, especially while they were working hard to adapt to, and find some foothold in, their new environment. In most cases this was not due to indifference or intended negligence, but rather was caused by the objective conditions these hard-working people had to face. After some years, when they had successfully settled down, most of them felt obliged to take care of parents and relatives in Germany. Contacts were renewed and material help was provided where needed and possible.

"How wonderfully conditions have changed since 1837!" exclaimed *Die Deborah* in an article of 1860:

> These unnoticed artisans, these youthful adventurers have since then become the supporters of their kinsfolk in their old fatherland. . . . How many parents who had to slave hard and and bitterly, and faced declining years full of cares, now live contented and carefree, through the largesse of their children in America. How many old fathers and mothers exclaim like Jacob in the joy and gratitude of their heart: "Oh, if I were granted once more to

embrace my child blessed of God, how sated with life I would then be able to die." And lo! Suddenly come the tidings: Your son is coming from America! And the youth who had departed as an ill-starred fellow, as a beggar, comes back for a visit to his paternal home. . . . And then there are other poor emigrants, who have written to their brothers and sisters, enclosing generous sums for passage in their letters. And they have married off their sisters well and taken their brothers as partners in their businesses, so they are all faring well. . . . And then one or the other of the sons went abroad and fetched the parents so that they might be able to rejoice in the good fortune of their children.

And the aged country Jews come; the father with his silver-plated pipe and the coat that he has been wearing for ten years, and the mother with her wig and her old *Mamma Tephillah* (women's prayerbook). Used to their quiet life in their old villages or market-towns, the marvellous and turbulent life of their "merchant princes" is so strange to them that they can never feel really at home. While they thank the providers of these unexpected blessings in their prayers, they try to continue their accustomed unpretentious way of life.[8]

This last, somewhat casual remark points to the often painful problematics of such a reunion. Although only ten or fifteen years had passed since the departure of the children, there was much that now separated them from the world of their fathers. As simple, hard-working people, they had tried hard to learn English and become "Americans." Religious observance was quite easily abandoned when it was felt to be a hindrance. The renewed contact with the families in Germany complicated the process of Americanization. It brought back childhood memories of forgotten customs and cultural patterns of Geman-Jewish life. The reunion with aged parents could create tensions about kosher diet or the observance of the Sabbath in the household.

This may have been the reason that the Americanized children, and probably also their parents, often preferred to leave their parents back home, and show their concern by supporting them financially. This help was proudly shown off also by the German-Jewish press. It seems to have been generally accepted that parents would remain in their old communities. In the 1840s a pedagogical controversy started about the continued usefulness of *Juedisch-Schreiben* (German written in the Hebrew alphabet) in the curriculum of the Jewish schools in Germany. Its proponents argued that for elderly parents it offered the only way of maintaining a correspondence with their grown children after their emigration.[9]

The sentimental attachment to the hometown or village remained with many of the emigrants for a long time. Some evidence of this has recently been detected in Bavaria: the Jewish cemetery at Buttenheim in Upper Franconia was restored around 1900 with a generous contribution from Mr. Levi Strauss, the famous inventor of blue jeans, who had emigrated from there as Loeb Strauss in 1849. And at the deserted cemetery of Reckendorf in the same region restaurateurs discovered a commemorative stone with an English inscription dedicated to the members of the Hellman family of Los Angeles, who emigrated from the village and were buried abroad.[10]

Contacts with the old country were in many cases extended beyond the close circle of the family. A communication of 1854 from the village of Randegg praised the

> four sons and a nephew of Mr. Moos, the local Hebrew teacher . . . , who live now in Cincinnati. They keep up a constant correspondence with their father and uncle, and have supported many other relatives and even the local Jewish indigent generally. . . . On the occasion of his birthday the local Rabbi . . . received from Mr. Moos on behalf of his sons a marvelous gold-plated silver goblet with the inscription: "Dedicated In Love and Respect from your Grateful Students." These good people appreciate the religious education they received twelve years ago! . . . This proves that the emigration does not cause as much slackening of Jewish sentiments, as some people often try to make us believe.[11]

This connection of familial and sentimental with religious ties and loyalties was by no means incidental. It expressed the firm conviction, shared for a time by many German Jews on both sides of the ocean, that American Judaism was a branch of the German-Jewish tree, drawing its spiritual strength from the common roots, and surviving thanks only to the continuous guidance by its intellectually superior leaders in Germany.

Americanization and German Judaism

In the first years of the mass emigration, Jewish congregations in America regarded their dependence on the Jewish establishment in Germany as natural, and did not hesitate to turn to it for spiritual guidance and even material help. In August 1838 the Jewish community in Hamburg received an appeal from Congregation Beth Elohim in Charleston, asking for financial contributions to help rebuild its synagogue, which had been destroyed by fire.[12] The letter to Hamburg was part of a general campaign among American and European congregations, but it was nevertheless not accidental. The Hamburg temple, dedicated in October 1818, had been the first greater Reform congregation in Germany. Charleston followed suit in 1824, and its congregation, Beth Elohim, is regarded as the cradle of the American Reform movement. Gustavus Poznanski, who became *hazzan* of Beth Elohim in 1836, was born in Posen, had studied in Germany, and had spent some time in Hamburg.[13]

The new synagogue, which was consecrated in 1841, was the first in America that contained an organ, and the often-quoted sermon of dedication by its *hazzan* became famous as one of the most radical programmatic statements in the dispute about religious Reform in America. In the focal and most controversial part of his sermon, Poznanski declared: "This synagogue is our Temple, this city our Jerusalem, this happy land our Palestine. And as our fathers defended their Temple, their city and their country with their life, so shall their sons fight to the last drop of our blood . . . for our religion and our country."[14]

Relations with the Jewish spiritual leadership in Germany were close, but the contacts gradually loosened with the growth and development of American Jewry and the establishment of its own institutions. From Germany, these developments were closely, and during the first decades also sympathetically, followed and commented on. For quite a time the rabbis, ministers, and lay leaders of the American congregations turned to their former teachers and acknowledged authorities of German Judaism for practical advice and spiritual guidance. When Isaac Leeser founded the *Occident* in August 1842, he informed Ludwig Philippson, adding that "not only have I taken the *Allgemeine Zeitung des Judenthums* as my example, I also count very much on your assistance . . . so that the truth of our religion may again be brought to the consciousness of the Jewish population here."[15] Many of the following issues of both papers bear evidence of this cooperation. Leeser reported on developments in the American congregations, differences of ritual, and so on, and Philippson volunteered his own opinions and advice.

Philippson's contacts and the influence of his paper were not confined to his personal relations with Isaac Leeser and Philadelphia. In September 1843 he published a "private communication" from New York announcing the establishment of a Jewish association with the aim of installing "an orderly service and assign[ing] an academically learnt rabbi to be called over from Germany. Meanwhile the ideas and notes presented in the *Allgemeine Zeitung des Judenthums* are made use of. A member of the association has presented it with two yearly volumes of the paper, and has been immediately asked to arrange a subscription on its behalf." Ten years later, in December 1853, the paper reported the foundation of a "Hebrew Young Men's Literary Association" in New York, which had "unanimously elected Dr. Philippson in Magdeburg as its honorary member."[16]

In June 1855 Philippson even addressed a personal appeal, in the leader of his paper, "To the American Coreligionists, in particular to the rabbis, preachers and teachers there." He had received information from America that many Jews there were unable or unwilling to circumcise their sons. Well aware "that many German Jews have even in America not forgotten this paper and its endeavors, and lend it a sympathetic ear," he felt free to express his concern and to forward practical proposals how to solve the problem by "travelling *Mohels,* [circumcisers] who would reach remote-living and impecunious Jewish families," and be financed by the more prosperous communities.[17]

In 1854 Philippson announced the appearance of I. M. Wise's *Israelite* in a reservedly well-meaning, somewhat paternalistic tone, expressing his hope "that this new paper [might] not be carried away by too extreme opinions."[18] When in 1855 Philippson established his *Institut zur Foerderung der israelitischen Literatur* (Institute for the Promotion of Jewish Literature), some American Jews subscribed to its publications. As late as 1867 the society's membership list of close to 3,000 names contained 60 members in the United States.[19]

These close connections continued for some more years, but discords came increasingly to the fore. We may assume that, but for the continuous influx of new immigrants, relations would have been even more consistently headed toward total separation. The clash of two such domineering and strong-headed personalities as I. M. Wise and Philippson aggravated the conflict but was not its cause. Personal differences and dissenting interests were, of course, involved, but the core of the conflict was the ongoing process of Americanization, on its way toward shedding the spiritual patronage of German Jewry.

One of the early open quarrels broke out over a virtually marginal matter. In 1857 Philippson's institute published an anonymous brochure, the "Deutsch-Amerikanische Skizzen für jüdische Auswanderer und Nichtauswanderer" (German-American Sketches for Jewish Emigrants and Non-Emigrants). The pamphlet was an account by a still unknown author of his personal experiences. Judging by its style and composition, it was written by an educated, apparently Orthodox man who had come to America in 1853 and who submitted his manuscript after his return to Germany. In America he seems to have met with no great success. It may well be that "some professional or personal failure catalysed his leaving, and that he was looking for a scapegoat."[20] But however accurate or biased these descriptions of the religious or social life in New York may be (there is no indication that he ever visited other Jewish congregations), their interest lay mainly in the reaction it aroused in the United States, and especially that of Isaac Mayer Wise.

A few examples picked at random may illustrate the malice of the author's criticism. In New York's Temple (Emanu-El) he had

found no true devotion. . . . Even on High Holidays. The atmosphere was more like a theater party than of worship. . . . The organ isn't played on Sabbath, but only because the choir director is still studying his music, or because some female choir member could not get away from her millinery shop. . . . This superficial and forcibly initiated reform has reached the point of absurdity. The audience belongs in a theater lobby. . . . "Reverends,"—rabbi, hazzan, shohet and shammash—go around cheating their unfortunate clientele. Remnants of offbeat student days at German universities have become doctors, preachers and rabbis in America. . . . "Reverends," even with the orthodox—use sacristies to don their robes of office. There are various head coverings and loosely fitting tunics. English churchyard-like pleats fill their robes. Their round, mushroom-like berets make them look like puffed-up, somersaulting peacocks. There is also the many-pointed hat and pleated coat of the Russian pope . . . the priestly garb will save Israel. . . . Superficial attempts at reform can take credit for such ostentation and aping of American Christianity. Even the crudest forms of orthodoxy have more character and conscience.[21]

No wonder that Isaac Mayer Wise was furious. But his main wrath he directed not against the anonymous author, who, he assumed, "lives in New York, belongs to the outstanding minds of the B'nai B'rith Order, apparently an orthodox-atheistic misanthrope . . . who never left New York, and writes (very upliftingly!) for a German readership." The greater part of Wise's article, and the most venomous abuse, was reserved for the publishers, and first of all for Philippson:

No wonder that Dr. Philippson has again lent his name to vituperate against the Jews of America. . . . [He is] a man who has served all masters, sworn to all flags, borne all colors, and has turned with every wind. He has assumed the role of a rabbi, and of the guardian of the Jews. He tries to reduce every higher-standing man to his own level; but most of all he disparages American Judaism at every occasion, because here his bottomless scribbling and concentrated gossips remain without attention, and his arrogant patronizing is contemptuously repudiated.[22]

Other commentators were more restrained and less personal. David Einhorn dedicated a short note to "this fabrication" in his *Sinai,* and he also added that it had "regretfully destroyed the interest" in the pursuits of Philippson's publishing institute.[23] Dr. Mayer of Charleston described the pamphlet, "which does not find a single good spot in all American Jewry," as the "creation of a disappointed man . . . who had remained without any attention in America and had turned his back to this blessed land of freedom." In a long-winded commentary Mayer tried to refute some of the specific arguments, mainly those that accused the German Jews in America of being unfaithful to their German cultural heritage in replacing the German by the English language, in the synagogue as well as in daily life.

Although Dr. Mayer did not explicitly blame the publisher, Philippson saw fit to add his own editorial remarks to Mayer's article, while no reaction from his side to the diatribes of I. M. Wise is on record. Denying first any responsibility for the contents of the institute's publications, he felt

nonetheless obliged to openly confess that what has so far come to our knowledge from America . . . generally creates the impression of conditions that are similar to those described in the *Deutsch-Amerikanische Skizzen.* If you, the bearer of modern Judaism, especially those of you who assume you are the leaders of Judaism in America, have nothing to show but narrow-minded careerism, you will soon be forgotten! German-American Jewry has so far shown nothing but ingratitude to its mother, the German Judaism. It has not supported any of its endeavors or institutions.[24]

Philippson did not specify the kind of support he expected to receive from America, but he left no doubt about the role that he enjoined on the German "mother": to guide and tutor her young offspring across the sea. Eight years later he still held the same opinion and clearly defined it in a leading article of his paper, addressed explicitly to "The German Jews in North America." The question he posed was clear and urgent: "Will the great and ever growing number of German Jews in North America keep closer contact with German Jewry and take a greater part in its endeavors and efforts than heretofore?" To illustrate his point, Philippson quoted a letter addressed to him by one Moses Ehrlich of New York, who had expressed his regret that

we lack here able Jewish personalities, who, like you, *Herr Doktor,* are earnestly concerned to raise the status of Judaism and to assure it more respect from in- and outside. . . . It is well-known that the Jews who emigrated to America preserve an extraordinary attachment to their relatives who stayed behind. In a rare loyalty they share with them the means they were able to achieve. In some places in Posen a considerable part of the Jewish community is living on what their relatives send over from America.

But does this loyalty relate also to matters of religion? Many people were concerned about the perseverance of Judaism in America because of the predominant materialistic attitude there, and the total licence in matters of religion. We mean not only the absolute division of state and church, but even more the breaking away of the individual from his family, and the neglect of all consideration and example. Both apprehensions have proved to be unfounded. Everywhere congregations and the necessary institutions are being established in growing numbers. But the German Jews in North America have preserved only a few connections with German Judaism. True, they send there for their rabbis, preachers and teachers, because they cannot manage otherwise, but this is all. No concern about, or participation in, any institute, purpose or undertaking in Germany.

Philippson's comments on this letter reflect the whole complex situation of an ongoing process, in which American Judaism proceeded to assess its own identity by gradually detaching itself from the "umbilical cord" by which it was still connected to the spiritual Jewish leadership in the homeland. Philippson, regarding himself as the foremost spokesman of liberal German Judaism, strongly opposed these endeavors, and not solely for personal reasons. His remarks deserve to be quoted at length:

> We have mentioned earlier a very peculiar phenomenon. The editor of this paper has for decades now sent quite a number of rabbis, preachers and teachers to North America, recommended them or even chosen them, when asked to do so by [American] communities and individuals. And not a single one of all these persons has written him a single line from the moment they reached the shores of the New World. . . . We are not offended, although there were some cases of insulting personal ingratitude. The experience of thirty years has blunted our sensitivity. We will not let this deter us from promoting the good wherever we are able to do so, and we are glad that in this instance two more able men are crossing the ocean by our offices. But as this is so consistent, one might arrive at the opinion that these men have found the ground over there extremely different from what they had expected. . . . They could at least have written us about their disappointment.
>
> But let us go further: All these many German rabbis, preachers, and teachers assume this same relation to Germany. We could name men who purposely take pains to totally estrange the Jews there from German Jewry. They go to great lengths to belittle and malign everything that happens in and comes from Germany. But we refrain from mentioning their names. The question is: Will these relations improve? Will a higher religious aspiration, a more spiritual conception of Judaism develop among the Jews in North America? We believe it will. But we ask the spiritual and religious leaders [there] to consider that they only condemn their own fields to remain barren, if they forego sowing them adequately in their anxious endeavor to spread into the ground only seeds from their own original sack.[25]

That Philippson's editorial stirred indignation, but also some approving argument in America, illustrates how strong the connections still were at this time. An unsigned "private communication" from New York, dated September 2, 1865, reported the

> great displeasure that your article aroused amongst some gentlemen, who pose as the most influential and active leaders of the American Jews, especially Mr. Wise in Cincinnati. You will not be surprised that this gentleman so furiously blows his trumpet. But you are in great company: He declares that all German Judaism is backward compared with the Americans. Moreover, he declares all of Europe to be dead.[26]

Whoever the unknown correspondent was, his comments were obviously welcomed by the editor. The next number of the paper brought another unsigned "private communication," this time from Philadelphia:

> You may know already that your article has tremendously enraged some of

the newspaper editors in this country. This only proves that it has touched on a sore spot. Therefore we have to declare, that these gentlemen do not represent the general opinion, at least on this issue. We very well know that their papers totally depend on the Jewish press and literature in Germany, and that nothing worthy of being returned to Germany has so far been produced here. Considering the age of American Judaism, this seems quite natural. In the same way we still have to bring our rabbis, preachers, and teachers from Germany. Still, this is not the first time that these people are throwing stones into the well from which they drank.[27]

In December of the same year one Ignatz Stein, president of New York's Congregation Ahavath Chesed, asked Philippson to propose a candidate to serve as "preacher, rabbi and religious teacher, whom both we and our children will be able to follow, neither too young for us, nor too old for our children." As reason for this request he declared that "the German Jews in America cannot yet dispense with the counsel and assistance of their coreligionists in the homeland, especially in matters of faith. As proud as I am to have become an American as a man and a citizen, I still would like to remain German as a Jew. In the house of God every Jew should feel at home as much as possible." Philippson printed the letter with obvious satisfaction as "a voice from the people."[28]

At issue, however, was not only the sentimental attachment of "the people" to the German language and the ritual of their old home. The assumption that it was mainly the more traditional circles that turned to Germany seeking assistance against the extreme, in their eyes too radical, reformers would be incorrect. Actually, some of the most extreme protagonists of the Reform movement also tried to base their argument on the rejuvenating spirit of German Judaism. A striking example is Bernhard Felsenthal, a former teacher from Bavaria, who in 1858 founded the Jewish Reform Society. In 1861 Felsenthal, "until then a learned layman but still only a layman," was elected to serve as the rabbi of the Chicago Congregation Sinai.[29] His ideologically conceived relation to German Judaism is recorded in a lecture presented on December 13, 1866:

Against the position that we should emancipate ourselves from German Judaism, and proclaim our independence, I declare: Woe to us, should we now free ourselves from German Judaism and its influence! The sun of Jewish science, which shone in Spain in the Middle Ages, shines now in the German sky. From there she sends her beneficial light to every Jew and every Jewish community to be found among the modern cultivated peoples. Germany has taken the place of *Sepharad*! . . . Should this turning away from Germany take place to a large, or even general extent, American Judaism would either lapse into orthodox ossification, or find its expression in an insolent and rude barroom wisdom.[30]

As we can see, Americanization was a complex and prolonged process and cannot be simplistically identified with the Reform movement. The continued immigration, interrupted only for a few years by the Civil War, brought to the United States an increasing number of educated people rooted in and proud of their German cultural background. This undoubtedly delayed the process of the cultural detachment of immigrant society from its German heritage. In matters of religion, however, traditionalists and reformers of every hue depended for many years on spiritual tutelage from Germany, whether they liked it or not.

In the end, the religious Reform movement in America gained much more ground and many more followers, and went to greater extremes in changing both rituals and content, than its German tutors had ever dreamed of. Rabbi Kaufmann Kohler expressed this aspiration in unmistakable terms. He was the son-in-law of David Einhorn and his successor at New York's Congregation Beth El. Kohler had come to the United States in 1869, after extensive study at German universities. In 1874, on the occasion of the obsequies held in Chicago after the death of Abraham Geiger, Kohler praised Geiger's contribution to reformed Judaism, but concluded: "In the end even he lagged behind the requirements of our times. The free, original land of America and its determined Reform leaders by far outdistanced his ever more moderate regulations. In the end his over-paternal tutelage somewhat estranged him from his closest spiritual associates and disciples." To which Philippson could not refrain from adding his own caustic last word: "Fortunately even in the 'original land America' one knows what to think of this usual *Humbug*."[31]

Language, Literature, and Loyalties

Most [of the earlier immigrants] had little time for matters either Jewish or German. They struggled to make a living and to improve their economic lot wherever possible. Their occupational situation required their gaining a basic knowledge of the English language, considerable freedom from ritual constraints, and full devotion to the great American enterprise of "making money." . . . In their initial drive to establish themselves economically, the early immigrants rarely looked back upon Germany with any nostalgia. They had never really identified as Germans either politically or culturally. Most spoke and wrote only Judeo-German [Yiddish], not the German of Moses Mendelssohn, and were not acquainted with the classics of German literature. Germany primarily represented for them the restrictiveness which they had been pressed to flee; positively, the old country meant little more than the landscape of their childhood.

Michael Meyer argues here that in the cultural as well as the religious sphere Germany became the model for American Jews only after the arrival of a greater number of university-educated intellectuals during the second half of the century. This does not mean that the earlier immigrants ceased to speak German. English had to be used in business, but German "was retained in the sanctuary of the home as the language of the family."[32] In this he is in accord with an earlier critical study by Bernard Weinryb, who already suspected that it was mainly the later arrivals, after the Civil War, who "created the notion that a Jew must necessarily speak German, and overshadowed the large masses of German immigrants who came to America up to the 1860's."[33]

In one of its first reports from America the *Allgemeine Zeitung des Judenthums* praised the newly established New York Sick-Care and Burial Society because its regulations demanded the exclusive use of German in all proceedings and correspondence: "Nowhere a more faithful tribe for Germany can be found than the Jew. He cannot help but carry the German fatherland with him, the same German fatherland that repels him in so many instances and denies him place and home."[34] It was, however, only after separate German congregations had been established that German became also the language of the synagogues. Even then, at least in one known case, at Rodeph Shalom of Philadelphia, records were written for several years in English before being kept in German.

On the occasion of the first services of New York's Congregation Emanu-El, then still on rented premises, the event was praised in Germany as the victory of the founders over the "hostile attitudes of those who prefer the old ritual (i.e., Polish singsong), be it because of entrenched bad habits, or the prejudice that the abandonment of disharmonic howling would de-nationalize Judaism." When the first service started, these adversaries were allegedly surprised to hear the new cantor, accompanied by a choir, pray in Hebrew, and not, as they had been afraid, in German. The sermon was, however, delivered in German by Rabbi Merzbacher. Two weeks later the reporter added a postscript, stating that other German congregations had also started to introduce similar reforms, "fearing that they would otherwise be unable to gain new members." He then went on to describe the educational achievements demonstrated by the pupils of one congregational school, adding that he could not comprehend "why a teacher of German origin has to force himself to provide elementary knowledge in English, why the German language is generally neglected, and even rejected by most congregations."[35]

Scholars versed in this field still argue about the "German" or "autochthonous" American roots of the Reform movement; I prefer to leave its spiritual aspects to the experts.[36] Most of them seem to agree, however, that the first steps of the movement were not primarily initiated by tendencies of "Germanization." When the first German congregations were founded, it was only natural that their members and officials should communicate and keep their records in German because this was the language they knew best. This was apparently usual in both traditional and more liberal congregations, except in the few old Portuguese synagogues. If sermons were delivered at all, or religious instruction given, it was also conveniently done in German. But we have ample evidence that this was often considered to be only a temporary solution, as long as no experienced English preachers and teachers could be found. In almost all cases when positions were offered in the German- or American Jewish press, knowledge of English was a requirement.

German Judaism quite naturally served as a model for the religious reformers, but not for them alone. Isaac Leeser and those who shared his more traditionalist views can be rightly regarded as American exponents of ideas previously developed in Germany by Zacharias Frankel.

> The extent to which [American] religious leaders minimized or maximized the German connection seems to have depended largely on how deep their own German experience had been. Neither Leeser nor Wise had German university training or much direct acquaintance with the intellectual ferment in German Jewry during the first half of the century. Most of those who were especially tied to Germany . . . had both.[37]

As many of the latter arrived in America with the second wave of immigrants, we may add that this was not just an accidental, personal phenomenon, but rather reflected the general changes in the life of the Jews in Germany and their whole social and intellectual development.

Our assumption that the process of Americanization was delayed by the continuous influx of new immigrants seems to be confirmed by the impact of these trends in the religious sphere. The most prominent and active of the early reformers, as well as the most enthusiastically American among them, was Isaac Mayer Wise. Arriving some years after Max Lilienthal, the "chief rabbi" of New York, Wise was the second ordained rabbi in America with a university degree, although both titles have been questioned. His first rabbinical activities in Albany, New York, seem to have been only moderately Reformist. In his Albany day-school, religious and secular subjects were taught in English and Hebrew only. He studied hard to perfect his English, became a member of an Odd Fellows Lodge, and cultivated personal contacts with local Christian clergymen, businessmen, and politicians—all alleged expressions of "his passion for Americanization."[38]

After taking office in Cincinnati Congregation B'nai Yeshurun, Wise became the leading promoter of religious Reform, although he never identified with its most radical wing. Like the majority of Jewish immigrants, he was ready to compromise on religious principles and improvise in matters of ritual and service, but was adamant in his commitment to the goal of Americanization: "The Jew must be Americanized, for every German word reminds him of the old disgrace. . . . The Jew must become an American in order to gain the self-consciousness of the free-born man."[39] Wise was, of course, aware that for the time being "Americanization" had to be propagated in the immigrant's own language. He preached and wrote in German, as well as in English, published a German paper, and participated in the cultural activities of Cincinnati's German community.

Compared with Wise, some of the later-arriving rabbis were the most "German" and became the most radical religious reformers. Most prominent, and spiritually the most influential, was David Einhorn, supported by his two sons-in-law Kaufmann Kohler and Emil Hirsch. Einhorn arrived in America in 1855 to serve as rabbi of Congregation Har Sinai in Baltimore. He was passionately attached to the German language and refused to preach in English, the use of which in the synagogue he regarded with suspicion. "German research and science," he wrote in his *Sinai* in 1859, "are the heart of the Jewish Reform idea, and German Jewry has the mission to bring life and recognition to this thought on American soil."[40] Ten years later a convention of Reform rabbis in Philadelphia discussed the theses Abraham Geiger had presented earlier in Leipzig. When the Philadelphia resolutions deviated from Geiger's theses, Einhorn called his disciples to order: they should "give up all petty jealousy toward the old homeland, . . . and rather recognize spiritual depth as it is nurtured in Germany."[41]

It was, however, the continued arrival of new immigrants that for practical rather than ideological reasons was responsible for the extended use of German in the synagogue. On the other hand, it became soon quite evident that the growing numbers of American-born members in the congregations required that sermons and other parts of the service be held in English. On the occasion of the cornerstone ceremony of of New York's new temple Emanu-El in December 1866, Philippson's correspondent expressed his satisfaction that "while only from one pulpit were German sermons delivered only two years ago, this is now being performed every Saturday in seven congregations." But he also explained that this was a temporary expedient because no English preachers were at the time available to take the place of those who retired.[42]

Over time, the request to replace the German language in the synagogue became even more urgent. In 1872 a German newspaper in Pittsburgh complained that the "Israelites of German descent show a tendency to emancipate themselves from remembering the German language, customs, and education. . . . Even in religious service German is progressively displaced and the ritual performed in English." The paper regretted this development, which it interpreted as demonstrating that the Jews in "this country have decided to eliminate any memory of German descent, language, etc., in the following generations. . . . Though one cannot take it amiss that the German Israelites break away from the language and national customs of a people amid whom they have to these days experienced all kinds of oppression and discrimination," they should still think to preserve among themselves the language of Moses Mendelssohn and Heine.[43]

The replacement of German with English increased with the growth in numbers of American-born members. In 1864 Isaac Mayer Wise complained that in only eight of eighty-four congregations were English sermons presented more or less regularly:

Till now we had to make do with immigrants because we are ourselves immigrants. [Now] most American congregations demand preachers and teachers versed in the English language and familiar with the expectations and requirements of American congregations. In the last ten years a generation of American Israelites has grown up that can find nothing to do with a European teacher or preacher, so that this youth is already found [to be] neglected. . . . In this way the synagogue becomes estranged from the fatherland and adolescent youth, as before in Europe, when a special jargon prevailed [in the synagogues].[44]

Three years later the issue was taken up in a circular letter of the *Grand Saar* of B'nai B'rith, the American-born scion of an illustrious Sephardic family, Benjamin Franklin Peixotto:

Our children grow up in ignorance of the great truths of Judaism, its glorious history, its precious literature and its sublime mission. We are lacking in adequate teachers, preachers and literature. . . . The present generation, being almost exclusively educated in the public schools of the country, is unable to read, think or speak in any but their native language.

He therefore proposed to establish a Jewish institution of higher studies to prepare the requisite staff of English-speaking rabbis and teachers. Philippson could not refrain from adding, on an editorial note, that the poor state of Judaism in America was certainly restricted to the English-American Jews, but more than compensated for by the growing importance of the German element in American Jewry.[45]

The tendency to introduce the English language in religious services and education gained general support. A communication "from the West of America" in 1867 stressed the need for

teachers that were educated here and are not only adequately versed in the language, but also in the sentiments of this country. It has always been a mistake in our schools to wish to Germanize the Jewish children. It was most of all religious instruction which suffered, as this must especially be conducted in a language which penetrates to the heart of the child, which is by no means the German language. . . . . Thanks to the endeavors of able men America will soon educate its own teachers and rabbis. If we, the adults, are today American citizens but German Jews, our children will be American citizens and American Jews. The future of Judaism will be securely preserved in their hands.[46]

On the traditional side, we find at the same time a similar appeal from S. M. Isaacs, the editor of the *Jewish Messenger.* At a conference of the Board of Delegates Isaacs warmly supported the establishment of a Jewish institute for higher studies: "The teachers and rabbis, most of whom have come over from Germany, are out to Germanize the country! This has to be stopped!" Isaacs then "emphatically asked" Marcus Jastrow, who had recently arrived in Philadelphia to serve at the pulpit of Congregation Rodeph Shalom, to learn English "so that his admittedly high contribution may even be improved." Jastrow replied, in a somewhat more moderate tenor, that for the time being America had little choice than to import its rabbis from Europe and first of all from Germany. "But teachers are needed for our youth," he added, "and must be familiar not only with the language, but also with the spirit and the conditions of the country, in order not only to teach but also to educate."[47]

As English gained ground in synagogues and education, German remained for a long time the language of the family. Newspapers and periodicals continued to appear in German as well, along with the older English publications like the *Occident* and the *Asmonean,* which were edited in the conservative spirit. I. M. Wise founded his English-language newspaper *The Israelite* shortly after his arrival in Cincinnati in 1854. But it is indicative that he soon added a German-language subsidiary, *Die Deborah,* which was intended to supply more popular reading, "dedicated to the daughters of Israel." Evidently it was no less widely read by male readers among the constantly arriving immigrants, whose English was yet to improve. The German supplement actually became an independent paper and continued to appear until 1905. Apparently it was of little avail that Wise used its pages to fight—in German!—for the purity of English:

"My children must speak only German at home" mothers tell us with special self-satisfaction. This is very fine not because in that way the children somehow learn German, but because the German woman's mind finds comfort in the homeland's sounds, because the German mother wants to know that she is loved in German by her children. But the drawback of the matter is that the children's bad English is not heard, consequently also not corrected at home, and that every child so brought up is forthwith recognized by the fact that he twists the everyday conversational speech and often Germanizes and distorts it to absurdity. . . . If we wish to bring up the youth for America and not for Germany or France, if we do not wish to make them ridiculous to their material detriment and stamp them as being [somehow] apart, then we must not tolerate jargon.[48]

The language and distribution of publications reflected the changing preferences of the immigrants at different stages of the immigration period. The first Anglo-Jewish periodical, *The Jew,* was published in New York City by the printer Solomon H. Jackson between 1823 and 1825, in an effort to counter Christian missionary activities. The English *Jewish Messenger,* founded by S. M. Isaacs, appeared from 1857 on. In 1849 a German weekly, *Israel's Herold,* was started in New York City by Isidor Busch; it ceased publication after only twelve issues, even though it was financially supported by B'nai B'rith. In addition to this, all earlier Jewish publications were in English. It was only after 1855 that the German-Jewish press expanded. Numerous publications appeared and increased their circulation, some as independent papers, other as supplements to Anglo-Jewish periodicals.

Most German publications were of a merely parochial character, dealing with congregational and other local affairs. A recent study counts forty-three German-language serials in the nineteenth century; some earlier estimates arrive at much higher figures. These apparently included many short-lived publications of a local character.[49] Some of the better-known German-language publications attained a remarkable cultural level and were widely read and quoted in the United States and abroad. Prominent among them was the *Sinai,* edited and published by David Einhorn between 1856 and January 1863. Devoted to the promotion of both radical Reform and abolitionism, it ceased to appear after Einhorn had to escape from Baltimore. *Der Zeitgeist,* a bimonthly published in Milwaukee from 1880 to 1882 by Isaac S. Moses and Rabbi Emil Hirsch, remained "a monument to the German-Jewish synthesis which was attempted but not achieved in Milwaukee."[50]

The demand for German-language Jewish journals created by the new wave of immigration after the Civil War was, however, taken into account by a part of the Anglo-Jewish press, who carried German supplements like *The Hebrew Leader* (New York, 1865–82). *Young Israel* (New York, 1871–1901) published a German supplement *Libanon* between 1875 and 1878. Other papers that were at least temporarily bilingual or had German supplements were *The Jewish Advance* (Chicago, 1878–82), *The Sabbath Visitor* (Cincinnati, 1875–95), and *The Hebrew* (San Francisco, 1863–1923).

However, most of the demand for German-language papers seems to have been satisfied by the long-lived *Deborah*. Originally a supplement to the *Israelite* (founded by I. M. Wise in 1854, from 1875 on *The American Israelite*) it soon became an independent paper under different editors. Its contents and intellectual aspirations changed with the times, as indicated by the changing subtitle. From 1855 to the first number of its fifth volume in July 1859, it was *gewidmet den Töchtern Israels* (dedicated to the daughters of Israel). From this issue on, the *Deborah* was edited temporarily by Max Lilienthal, and bore the obviously provocative subtitle *Allgemeine Zeitung des Amerikanischen Judenthums* (general newspaper of American Jewry). Later it became *Eine deutsch-amerikanische Monatsschrift zur Förderung Jüdischer Interessen in Gemeinde, Schule und Haus* (A German-American monthly for the promotion of Jewish interests in the community, school, and home).

The remarkable fact is that only thirty years after the start of the German immigration, a noteworthy German-Jewish press appeared on the scene. Rabbi Hochheimer, writing from Baltimore in 1849, explained why it took so long: "Jewish journalism does not fare so well in America. Especially papers in German have no long existence. Isidor Busch was forced to discontinue his excellently edited periodical for lack of interest." Hochheimer praised Leeser's *Occident* as "containing many worthy and genuine materials" and also mentioned

> the *Asmonean,* edited by a number of scholars in New York; there you have the whole of Jewish journalism existing at the moment in America. The explanation for this lack of interest is to be sought in the fact that the major part of the American Jewish population is not to be counted among the intelligentsia. Those intellectuals who are interested are mostly content with the American journals, that bring much about the Jewish affairs, and sometimes even reprint whole sermons.[51]

That most of early immigrants did not exactly belong to the intelligentsia is certainly true. But at least their greater part was not illiterate and could read German before they became fluent in English. However, the delayed appearance of a German-language press was undoubtedly caused by the changing cultural requirements of the immigrant society. There were two main reasons for this. First was the settlement and the achieved economic security of the first-generation immigrants, and the higher educational level of their mostly American-born offspring. Second, and probably more important, were the intellectual needs and creativity of the new arrivals. An additional reason was "the rising respect accorded German culture in the United States." Before the 1860s German, as well as German-Jewish, immigrants rarely demonstrated pride in their origin, at least in public. "Thus, while earlier Yiddish-speaking Jews had no support in the American context for retaining their language—and as a result Americanized very rapidly—German-speaking Jews were part of a larger language group which encouraged their endeavors to preserve the German heritage."[52]

As we shall see, relations between Jews and Gentiles inside this German "language group" changed over time. The same relates to the German Jews' sentiments toward their "German heritage," in a cultural, political, or historical sense. They were complex and often ambivalent attitudes, influenced by developments on the American as well as the European scene. There is, however, no doubt that the period between mid-century and the late 1870s was the heyday not only of the German-language press, but also generally of German cultural activities in America. The role of the Jews in these ventures, as producers and performers and even more as financially supporting audiences, was outstanding. Rudolf Glanz's evaluation of the Jews, especially in New York, as "a bridge between German, or even European culture and American culture," may be somewhat overrated, but it contains certainly more than a grain of truth.[53]

In addition to the theater, literary societies, and clubs there was another instrument to satisfy the cultural needs and leisure-time recreation in German. B'nai B'rith lodges and other fraternal organizations took the lead in promoting these pursuits. In 1850 the order established the Maimonides Library Association in New York, running a reading room and a lending library. In 1855 it had 150 members and a collection of 800 books, and conducted a weekly series of social and cultural meetings. Most lectures were delivered in German by well-known, mostly Jewish speakers and included topics of religious and general knowledge. Another cultural institution in New York was the Harmonie Club, founded in 1847 by a group of German Jews. Its activities resembled those of the Maimonides Library, but seemingly on a more exclusive level. The club's membership seems to have been composed mainly of the elitist and snobbish members of Congregation Emanu-El, who refrained from publicizing its activities.[54]

Similar organizations were formed in all larger, and sometimes even in small, communities. Lodges and benevolent societies occasionally also organized lectures or amateur theater performances in German. Isaac Mayer Wise, despite all his efforts promoting Americanization, followed these cultural activities with sympathy. In 1871, summarizing one of his frequent tours of congregations, he reported in the *Deborah* on the three congregations of Albany, New York, stressing the fact that only once every month an English sermon was delivered "for the benefit of the upgrowing youth." Still, he was full of praise for the cultural activities performed in German: "In the literary association *Harmonia* the German language and literature are carried on in a very restful manner. Lectures and discussions, dancing circles and small-talk are the main activities. In the 22 years since its foundation the association heartily preserved its German character, without resorting to cards or billiards."[55]

These activities were followed with interest by Jewish intellectuals in Germany who regarded the American Jewish community as a branch of German Jewry. They shared the general estimate of their homeland as the "Land of Thinkers and Poets" and were rightly proud of the German-Jewish scholars and institutions prominent in modern scientific Judaistic studies. No other country, not to mention America, could at the time show anything comparable to the achievements of men like Zacharias Frankel in Breslau, or Abraham Geiger or Leopold Zunz in Berlin, to name only three of the most prominent. This explains the satisfaction with which Philippson reported in 1867 the request forwarded to him by San Francisco's B'nai B'rith to assemble a selection of scientific, popular, and belletristic books in German. In his editorial remark, he expressed his hope that this initiative from the West of America might soon move eastward to include the "many literary associations, of whose relations with Europe and European Jewish literature we have so far little heard. The effect would be twofold: the distribution and influence of this literature on our American coreligionists, as well as its powerful [financial] support."[56]

The rising German nationalism after 1871 also influenced many Jews in Germany, and reflections of this spirit can be detected in some communications from America. One report from Cincinnati in 1878 proudly noted the contribution of the Jewish teachers in American public schools, "most of them entrusted with the instruction of the German language, who are active in the establishment of a German teachers' seminary in St. Louis. The venture is almost exclusively under the management of Jewish teachers."[57] Some years later, mention of the Jew's contribution to the preservation of German language and culture in America sounded unmistakably apologetic, as in a report from New York of October 1887:

The fanatic endeavors of the anti-Semites in Germany to classify the Jews as a foreign element in the German nation are regarded by Americans as very strange indeed. . . . Among all immigrants [here] the Germans are the first to renounce their nationality. As soon as possible they try to speak broken English, decline from speaking German at home, as if they were ashamed of their German origin. Their children attend public schools and most do not understand a single German word. The only exception are the German Jews, who over generations preserve German as the language in the family. This is so generally the case that in this country the Jews are always being counted as Germans.[58]

The tenor of this report so much resembles the apologia of Jewish spokesmen in Germany that one may wonder about the genuine source of its style and wording, at least.

Some years later original utterances from America sound extremely different. In 1893 Dr. Deutsch of Cincinnati, in contrast to the above-quoted report, stressed the function of German Protestant and Catholic churches in America as the preservers of the German language, "only the Jews are the quickest to change." The reasons he gave for this difference are very enlightening:

The German Christian who keeps to his home-tongue is called a German, while the Jew who does the same remains a Jew, or at best politely a Hebrew. . . . If therefore the Jew wants to be considered a genuine American he has to speak English. A second reason is the anti-Semitism in Germany. This movement has caused many Jews not to want to be reminded of the old fatherland. . . . Practical considerations may be added, according to which a *permanent* conservation of German is unthinkable, while good English without an accent is an unavoidable condition for advance in this country.[59]

That same year the *Jewish Voice* of St. Louis reported the fiftieth anniversary meeting of the city's B'nai B'rith lodge. Speeches were held in English, but stressed the German origin of the order's founders, and greetings were sent to the sister lodges in the old country. "Following a vocal solo, Rabbi Spitz of Congregation B'nai El was called upon to deliver an original German poem which had been written for the occasion." Apparently the audience could still understand the language and cherished its German cultural heritage, although "the Jews of St. Louis were well on their way toward the goal of Americanization, and the nostalgia for the old 'Fatherland' was soon to be permanently left behind."[60] Actually, 1893 was one of the peak years in the development of political anti-Semitism in Germany. What happened in Germany did not pass unnoticed by America's Jewish community. As we shall see, it left its impact not only on Jewish attitudes to the language and culture of the "Old Fatherland" but also on relations with non-Jewish German society in America.

Jews and Other Germans

The German Jews, as we know, came along with the general stream of emigrants from Germany, and together with it they penetrated into the interior of the country. . . . These familiar German surroundings translated into the new world, in part with identical economic functions, provided the Jews with a solid footing in the early years. A second important factor was the German language, which kept the field among the German immigrants in the new home and aided the German Jews considerably in taking root in their first occupations.[61]

This statement, in one of the earliest works of Rudolf Glanz on the German-Jewish immigration, tried to explain the complex relationship between Jews and other Germans in America. Almost half a century later the subject still awaits a more profound evaluation. This may explain the categorical criticism of one recent writer who speaks of a "sixty-year-long 'German Jewish nexus' of identity" and of the "organic unity" of the two communities, which he believes to have been ignored by most historians for too long.[62]

In my opinion, most relevant scholarship still suffers from an optical illusion created by the historiographic focus on the midwestern Jewish communities. In this region, and for a limited period of time, the relationship may indeed have been as defined by Rudolf Glanz. But the majority of German-Jewish immigrants settled, as we have seen, in the older established Jewish communities of the East Coast, in New York—the City and the State—in Philadelphia and Baltimore, and in the new communities established in these cities. For them the first "footing," or the "surroundings of their economic activities," were rarely the Gentile German immigrant society. Their tutors and early guides were mainly German-speaking Jews, and their customers were the ethnically mixed population of wherever they started business. Among them were, of course, also many Gentile Germans, with whom the Jewish peddler or shopkeeper had easier contacts. However, social and personal relations were a different matter. Not always was the common German background necessarily helpful, and not everywhere did it create an "organic unity."

First encounters of American Jews with Gentiles from German-speaking countries in America started with a hopeful accord. Around 1734, groups of Lutheran peasants, expelled by the Archbishop of Salzburg, arrived in Georgia after having traversed large regions of German territory. On many occasions they had been helped by Jewish communities during their long and destitute voyage. In a report by their pastors we read that the refugees were

> so hated by the Roman Catholics that the latter deny them the hospitality which they practice toward Jews and other unbelievers. . . . The priest of Klein-Noerdlingen forbade his congregation to give these people a drink of water or to do them the least favour, as he considered them heretics and dogs. They removed the buckets from the wells and refused them water even for money, although the weather was warm. But the Jews proved to be more compassionate than the Christians. They led the emigrants to their wells and handed them vessels to draw water for themselves and their horses. They also presented them with bread, beer, and a little money, as far as their meager means would permit.

Similar incidents are reported from Hannover, Frankfurt am Main, Berlin, and other places. Reports on the Salzburgers' settlements in Georgia published in Germany in the 1740s reflect a neighborly, although distanced and sometimes critical, attitude toward the small Jewish community of Savannah.[63]

The same aloofness divided the Jewish immigrants from the early Gentile German settlers of the colonial period and far into the nineteenth century. The cultural attachment, nostalgia, or mere loyalty of Jewish immigrants to the cultural heritage of the old homeland was a later phenomenon. It required a higher level of education and of sentimental identification than could be expected from the underprivileged youngsters of the first wave of immigration. What they had left behind evoked occasional homesickness but no patriotic or cultural yearning. They had very little in common with the German settlers of Pennsylvania and other German settlements, who lived in huge German ethnic-cultural enclaves, used the German language exclusively in their own press, newspapers, and schools, and cultivated their own art, literature, and pastimes. German street signs and other public announcements demonstrated their attachment to their cultural heritage, so much so that for a time Benjamin Franklin distrusted them and questioned their political loyalties. In contrast, the early Jewish immigrants tried to acculturate and adapt to the language, culture, and ways of Anglo-American society.[64]

With the mass immigration starting in the 1830s, some change in the mutual attitudes can be observed. A great part of the German Gentiles settled in the open frontier regions of the Midwest. Those Jewish immigrants who ventured to the same area found them to be more easily approached as customers, more familiar than others. Economic grounds, more than anything else, caused these Jews to "stay close to the new German settlement concentrated around the Cincinnati-Milwaukee-St.

Louis triangle, where they enjoyed the security of a common language and origin."[65] We have, however, to keep in mind that this concerned only a part of the Jewish immigrants and was for many of them only a transitory stage before they moved on west or back to the East Coast cities. Those who permanently stayed in the communities of the "triangle" established a permanently settled German-Jewish society. But does this necessarily imply that they were really integrated into Gentile German immigrant society?

Most existing studies suggest the opposite. Stephen Mostov's informative analysis led him to conclude that "a desire on the part of Cincinnati's Bavarian Jews to live near non-Jews from the same region remains a purely theoretical assumption." The social interaction between the two groups in Cincinnati remained limited. For the Jews, group cohesion according to place of origin was far more important than their connection with Gentile Germans. In Germany as in America, differences of economic pursuits, not to mention religious and social dissimilarities, worked against the establishment of a unified Gentile and Jewish German society in the social or even cultural sphere. Once established, the large Jewish community of Cincinnati exhibited a high degree of self-sufficiency, although not in total isolation from the Gentile German society.[66]

In Milwaukee relations seem to have been somewhat closer, with Jews considering themselves more than elsewhere to be a "part of Milwaukee Germandom." In 1845 one-third of the city's population was German, and by 1870 Germans constituted a large majority. This was partly a result of close contacts with the homeland. Sympathetic reports in the German press and deliberate action by the city and the state of Wisconsin attracted many German settlers during the 1850s and 1860s. The first Jewish immigrants arrived in 1844, and by 1875 the city's Jewish community amounted to about 2,000 souls. Seventy-eight percent of the foreign-born Jews came from Germany, Austria, and Bohemia. Most of them resided together, in close neighborhoods of Milwaukee's "German town." Jewish candidates for public offices enjoyed the support of Gentile German voters, and Jews served in German units during the Civil War. But there were also differences and tensions, as in 1858, when the German-Catholic press openly defended the kidnapping of the Jewish child in the famous Mortara case.[67]

Milwaukee's Jews participated actively in the cultural activities of the German population in America's "Deutsch Athens." Some were prominent in the German press and theater, and taught German in the schools. Many merged with the city's German community, to an extent, regarded as "the major source of 'leakage' [that is, dissociation and exogamy] in the nineteenth century." But even here "the new century opened a wide gulf between Germanism and Jewishness."[68] Similar developments seem to have been typical also for other cities, such as Detroit, with a large German population.[69]

Ambivalent relations are recorded for Atlanta, Georgia. Jews participated in some nonsectarian cultural and social organizations, and some Gentiles sent their children to the "English-German-Hebrew Academy," founded in 1869 by Rabbi David Burgheim. On the other hand, the *Atlanta Deutsche Zeitung* charged in 1871 that the Jews of the South "care but little for German immigration and the German element, desire to make political capital amongst the native population, and impede the progress of the German element." Steven Hertzberg concludes that toward the end of the century the German Jews in Atlanta had become Americanized and "had little in common with the young, mostly working-class newcomers from Germany, many of whom had been influenced by the resurgent anti-Semitism that blossomed in the fatherland after 1877. Moreover, the creation of new Jewish organizations and the improvement of old ones satisfied their associational needs to a fuller extent than could the German clubs."[70]

Contradictory contemporary statements on mutual relations can be found wherever Jews lived side by side with larger Gentile German communities. In April 1872 the Chicago *Illinois Staatszeitung* reported on the Jewish community of the city in an objective and even sympathetic manner, stressing the internal differences between German and "Polish" congregations. "The two essentially different tribes are living together and among themselves. . . . The local Jews have gradually found their place in commercial life. In social life, however, they have remained aloof from the Germans and the Americans and keep totally to themselves." At the same time the article reported the many activities of associations founded by the German Jews "merely for pleasure" and bearing German names like *Standardclub* or *Harmonie.*[71] This should cast some doubt on the tendency to take the existence of literary clubs and similar organizations performing in German and bearing German names as proof of cooperation between Gentiles and Jews.

During all this time New York City was the home of the largest Jewish community, as also of a considerable German ethnic group. How large the Jewish population really was and what exact percentage of New York's German population it constituted are still matters of dispute. Differences of estimates seem largely to depend on the diverging answers to the eternal question "Who is a Jew?" Minimalist numbers are usually based on official or congregational data of synagogue seats or memberships. Maximalists arrive at their results by accounting for a high percentage of immigrants who did not join congregations or any other Jewish association, sometimes assuming it to reach as much as one-half or even more of all German-Jewish immigrants. By this method a recent study arrived at no less than 35,000 Jews, or 17.5 percent, in 1860, and thus has them constituting an organic part of the German ethnic group of the city. By 1870 outsiders "had taken to calling the main German neighborhood 'New Jerusalem' instead of 'Dutchtown.' *Kleindeutschland* and New Jerusalem were seemingly one and the same."[72] Proceeding from here the manifold participation of Jews in various German circles and associations, from the early German-American labor movement to the criminal underworld, are assumed to prove that "these two groups were inextricably mixed on all social levels, from the elite members of the *Liederkranz* and *Arion Gesangvereine* to the members of the Dutch Mob."[73]

Quite evidently, the differences of estimation are no mere matter of diverging statistical methods. They reflect conceptually contradictory approaches to the definition of the individual members of a group that had to grapple with a problem of dual ethnicity. Personally, I believe that the answer to "Who is a Jew?" is to be decided empirically, according to what is being investigated. The comparative evaluation of the legal and social opportunities and mobility of Jews in a given country or time should necessarily include all people of proven Jewish descent, whatever their institutional, social, or even religious affiliation. But when we are exploring developments and characteristics internal to the group, as in the case of ethnic and cultural adherence, the determining criteria have to be different. In my opinion, under conditions of absolute legal freedom of choice no other standard than the individual's self-determination is admissible. The American Jews who by their own free will decided to join congregations or other Jewish associations did so in order to preserve their Jewish identity, and with them alone are we concerned in the present context. Those who remained outside of, or severed their ties with, the Jewish community chose to affiliate themselves, with varying degrees of success, with other ethnic groups, be they Germans or Anglo-Saxon "Americans." Their activities and careers may be taken as evidence of America's open society. They tell us nothing whatsoever about the internal developments of the Jews as a group, or their collective relations with other groups.

It stands to reason that the anonymity and the scale of opportunities of metropolitan New York induced a larger rate of Jewish disaffiliation than elsewhere. Naturally, German-speaking Jews sought to assimilate into the large German immigrant society of the city. Many of the intellectuals among them, the politically active, or the criminally inclined certainly played their role—but as Germans, not as Jews. It is therefore understandable if an author who is out to prove "the Germanness" of the German Jews complains about the "concentration on collective activities of German American Jews" and pleads that "as soon as the focus is broadened to the individual participation of Jews in the German-American communities, the evidence for large-scale participation and integration becomes overwhelming."[74]

The main point is, however, not the integration of individuals, which in many cases was accompanied by their dissociation from the Jewish community. For the Jewish group as a whole, as defined by its members' own choice of affiliation, the "Gentile-German Jewish symbiosis" was at best a transitory stage, for which I believe Moses Rischin's analysis of 1962 to be still valid: "As they became Americanized, their ties with the German community in New York became less pronounced and they, along with Jews of American origin, were discovering a common identity as Jews that they had not known earlier."[75]

Joint membership in German literary circles and other associations is recorded for almost every place of settlement with a larger German— Gentile and/or Jewish—population, mainly in the first years of the immigration. The small influx of intellectuals in both groups around 1848 apparently induced closer contacts, at least temporarily and in limited social strata. This was especially the case among the educated circles, in which "the Christians who took the initiative to leave Germany were less likely to have harbored anti-Jewish prejudices than those who remained." This can hardly have been the attitude of the millions of German peasants or artisans who constituted the bulk of the German emigration. But in the confines of the educated urban middle class it seems plausible that "when Jews with German professional training reached America, having fled German discrimination, they were, ironically, hailed as representatives of superior German university training. With few exceptions, Gentiles welcomed Jews into German cultural societies whose counterparts in Germany would have most likely excluded them."[76]

Leopold Mayer, who arrived in Chicago in 1850 and started as a teacher, became one of the leading Republicans among the Chicago Germans. According to his own testimony, he soon adopted the doctrines of the Free-Soilers, "as they coincided closely with the ideas of liberty I had imbibed in Germany during the stormy times of '48." Recounting his early experiences some fifty years later, Mayer emphasized that "the relations between Jews and non-Jews were cordial, and many of the former not only belonged to the various political and fraternal organizations, but also held offices therein. . . . The Germans, Jews and non-Jews, were one, and the prejudices from the fatherland, if not dead, were at least hidden."[77]

There is some indication that German Gentiles and Jews of this early period created common associations in defiance of the older established Anglo-Saxon organizations, which remained closed to both of them. The Cincinnati Pioneer Association admitted only members who could prove they had resided in Ohio before 1812. Later the date was brought forward to 1815, but the roster of the society contains no German-sounding name. Evidently, few Germans or German Jews could prove that they had come to Ohio before 1815.

Consequently, the Germans founded their own *Deutscher Pionierverein*, as well as other lodges and associations where Jews were admitted, although not always welcome.

> The leaders of the pioneer societies were educated and eminently practical Germans, often former revolutionaries and lifelong liberals by conviction . . . although their anti-Jewish sentiments forced them into a dubious position. They were ready to admit Jewish intellectuals . . . but for the most part they had to deal with Jewish pioneers who by dint of hard work had prospered in their vocations but who possessed little education. Toward such Jews they were stiffly formal; one praised them formally, but there was no inner warmth behind the words. . . . If the sentiments of the leadership were ambiguous, those of the led masses manifested themselves in undisguised hatred.[78]

One may have some doubts about this statement—which was written, as is well to remember, in 1947—but it nevertheless contains more than a grain of plausibility. Openly demonstrated anti-Semitism was, however, essentially a later phenomenon, keeping pace with, and influenced by, political developments in the fatherland. Before and during the Civil War, the cooperation of German Jews and Gentiles was often a matter of mutual interest and necessity. To the exclusiveness of the Anglo-Saxon society we have to add the convenience of a common language and background in cases where concerted action was unavoidable. How else could we explain the establishment of military units in which German Gentiles and Jews fought side by side, sometimes under the command of elected Jewish officers? In 1863 the officers of the 54th New York Volunteer Regiment elected the Jewish Reverend Ferdinand L. Sarner to serve as the regiment's chaplain on the recommendation, among others, of the Prussian ambassador in Washington. This regiment, known also under the names "Hiram Barney Rifles" or the *Schwarze Jäger* (black hunters), apparently contained some Jewish volunteers, but the majority seem to have been Gentile Germans. Still, the "regimental officers were more concerned to secure the services of a cultured German than of a chaplain of a particular denomination." Sarner, who had studied at two German universities, seems to have performed in a satisfactory way, providing, as was usual in many other units, "a non-denominational worship and ministration with, perhaps, occasional Jewish services."[79]

Jewish-Gentile cooperation was generally intensive during the first years of settlement in a new community and tended to decline as both groups established their own cultural and social institutions. When I. J. Benjamin visited San Francisco in 1861, he was enthusiastic about the many German associations of the city, and the fact that some of them had Jewish presidents and officers. The city had at this time over 20,000 German inhabitants, of whom an estimated 5,000 we can assume to have been Jews. Benjamin was impressed by their various intellectual and social activities, and described in detail the May festival of 1861 as an example of "the Germans' unextinguishable loyalty to the customs and traditions of their dear old fatherland." It was organized by the German General Aid Society, which had been founded in 1855 and had several Jewish officers on its board and Jewish doctors among its hospital staff. But Benjamin also expressed his hopes, vaguely and without being very concrete, that "the dissonances that now and then . . . disturbed the unity of the German people in California will certainly be silenced for a long time under the influence of this festival, and . . . will never again find expression."[80]

Cordial relations persisted in San Francisco for quite a time, especially in intellectual circles. German newspapers like the California *Democrat,* one of the most influential German newspapers on the Pacific Coast, or the daily *Abend Post,* were owned or edited by Jews, who were also in leading positions in "high-brow" associations like the literary San Francisco Society or the Natural History Society. They appear to a much lesser extent in the rosters of the athletic clubs and the male or mixed choral societies.[81]

For their social and recreational needs San Francisco's Jews apparently preferred their own B'nai B'rith lodges and other associations. In some cases the names of clubs like Concordia or Eureka can be misleading. In San Bernadino the local *Turnverein* organized a May Festival in 1870. The report in the *Los Angeles Star* praised the organizers, promoters, and speakers of the festival, who, according to their names, were exclusively German Jews.[82] In 1864 a report from New Orleans tells of an association called *Deutsche Compagnie* founded the year before. Its declared aims were the promotion of literature, art, and the sciences among its members, "as far as their vocational pursuits allow," as well as the organization of a "charity ball for the Home of Jewish Widows and Orphans which brought in a fine amount of money. As all 71 members, with one exception, belong to the Jewish faith, the aim of elevating Judaism is never lost sight of."[83]

Choral and athletic societies were a genuine, traditional German pastime and flourished in all centers of German settlements in the United States. Among most Germans they were far more popular than the intellectually pretentious literary and theater clubs, which were for a time the main meeting place of German Gentiles and Jews. They seem also to have been far less eager to receive Jewish members, who sought admission as a way of achieving social recognition. In some cases these attempts were temporarily successful, only to give way to anti-Semitic discrimination in later years. A notorious example was the prestigious German choral society Arion of New York. In the first years after its foundation in 1853, some prominent Jews were among its leading members and promoters, and Jewish artists appeared on its stage. But by 1868 the club had changed its by-laws and had barred Jews from membership. The public scandal following this decision seems to have benefited, rather than harmed, the *Gesangverein:* "its ranks were swelled by an influx of all the elements who thought that they would feel more at home in a *judenrein* [Jewless] society, and that the genuine German art of singing could be better developed there."[84]

The Arion case was no exceptional occurrence. It is found repeated, although mostly in a less provocative manner, in other organizations and other cities. In Cleveland Jews were active in the German press and in German-American societies as late as 1890, and some remained members of the *Gesangverein* as late as 1883, although Gentile members of the club systematically blackballed Jewish applicants. Rabbi Samuel Wolfenstein, the director of the Jewish Orphan Home, was praised in the press "as a representative German of our city, having always taken a great interest in the welfare of our German citizens." In 1893 Wolfenstein presided over the North American *Sängerfest* and in his opening speech declared that the "German-American has become conscious of his new and well-loved fatherland . . . [and] must lend to the American genius the mightiest force and the finest products of his own, the German genius." Lloyd P. Gartner, who quotes this speech as the "farewell song of Jewish Germanism in Cleveland," adds some significant comments:

It is truly noteworthy that this address included no reference to Germany itself. Quite possibly, Wolfenstein, like many liberal German-Americans, regarded with profound disillusion the authoritarian regime which had unified and now ruled Germany. The German anti-Semitic revival of the 1880's must also have dampened enthusiasm for the native land, especially among Jews. What was treasured in the German heritage was therefore spiritualized, detached from German soil and government, and adapted philosophically to American life.[85]

Not all Jewish liberals reacted in the same way to what was going on in the old fatherland. Isaac Löw Chronik, born 1831 in Posen, had arrived in Chicago in 1866 after a stormy career as a gifted orator and publicist. He was apparently recommended by Abraham Geiger and invited to serve as "rabbi and teacher" in Chicago's Congregation Sinai, but extended his activities to the city's whole German population. In January 1869 the first issue of his magazine, *Zeichen der Zeit* (signs of the time), appeared. Chronik took an active part in the German community's fight against the "temperance and Sunday closing Bill," which they felt encroached on their traditional right to gather on Sundays in beergardens. Chronik lent the campaign an intellectual dimension by quoting Immanuel Kant's praise of drinking. But Chronik can hardly be considered typical for most German Jews or even intellectuals in America. In 1871 or 1872 he returned to Germany, while Sinai was changing from a German to an English-speaking congregation. Whether this was the reason for Chronik's return, as he refused to preach in English, is not clear.[86] Rabbi Samuel Hirsch of Philadelphia bade him farewell in a melancholic letter: "It is a comfort that you longingly return to the beautiful Berlin. There will be the proper soil for your *Zeichen der Zeit,* while here, as I told you before, the number of those who can appreciate such achievements is still too small."[87]

In Milwaukee the "doors of Germandom" were supposedly more open to Jews than elsewhere. Many Jews participated actively, and sometimes in leading positions, in German lodges and other organizations. The insurance fund of the "Order of the Sons of Hermann" was headed by Jacob Brandeis, president, and Rabbi Emanuel Gerechter, vice president. Brandeis also presided over the order's choral group. Other Jews were among the leaders in the local lodges. In 1873 Rabbi Elias Eppstein was the speaker of the day at a picnic of "800 blue-eyed sons (of Hermann), commemorating the Cherusker's victory in the Teutoburger forest in pagan Germany." His speech was a declaration of loyalty to the old fatherland:

We are Germans by tongue; Germans by will of reasoning our way onwards;
. . . Germans by the desire to seek knowledge and wisdom and foster them;
Germans by uniting in social life; and Germans by assisting each other in
times of need. . . We are Germans, but American Germans, who are willing
to amalgamate the good which we have brought from Europe with the good
we have found here.[88]

Gentile-Jewish companionship in lodges, musical and theatrical associations, and even in the *Turnverein* was certainly not brought from Europe. In Germany these organizations were a hotbed of anti-Semitism, and most Jewish members of these associations in America were quite separated from organized Jewish life. Even they seem to have dropped out in later years, "because of Jewish assimilation into Anglo-Saxon Milwaukee and the *Turners* [gymnastics] movement's growing anti-Semitism." Generally, after 1890 "the German sphere and the Jewish sphere hardly overlapped, and few Jews attempted to keep one foot in each."[89]

There is some indication that in places of later and smaller settlement, mutual relations remained friendly over a longer time, if only for convenience. In Kansas City Oscar Sachs was for thirty years secretary of the board of directors of the German hospital, and was appointed German government consul as late as 1909. Fund raising for charities was sometimes started as joint ventures, as in one opera performance in 1890, whose proceeds were divided between the German hospital and the Jewish charities. But even here Gentiles and Jewish institutions remained separate.[90]

From the late 1870s on, the ties between German Jews and German Gentiles dissolved. By the 1880s the contacts were already largely reduced. The rise of political anti-Semitism in Germany certainly played a role in enhancing this process, although somewhat delayed in America, of separation and estrangement. How much of this was the result of political influence from overseas or of genuine American developments inside both groups is still open to systematic investigation. Here we can pay it only cursory attention.

Early contemporary observers had no doubt that Jew-hatred was of German import. A report from Boston of November 1840 quoted the *Volksfreund* of Lancaster, Ohio, as an example of how some "hungry journalists try to exploit the Jew-hatred imported from Europe." The paper had accused the Jews of avoiding agricultural work, "claiming to be scholars, preachers or poets . . . and (as peddlers) ever ready to cheat Christians." The reporter's conclusion: "You see from this that Jew-hatred can enter the hearts also under the American sun, but not American hearts, if you see what I mean."[91] Twelve years later a visitor from America complained about the "many malicious reports on 'The Jews in America' that are being printed in German newspapers," especially about the Jewish clothiers on Chatham Street. After citing at length some fraudulent actions of Gentile-German immigrants involving, among other people, the superintendent of the German Customs Union in New York, he concluded: "Imagine with what pleasure *good* German papers would have reported these news if the thieving superintendent had been a Jew!" Unfortunately, most German-American journalists were Gentiles, and therefore "most of them share the judeophobic sentiments of their colleagues in Germany."[92]

The American Jewish press usually attributed anti-Semitic outbursts of any kind to the fanaticism of the Germans. In 1856 a German Jew, Eduard Kanter, was elected in Detroit on the Democratic ticket despite an openly anti-Jewish campaign. A Republican German-language paper had some days before the election cautioned the city's "free German workers to keep their eyes open and beware of the Jews!" A Jewish Republican who reported the incident commented resignedly on the "fanaticism with which our brother-tribe spoils everything. . . . He is fanatical in darkness as in the light. If only he would learn some moderation from his neighbor, the Anglo-Saxon American!"[93]

That same year the *Sinai* reported the attempted crucifixion of a Jewish boy in Philadelphia: "In this way the Germans transplant their bloodthirsty fanaticism even across the ocean, to this sacred sanctuary of religious liberty!"[94] Almost ten years later the *Deborah* quoted rumors about the burning of a synagogue in St. Joseph, "allegedly set on fire three times by German fanatics. . . . That Germans should burn the synagogue of their own *Landsleute* out of pure fanaticism is hardly believable in our enlightened times."[95] Similar comments appeared time and again in the Jewish press of America and were reprinted in Germany. Rightly or not, most contemporary German Jews apparently believed that "we have to thank [extremist Germans] for all the *Rischus* [i.e., anti-Semitism] in America. Originally the American knows nothing of it."[96]

It stands to reason that the political anti-Semitism that gained increasing influence in Germany was transplanted to America with the continual stream of immigrants. The German press and literature, widely distributed in the German immigrant society, was certainly responsible at least to some extent for the rising anti-Jewish sentiments among Gentile Germans. At the same time as the Jewish community in America grew in numbers and property, and built ostentatious synagogues, theaters, and clubs, it became ever more conspicuous and open to envious ridicule. The position of some Geman Jews in the ready-made clothing industry added a new dimension to the old deep-rooted prejudice. The fact that they employed a considerable number of Gentile workers in their factories and shops almost inevitably provoked deliberate and bigoted political manipulation. As German workers were first to create unions and organize strikes in New York, Philadephia, and Cincinnati, it was almost unavoidable that anti-Jewish invective should be part of their campaigns.[97]

The exclusion of Jews from cultural and social clubs had its counterpart in the economic sphere. In 1867 the New York fire insurance company Germania advised its agents that every application by a Jew had to be submitted for special approval. Answering critics in the German-language press of New York, Germania's director explained that although "all respectable New York Jews are insured with us," the instructions were necessary as a protection against "second-hand goods dealers, hucksters, adventurers, Jewish war profiteers." The incident soon expanded to become a major issue and was taken up in the press and on the satirical stage. The image of Shylock, or of the criminal Jew who was setting fire to his stores in order to collect the insurance money, reappeared constantly in the German- and English-language press, and in the carnival-books of New York's Gentile-German society.[98]

In 1872 a series of anti-Semitic articles in the *Gartenlaube,* a popular middle-class magazine widely distributed in Germany, was immediately reprinted and discussed in the American German-language press. The main accusations were copied from the German original: the "unproductive" economic pursuits of the Jews in the Old and in the New World, their concentration in finance and commerce, and their absence from agriculture and handicrafts.[99] As readers, and sometimes editors, of German newspapers, the influence of American Jews could generally prevent the reprinting of the most extreme anti-Semitic invective, but not always, and with diminishing success as the years passed.

In 1875 some Catholic German-language periodicals started a political campaign against liberal German Democrats. The attacks resembled a practice already well-known in Germany: liberalism was stamped as the invention of Jewish "power-greedy vampires" all over the world. Often the political strife among American Germans was the occasion to give vent to anti-Semitic sentiments in the press. In 1876 the Republican *Westliche Post* of St. Louis repeatedly referred to the Democratic presidential candidate Samuel Tilden, a Gentile, as *Shmul* in contemptuous German derision of his first name. The rival Democratic German newspaper did not lag behind. It started a frontal attack on the *Post's* editor Carl Schurz, who "judged by his principles was always a Jew; he never acted otherwise than a Jew; he was the representative of European Jewry in America."[100]

If the intensified anti-Semitism in America toward the end of the century was not exclusively imported from Germany, it certainly had its "German connections." Prominent German anti-Semitic politicians and ideologists like Adolf Stoecker or Hermann Ahlwardt visited the United States in the 1890s and were applauded by attentive German-American audiences. The latter even founded two anti-Semitic papers—in German and in English—during his two-year stay in America, and claimed to have had influence in Congress in favoring restrictive legislation against the immigration of Russian Jews.[101] In Milwaukee a former editor of a German paper, accused of having invited Ahlwardt to America, denied his initiative. But he also declared that he was "an earnest anti-Semite" who had learned from Ahlwardt "that it would be a good thing if the eyes of the American people were opened to the fact that the Jews were rapidly ruining the commercial interests of the country, and robbing the Christians on all sides in the highwayman style."[102] Even the academic sphere was not immune: some honored American professors who had obtained their degrees at German universities now were teaching Social Darwinism and racist theories at Johns Hopkins and Columbia University.[103]

It is not easy to reach a conclusive evaluation of the relations between German Jews and Gentiles or, which is probably more important, of the way in which the German Jews came to terms with their dual ethnicity. Attitudes on both sides were complex and ambiguous, and changed over time. For the first-wave immigrants the problem seems to have been easier, if it concerned them at all. In these early years, even those Jews who were inclined to identify themselves as Germans were not encouraged to do so by the general American attitude. American nativism regarded the Germans as unwelcome intruders, associating the "German name with beer and sauerkraut." Germans were not regarded as pioneers. "Where the German comes in, the Yankee goes out" was a popular slogan. For some time "they had created a scarecrow, namely, that all America was being Germanized. In the end all that was left to Germans was a fight for minor habits of living, which were more or less willingly conceded to [them]."[104]

Had German-Jewish immigration stopped at mid-century, the problem of mutual relations and dual ethnicity would probably have been solved at this point. But after the Civil War the renewed immigration of both Gentiles and Jews from German-speaking countries complicated the issue. Jews were more conscious of their legal and cultural achievements in the homeland. Both groups were not unaffected by the rising nationalism in Germany and were susceptible to an at least cultural German patriotism. Jews were now eager to participate in German cultural and social activities, or to practice their own independent activities in German. On the other hand, Germans regarded the accomplishments of German Jews in the cultural—and sometimes even in the economic—sphere as part of the strengthened German position in the United States. As late as 1891 a German publication praising German achievements in New York City included a number of prominent Jews in "the row of distinguished personalities who have brought recognition and honor to the German name in all fields of science and the arts, politics, industry and commerce."[105]

The change of attitude is illustrated by some critical remarks from both sides regarding the other group's loyalty to the German language and culture. In 1857 a letter from San Francisco published in the *Augsburger Allgemeine Zeitung* described, in not exactly sympathetic terms, the impressive economic success of the city's Jewish population: "The people of Israel flourishes here unhampered and without any obstacles. I have noticed how quickly the Jewish population tries . . . to cast off everything Israelitic, to speak preferably English and to praise everything American."[106] But fifteen years later the visiting president of New York's Geographical Society emphasized in a lecture in Berlin that the German Jews in America "preserve the German language and modes in their families much longer than the rest of the Germans."[107]

We have no way of comparing the actual loyalties of the two groups, but individual Jews are on record as having been active in promoting the German language and German studies even in later years. Max Winkele headed the German faculty at the University of Michigan in 1909, and Kaufmann Kohler, president of Cincinnati's Hebrew Union College, was in 1913 elected president of the city's *Deutscher Literarischer Verein* (German literary association).[108] David Einhorn regarded the German spirit to be "the bearer of Reform Judaism," and as late as 1901 Bernhard Felsenthal declared himself to be "racially a Jew, for I have been born among the Jewish nation. Politically I am an American as patriotic . . . as it is possible to be. But spiritually I am a German, for my inner life has been profoundly influenced by Schiller, Goethe, Kant and other intellectual giants of Germany."[109] But by no means can these individual positions be generally regarded as representative for the bulk of German-Jewish immigrants, and even less so for their second- or third-generation descendants, who had not been as intensively trained in Schiller, Goethe, and Kant.

There is quite contradictory evidence suggesting that the process of advanced Americanization, and the disillusioning symptoms that changed the political atmosphere in Germany, combined to pull German Jews and Gentiles apart. Naomi Cohen's distinction between the rural "church Germans" and urban "club Germans" may have its merits in explaining the relationship up to this time.[110] Afterward, the most liberal "club Germans," and certainly the American Jews, were increasingly influenced by the winds that blew from across the ocean. An article in the "American Correspondence" of December 1880 reported rumors of a semi-official intervention by the American minister in Berlin "with regard to the present anti-Semitic crusade." Doubtful as this may be, the paper's own comments are informative: "Public opinion on the Israelites in the United States is generally very favorable. . . . Some of them were till a short time ago more German than American . . . but these were only a small minority, who may now very much regret having held the '*Vaterland*,' personified by Bismarck and the Kaiser, in such high esteem."[111]

Over time contacts with "the other Germans" in America loosened and were eventually abandoned. The ties with relatives in Germany lost importance before they gained a new tragic significance in the 1930s when German Jews sought to be rescued. The main identification of this group was now with itself, and the "German heritage" continued to inspire its self-esteem as a distinctive, and for some time and in certain aspects separate, group of American Jews. Many of them considered it as an important privilege in their confrontation with the assertive and dynamic East European Jews soon to become the overwhelming majority of American Jewry.

8

German and Other Jews

Between 1880 and 1914 some 2 million Jews immigrated to the United States, close to 650,000 in the five consecutive peak years from 1904 to 1908 alone. Three-quarters of them arrived from Russia, the rest from Rumania and other Eastern European countries. These Jewish immigrants amounted to over 9 percent of the total immigration, and the Jewish population in the United States now increased from 0.6 percent to about 3.5 percent.[1]

This influx of 2 million poor East European Jews, the tenfold growth of the Jewish population in the span of one generation, by far exceeded the "critical mass" for revolutionary change. It would have generated tensions and taxed the financial and spiritual resources of the German-Jewish community even if these immigrants had been more similar to them than they actually were. In a relatively short time the structure and the spiritual image of American Jewry was radically transformed. Up to 1880 its residential distribution had been quite balanced throughout the country. Now it became compactly concentrated in the Northeast, with almost half living in New York City. At the same time the group's social and economic situation—if we continue to deal with the whole body of American Jews as one socioeconomic entity—deteriorated. Prior to 1880, most Jews were engaged in commerce as independent, self-employed people. Now, after the first years of the new mass immigration, the occupational structure was diametrically different. In 1900 three out of every five of the Russian Jews were workers, and more than half of them in a single industry: the manufacture of ready-made clothing.[2] And to make things worse, with the one exception of their religion, and even here much unlike themselves in their ways of religious observance and worship, the new immigrants were incomparably different from the Americanized German Jews in almost every way; in their language, dress, family life, customs, and manners. Under these circumstances the shock of the confrontation was inevitable.

In earlier American Jewish historiography much ink was spilled in emphasizing the least appealing aspects of this confrontation; the German

Jews' alleged efforts to stem the flow of the immigration, their grudging and reluctant assistance to the immigrants, their condescension and patronizing, reserved attitude. The other side of the account is the contempt reciprocated by the East European immigrants, their hurt pride, their resentment at being dependent on the charities of the assimilated *Yahudim*. There is, of course, more than a grain of truth in this picture, but in recent years a more contemplative research has weeded out many distorting exaggerations to paint a more balanced picture. Historians of the American Jewish experience, trying to cope with the problems of intragroup tensions and the relations between German and East European Jews and their American-born descendants, admit that "there is need for further study . . . genuinely sensitive to the pluralistic complexity of American society."[3]

Facing the Tide

A constant trickle of Prussian-Polish, Austrian-Galician, and Lithuanian Jews arrived in the United States as early as the 1860s and 1870s. According to one estimate their numbers approached as much as 70,000 to 75,000 before the start of the mass immigration of the early 1880s. Like their German coreligionists, they settled mainly in clusters, establishing their own congregations and mutual aid associations wherever possible. In Baltimore East European Jews separated from the German congregation in 1865 and founded their own mutual aid association. From this a group of Lithuanian Jews seceded in 1873, to establish a *"Russishe Shul"* (Russian synagogue). Two years later it was followed by a *"Byalistoker Shul."*[4] Similar developments are recorded to have taken place in most greater Jewish communities, apparently without creating any serious, lasting discord.

The process by which the whole fabric of American Jewry was to be so dramatically transformed had been brewing in Europe for a long time. In the Russian "Pale of Settlement" and the neighboring countries an unprecedented demographic growth had increased the Jewish population from an estimated 1.5 million in 1800 to almost 7 million a hundred years later.[5] The economic backwardness of the region and its political developments combined to make emigration the only possible way of survival for many Jews. The Western European countries absorbed the first waves of the East European Jewish emigrants, but very soon America became their main and foremost destination.

In 1870 a conservative Jewish periodical appearing in Breslau published a "very distressing piece of news":

The executive committee of the [American] Board of Delegates passed a resolution on January 25, to inform Mr. Crémieux that the American Jews are not willing to favour the immigration of Russian Jews, but indeed want to collect money for their migration into the interior of Russia. . . . In California the attitude is better; Mr. Peixotto in San Francisco has expressed himself to Crémieux warmly in favor of immigration and has raised his voice for it in the press.[6]

One year earlier the New York Herald had, on the other hand, published an editorial in favor of "Hebrew Immigration," calling on "our rich Israelites to bring their oppressed brethren to this new land of promise. Here, at least, they will be free men, and milk and honey will not be found wholly wanting."[7]

Disregarding the Board's opposition a group of 114 grown persons and 22 children embarked from Hamburg in March 1870. They were taken care of by the "Central Frontier Committee" in Königsberg, East Prussia, a body established by some German-Jewish communities and the Alliance Israélite Universelle, known worldwide, shortly, as the Alliance, which paid for the crossing.[8] Their arrival in New York alarmed some representatives of the Board of Delegates, who convened informally with leaders of the Hebrew Benevolent Society and together issued a circular to the presidents of "Hebrew Congregations and Charitable Societies in New York and Vicinity" dated April 27, 1870:

Notwithstanding our urgent remonstrances against indiscriminate immigration . . . hundreds of Israelites are here, despatched by the Koenigsberg committee and utterly penniless. We cannot see them starve . . . something must be done for them. . . . Please take up a collection among your members at once, as we need a large amount to give temporary relief to those here and soon to arrive.[9]

The incident stirred a good deal of opposition in the American Jewish press. The Königsberg committee defended itself against the accusation that it had "sent away the sick and the crippled,"[10] and continued its activities over the following years, against the undiminished opposition of the American Jewish establishment. Early in 1872 it published a letter from New York by an unnamed, but, according to the editor, "very distinguished personality of sufficient standing." This writer underscored the fact that "the immigration [of West Russian Jews] is undesired by the Jews of this country . . . but can be only beneficial for these people themselves, provided you send only young people between 16 and 35 with not too large families."[11]

The issue was publicly taken up in 1871 after the pogroms in Rumania. This time it was brought to the attention of Congress and the press by an initiative of Arthur Wellington Hart and Benjamin Franklin Peixotto, at the time American consul in Bucharest. Both men proposed to initiate a massive immigration of Rumanian and other East European Jews, and to settle them on the land. The latter even brought his proposal to the agenda of what is considered to be the first international Jewish conference held in modern times: a meeting of forty-five prominent bankers, politicians, scholars, and writers who were invited by Gerson Bleichroeder and met in October 1872 at the home of Jonathan Bischoffsheim in Brussels, to discuss the situation of the East European Jews. Peixotto's settlement plan was, however, unanimously rejected. In America the plan gained a more positive reaction. An editorial of the *Philadelphia Inquirer* of April 24, 1873, reported the arrival of "several wealthy Rumanian Hebrews . . . to make arrangements for the reception of their oppressed coreligionists, who, to the number it is said of fifty thousand, desire to seek refuge in our broad, free land." Actually some 150 people arrived in small groups by August 1873. Leopold Bamberger, the president of the Rumanian Emigration Society, which had been established by the Board of Delegates, complained that the majority were paupers and asked Peixotto to send no more such persons.[12]

The number of Russian and Polish Jews who arrived before 1880 was too small to generate serious conflicts or clashes of mentality. The real confrontation started with the unexpected mass immigration in the wake of the violent pogroms in Russia that started in 1881, and continued in sporadic outbursts into the twentieth century. Initiated or tolerated by the government and the church, violence became an ever-present threat to every Jewish community in the "Pale of Settlement." Legal discrimination limiting Jewish economic pursuits and places of residence reached its peak with the expulsion of the Jews from Moscow in 1891. These planned as well as spontaneous developments caused the deterioration of the already destitute economic situation of the Jews. The targets of the Jew-haters, and the victims of the riots, were masses of hungry people, poor families with many children, living in the overcrowded, unsanitary ghettos of small and middle-size towns and in dilapidated shacks in the villages.

The Russian Jews' first reaction to the pogroms of 1881 was horrified flight. Many thousands of refugees took to the roads and flocked into the town of Brody, on the Austrian-Polish border. They were acting on rumors that Western European Jewish aid committees, with allegedly unlimited funds, were awaiting them there. In the spring of 1882 this township of no more than 15,000 inhabitants housed over 20,000 refugees. These starving people, forced to sleep on the streets, and ill-treated by the Austrian authorities, could not be taken care of by the small Jewish community of Brody. They presented an immediate problem for the entire Jewish population of Europe. Jewish institutions like the Baron de Hirsch Fund and the Alliance Israélite Universelle tried to help, but could hardly cope with the situation. Only slowly did relief reach Brody. Refugees were directed to Hamburg and Bremen, where temporary and inadequate quarters were set up. "What had at first been envisaged as a limited relief operation by the Alliance now began to confront the Jews of Europe as the task of coping with a mass exodus."[13]

Naturally, the issue soon became a major concern for the Jews of America as well. At first they seem to have been taken by surprise and were uncertain how to react. The problem was on the agenda of the Union of American Hebrew Congregations (UAHC), the national organization of Reform Judaism, which convened in Chicago in 1881. But

like all Jewish associations this forum also had to admit its helplessness in the face of these outrageous occurrences. . . . A letter of the Anglo-Jewish Association seeking information about what the American coreligionists may be able to do for the immigration of Russian Jews . . . remained for the time being without response, as indeed it requires earnest consideration.[14]

Interestingly, the reaction of the traditionalist leadership was different. In 1878 the former Board of Delegates of American Israelites, representing mainly Conservative or Orthodox congregations, had been formally integrated into the larger Union of American Hebrew Congregations. It did, however, continue to exist as a separate body until 1925, and was now named "The Board of Delegates for Civil and Religious Rights." It was this Board that was approached by the Alliance and other European Jewish institutions in the matter of the refugees in Brody and elsewhere, and in contrast to the UAHC it at least responded to the appeals. For some time the Board therefore served as the main line of communication regarding the Russian-Jewish immigration.

This does not mean that it encouraged these efforts from the start. In 1878 Meyer S. Isaacs of New York, active in communal philanthropies, reported to the Board that "the dispatch of poor emigrants to America has long constituted a burden. . . . It is habitual with benevolent organizations in certain cities in Europe to dispatch utterly helpless Jewish families to America—only to become a burden upon our charities."[15] A similar communication by another member of the Board of Delegates, Mr. Meyer Stern, was forwarded in the same year and repeated in October 1881. Stern pointed out "that there is great poverty in America. Alone in New York a population of 10,000 souls is living on charity. Therefore great care should be taken to choose only young, healthy and work-able emigrants, especially those who can pursue some craft."

The report of the Central Committee of the Alliance, which quoted these communications, was nevertheless full of praise for the efforts of the Board, which had called for "the establishment of local committees in order to contribute to the costs of the absorption and accommodation of the emigrants." The report went on to describe in detail the efforts of the Alliance, specifically those of Charles Netter, its representative in Brody, in the selection of the emigrants, which resulted in the emigration of 450 persons to the United States. Directly following this report the Alliance published an official communication of the New York Board, signed by Isidore Loeb, declaring that it "would admit only a limited number of emigrants selected by the Alliance Israélite. Nothing is promised by the Board to all others, notwithstanding any assurances from Berlin or elsewhere."[16]

There is room for some speculation about the reaction of the Board, representing the religiously more conservative American Jewish element, as compared with the Reform-oriented UAHC, in which German Jews were dominant. Before long, however, the Union could no longer stand apart. In early 1882 it decided to send Rabbi Max Lilienthal of Cincinnati and Moritz Ellinger, the editor of the radical-Reformist *Jewish Times* of New York, to Europe "to negotiate appropriate measures for the continued expedition of refugees, and also to mobilize in Europe the necessary financial means." This was probably an indication of the sentiments of many American Jews who felt that Western European Jewry, at the time by far larger and more prosperous than themselves, should contribute a more substantial share to aid the refugees. However, the Union at the same time decided to collect funds by the emission of "certificates of 5 Dollars each, to the total amount of 200,000 Dollars, to be used for the agricultural settlement of Russian Jews."[17] We have no information about the results of this collection, and to what purpose its proceeds were actually put to use.

In any case the first endeavors to stem the flow of the immigration soon gave way to a more realistic attitude. "The refugees ceased to be respected objects of sympathy and became pathetic objects of charity. Some American Jews never gave up hope that the tide may be dammed up, or, at least diverted. Yet the obligation to aid those here was not shirked."[18]

Twilight of Charity

The German Jews' fear of the undesirable influences of the mass immigration is understandable. Like their relatives in Germany, they were aware of growing anti-Semitism endangering their economic and social comfort. "What benefits could they foresee, what but certain embarrassment and probably burden, from a descent of thousands of penniless Jews whom they supposed to be steeped in medieval superstition when not possessed by wild radicalism?"[19] As late as 1889 these apprehensions came to the fore in a letter to the Alliance from the United Jewish Charities of Rochester, New York: "The refugees are a bane to the country and a curse to the Jews [who] have earned an enviable reputation in the United States, but this has been undermined by the influx of thousands who are not ripe for the enjoyment of liberty and equal rights, and all who mean well for the Jewish name should prevent them as much as possible from coming here."[20]

At that time there had been several years of quite formidable immigrant assistance from Jewish organizations. The United Jewish Charities of New York alone spent an estimated annual amount of half a million dollars between 1881 and 1889. Its representative, addressing a conference of European Jewish leaders in 1891, explicitly confirmed that America was indeed the best destination for Russian-Jewish refugees.[21] Similarly contradictory statements and actions occurred almost everywhere. The first act of the secretary of Baltimore's Emigrant Aid Society, which had been established in 1882, was to induce refugees to return to Europe, providing them with the necessary funds. He then informed the New York committee that those refugees who came to Baltimore could find no work and were eager to return to Europe. It would therefore be much more economical to send them back "home" directly from New York. Yet the Jews of Baltimore went out of their way to assist the many thousand immigrants who disembarked at its port. Those who continued to other locations were met at the boat and provided for, while those who stayed were helped to find work and funds in the city until they could become self-supporting.[22]

The first attempts at organized and coordinated immigrant assistance were undertaken by the Russian Refugee Aid Committee, which had been established in 1881 by the Alliance, together with Jewish institutions in England, France, and Germany. The Committee maintained branch offices in New York, Chicago, Philadelphia, and other large cities in America. In December of the same year American Jewry set up its own organization, the Hebrew Emigrant Aid Society (HEAS). (This is not to be confused with the still-existing HIAS, the Hebrew Immigrant Aid Society, founded in 1889 by a predominantly East European leadership.)

Before long, letters about the harsh, condescending, and bureaucratic attitude in the organization's immigrant hostels appeared in the Jewish press in Russia. Abraham Cahan, soon to become a prominent figure in the early Jewish labor movement of America, had arrived in June 1882, and recollected the prevailing atmosphere in his later writings as "a cross between charities and an army barracks." The Committee members allegedly considered the immigrants to be "wild Russians." No one was allowed to leave the immigrant hostels "without express permission. The food was miserable, the immigrants were generally disdained as 'worthless rabble and *Shnorrers.*' Tension among the immigrants themselves was high, and quarrels were the order of the day."[23]

The tensions between the immigrants and the officials of the HEAS reflect the shortcomings of charity—however willingly or reluctantly granted—in the face of the needs of so many immigrants. In October 1882 violent riots in the Schiff Refuge on Ward's Island in New York required the intervention of the police. Emma Lazarus commented on the incident in the *American Hebrew:* "Given between six and seven hundred people subsisting month after month upon public and private charity under a single officer and one inefficient assistant, . . . the unavoidable result of utter demoralization and mutiny becomes simply a question of time."[24] HEAS soon proved to be utterly inadequate. In its single year of existence between December 1881 and 1882, it took care of about one-half of the recorded 20,000 East European immigrants, spending some $200,000. More than half of this money was contributed by various European Jewish funds. After 1882 all immigrant aid was taken over by the United Hebrew Charities (UHC).

Despite some efforts to "repatriate" a part of the Russian refugees, sending them back to be taken care of by the Jewish organizations of Western Europe, the record of UHC is generally positive. The German-Jewish leaders organized effective relief in the larger American cities and engaged in a consistent struggle against restrictive legislation. Outstanding figures like Jacob Schiff and Louis Marshall demonstrated the general Jewish solidarity in their commitment to support the masses of Jews pouring in from Eastern Europe.[25] Later historians, especially those of East European origins, used to stress the "extent to which the inevitable harshness and difficulty of a transition from one world to another were compounded by unnecessarily callous, bureaucratic treatment." They had to admit, however, that the misunderstandings were not entirely one-sided:

The immigrants were greeted by an attitude of superiority; they felt that they were regarded as objects of experimentation in repatriation and colonization, and their "ghettos" as a threat to the security of the Jewish arrivals of a generation or two before. On the other hand, there were doubtless a number who regarded "Eighth Street" [the location of the UHC] as a "Gentile institution, which it is a *mitzva* to exploit."[26]

Writing in 1973, Zosa Szajkowski confessed that he had earlier "helped perpetuate the negative view of the . . . wealthy 'Uptown Jews,' the *Yahudim* as they were called derogatorily by the East European Jews," which he now felt he had to reappraise. Reconsidering issues like the activities of the Industrial Removal Office, or Jacob Schiff's Galveston project, he came to the conclusion that "though it is true that [the German-Jewish leaders] did not mix socially with immigrants from Eastern Europe . . . the German Jews did everything possible for their East European brethren who came to these shores, defending them in individual cases and fighting restrictive legislation."[27]

As most of the East European immigrants—as much as 90 percent by some estimates—settled in New York City, almost all the earlier and ongoing arguments about the mutual relations between these two constituting components of American Jewry is centered on this East Coast megapolis. In his study on the "Promised City," Moses Rischin dedicated a whole chapter to the controversial subject of "Germans versus Russians." His conclusions are a well balanced evaluation of an objectively very complex situation:

> Uptowners, taken unawares by the heavy immigration of terror-stricken refugees in 1881 and fearful of a pauper problem, attempted to restrain further immigration. But as the tide could not be stemmed, the Jewish charities of the city, aided considerably by West European Jewry, chafingly accepted their new responsibilities. . . . German Jews devised comprehensive schemes to divest downtown brethren of the marks of oppression and to remodel them in the uptown image.[28]

A rather ludicrous expression of this intention was the publication of a weekly, *The Jewish Gazette,* in German, and not in *Jargon,* or Yiddish, as the report underlined, but written in Hebrew letters. This should "enable the older generation coming from eastern Europe to adjust to the language and manners of the country."[29] In the eyes of some later critics "the intensity of German Jewish hostility produced a well-funded, highly organized movement to shape the newest members of a minority group into the mold of the established community." But, as Rischin rightly counters, the effort to "Americanize" the new immigrants was by no means a uniquely German-Jewish endeavor.[30] He could have added that it was in fact also an objectively inevitable condition for the integration of East European Jews into their new environment. They certainly resented the patronizing attitude of the officials and the social barriers most German Jews maintained for a considerable period of time. But they also understood the need for "Americanization," although they sought to perform this in their own way, by their own educational efforts, preserving their own Jewish cultural identity as they conceived it. This was, however, a much later development and reflected the formation of a large, concentrated, culturally and socially self-sufficient, East European Jewish society. In the early 1880s the Russian Jews depended, however reluctantly, on the help of the *Yahudim* (the Russians' snide term for the German Jews), for whatever reasons it was granted. Possibly only a small part of the immigrants profited from these activities. The majority were self-sufficient, starting work as unskilled "Columbus tailors" in the city's sweatshops soon after their arrival.

The establishment's main efforts centered on education. Day nurseries, kindergartens, and afternoon schools were organized by the Hebrew Free School Association in an attempt to discourage Christian missionaries. The Hebrew Institute, established in 1889 and occupying an impressive five-story building, was a joint project of Jewish organizations and was known from 1893 on as the Educational Alliance. The house contained classes and meeting rooms, an auditorium with seven hundred seats, a library, gymnasium, shower baths, and a roof garden, and entertained a wide range of activities. While adults learned "the privileges and duties of American citizenship," youngsters took part in vocational courses, classes in English, civics, American history, and English literature. The hurdle of "Americanization" was expected to be taken in one vast stride, the old ways and customs shed on the way as just so much hindering dross. "Not until the first decade of the twentieth century was the Educational Alliance to bridge the gap between modern, urban New York and the psychological world of Torah and ghetto by conducting its courses in Yiddish."[31]

Like most Jewish philanthropy and many other Jewish communal activities of the time, the tone and perceptions of immigrant assistance were set by a small group of wealthy and influential personages. The communal stewards, men of economic and political influence, felt both entitled and obligated to take on the burdens of the community. By virtue of their economic standing or official posts they gained access to political power-brokers and opinion-molders, and were able to mobilize attention and support for the assistance of the immigrants. "Within the Jewish community they determined policy for the philanthropic and defense organizations as well as strategy for singular crises. . . . They made little pretense of consulting the constituency they represented. Undemocratically, but out of a sense of noblesse oblige, they defined the needs of the American Jewish community."[32]

The most important "stewards" of the time were Jacob H. Schiff and Louis Marshall. Differing from each other in many ways, they divided between them the various legal and social aspects of immigrant care.

Schiff, the scion of a wealthy Jewish family in Frankfurt, had first come to America in 1865, and had returned to the United States in 1875, after two years absence, to become the leading partner of Kuhn, Loeb & Co. Marshall was nine years younger, the American-born son of German immigrants, and had made his career as a lawyer. Both men belonged to the German-Jewish elite and were prominent members of Temple Emanu-El and cofounders of the American Jewish Committee, whose philosophy and strategy they determined for a long period.

Schiff's wealth and generosity, matched by his untiring and assertive energy, made him the central figure in Jewish philanthropy, in fact in most community ventures. He was the unofficial head of American Jewry, honored and obeyed by the already established Germans as well as the newly arrived immigrants from Russia and Poland. Marshall, on his side, was for many decades the leading, if not always uncontested, spirit in the legal and political representation of American Jewry. As an experienced and successful lawyer he believed more in quiet negotiation than in public demonstrations. His field of action was intensive private lobbying, the interplay of political interests and personal contacts. Both men played an important role in the struggle for unrestricted immigration of the East European Jews and assisted them in their first steps in their new country.[33]

Tendencies to restrict immigration had become a matter of public debate by the early 1880s, but most initiatives of restrictive legislation were repelled. In 1882 an act excluding "any person unable to take care of himself or herself without becoming a public charge" was finally passed in Congress, and then became a major cause of dispute between immigration authorities and immigrant-aid agencies. With ever more immigrants seeking entrance, more serious restrictions were legislated in 1891. "Paupers or people suffering from a loathsome or dangerous contagious disease," as well as those whose tickets had not been paid for by themselves, were added to the list of the "excluded classes." All these provisions led to severe harassment of poor immigrants, who feared to be sent back to Europe, as indeed quite a few actually were.

The ambiguity of reluctant, but nonetheless self-imposed solidarity is best demonstrated in the German-Jewish establishment's fight against restrictionism. In 1891 representatives of the UAHC met with Charles Foster, then secretary of the treasury, to guarantee that Russian-Jewish immigrants should not be treated as "paupers" or "excluded classes" as defined by the legislation. They assured the secretary that the Jewish community was prepared to make sacrifices in order to "help the immigrants attain the reputable status of American citizens, without becoming a burden to national or local relief agencies." Foster expressed his hope that conditions abroad would soon change "to make any mass-emigration of Russian Jews unnecessary. The American Jews were acting both patriotically and humanely, dissuading more Jewish refugees from coming, but at the same time assisting those who do eventually arrive, to become independent people." Accordingly he asked the petitioners to "use their influence in Europe, so that by no means should a mass emigration be directed to America." Directly following this information the editor of the German-Jewish paper attached a communication from Boston warning immigrant-aid agencies to let all ship tickets be bought by the immigrants themselves, else they might be repulsed as belonging to the "excluded classes."[34]

In the same interview Foster also praised the efforts of the Jewish immigrant-aid associations to "direct the emigrants to such areas where they can really help to meet an existing demand." Such efforts were indeed undertaken from the first beginnings of the mass immigration. In 1882 the Hebrew Emigrant Aid Society sent groups of immigrants without previous notice to inland Jewish communities. Forty-seven Russian refugees arrived in Cleveland "entirely destitute and helpless." The following spring, community officials complained that "about two hundred and fifty [Russian Jews] . . . are not merely a great burden to the Cleveland Hebrew Relief Society, but they give great trouble also to the Distributing Committee."[35] Small numbers of East European immigrants are reported to have arrived around 1900 in remote places like Kansas City, Missouri, and were taken care of by the earlier German-Jewish settlers. The community's women assumed the practical and financial responsibility for helping the Russians by renting an empty loft and providing beds and household goods. Later they helped the newcomers find employment.[36]

Here as elsewhere greater numbers of new immigrants started to arrive at that time due to the organized efforts of the Industrial Removal Office (IRO). This office was established in 1901 by the Baron de Hirsch Fund, in cooperation with B'nai B'rith and the UAHC, in order to disperse the immigrants crowding into New York City. Local agents and committees searched the country for employment opportunities and "qualified newcomers," or those assumed to be qualified, were directed there. After their arrival, the local communities assisted them until they adjusted to the new jobs and environment, while the IRO covered the basic costs.

The IRO's activities aroused objections from some of the Jewish communities. Most immigrants mistrusted its efforts and preferred in any event to stay together on the Lower East Side of New York and other gateway cities on the East Coast. Yiddish-speaking rabbis who were posted by the IRO on Ellis Island mostly failed to convince them. After the traumatic experience of crossing the ocean in steerage, they were frightened of further travels. The 50,000 reported to have been relocated until 1910 by the IRO was a number far below its annual target figures. Still, its activities helped to disperse at least some of the immigrants, and, as far as can be told, mostly to their advantage.[37]

The "Galveston plan" of 1907, initiated and financed by Jacob Schiff, tried to overcome the obstacle of a "second uprooting." Immigrants were told they should disembark in Galveston on the Texas coast. Los Angeles and some other communities on the West Coast that began to expand at this time benefited from the efforts of both the IRO and the Galveston plan.[38] Yet, on the whole, only several thousand immigrants arrived in Galveston before the outbreak of World War I. In addition to the opposition of some of the major immigrant associations, the deportation in 1910 of a large number of immigrants who had entered by this port curtailed these efforts. On the other hand, the East Europeans resisted all these German-Jewish initiatives to "remove" them as far away as possible.

There was at least one attempt to create a unified organization of Russian and German Jews in order to coordinate all activities of the absorption and dispersion of the new immigrants. When the Baron de Hirsch Fund was founded in February 1891, the Jewish Alliance of America, initiated by some prominent Russian Jews, held its first and last national meeting in Philadelphia, and was attended by representatives from both camps. The organization proclaimed its aim to change the lopsided occupational structure of the immigrants. Immigrants should be settled and employed in agricultural occupations all over the country. The machinations of philanthropy should be redirected "to instruct Hebrew immigrants in the duties and obligations of American citizenship, and to fit them for the loyal discharge thereof." But although over thirty local branches of the Alliance were set up after the Philadelphia convention, unity failed to materialize, and cooperation soon collapsed.[39]

An article in Philadelphia's *Jewish Exponent* reflects the viewpoint of the established German-Jewish community. The Baron de Hirsch Fund was warmly welcomed as being "the soundest basis for the solution of the much-discussed Russian problem." Immigration should be neither stimulated nor encouraged, and funds were to go for proper and quick settlement and to the immediate transfer of new arrivals to final destinations.[40] In the following issues the argument about the solution of the immigrant problem went on, with some dissenting voices protesting against the general trend toward "ruralism." Henrietta Szold requested more sympathy for the immigrants instead of the prevailing charitable attitude, stating that the German Jews should put themselves in the immigrant's place with "sympathetic imagination."[41]

The formation of the Jewish Alliance presented another occasion to express the paper's support for the idea of dispersion. One of its directors, Louis E. Levy, set the tone in an article of August 1891, and three months later in an address to the Association of Jewish Immigrants: "There is no subject of more far-reaching consequence than the present and final disposition of the Russian-Jewish refugees . . . [by] diverting the stream of immigration away from the great and overcrowded centers of population, to the benefit of the immigrant as well as the community."[42]

With regard to the most crucial issue of restrictive legislation and policies, the resistance of the German-Jewish establishment was consistent and unbending. Political pressure and lobbying were especially called for in 1907, when Congress created the Dillingham Immigration Commission. During the investigation, and after the Commission came up for a policy shift from regulation to open and discriminating restriction, the Jewish press and organizations unanimously rejected these proposals. In the center of the legal campaign stood Max Kohler, the son of Kaufmann Kohler and the grandson of David Einhorn. As a successful lawyer Kohler led the campaign on the general level of the constitutional rights of all minorities. His report to the Dillingham Commission, which concentrated on the negative effects of the proposed legislation on the Jewish community, was submitted jointly by the American Jewish Committee, B'nai B'rith, and the Board of Delegates. Kohler also led the vigorous campaign against William Williams, commissioner of immigration at the port of New York, who was accused of having ordained anti-Semitic directives on Ellis Island.[43]

Not all of these efforts ended in success. The adoption of the most extremely discriminating immigration quotas was postponed for several years, but the inclusion of the contested literacy test in the immigration act of 1917 was not prevented. But in these campaigns American Jewry closed its ranks to face the increasingly anti-Semitic undertones of restrictionist propaganda. "Unlike their predecessors before 1881, the immigrants from Russia and Rumania now appeared to the American Jewish public as victims of religious persecution who had a special claim upon the sympathy and support of their American coreligionists."[44]

In the fight against restrictionism, cooperation between German and East European Jews was both necessary and possible, despite different attitudes of political action. The established Jewish leaders who chose to fight restrictionism went against the general trend of American public opinion.

In this matter they compromised their usual accommodationist posture in favor of Jewish needs. . . . Their work drew them no closer physically or emotionally to the East Europeans. On a deeper level, they needed to assume the responsibilities of kinship for their own psychological well-being as much as for the needs of the refugees.[45]

In a sense these attempts were guided by more than mere psychological self-esteem. A growing awareness of Jewish solidarity did not allow the German leadership to accept these openly discriminatory restrictionist policies. Inconspicuous internal efforts to stem, or at least to regulate, the increasing flow of immigrants continued, but were mostly ineffective. Everything possible was tried to remove the new immigrants from the fast-growing ghettos of New York's Lower East Side and other big cities. As far as these endeavors succeeded, they were not necessarily detrimental to the immigrants' own interests. When they proved to be impracticable, "Americanization" became the main concern. The now urgent aim was to "wean" the newcomers, or at least their children, from their alien ways of dress, speech, and behavior, to immerse them as quicky as possible in their new environment. The underlying fear was that the xenophobic sentiments presumably evoked by the East European Jews would endanger the social status and achievements of the whole community. In any case, the German-Jewish leadership did not shirk its responsibilities in the communal and educational sphere. Here the Jewish tradition of *Tsedakah* merged with the American ethics of private philanthropy as well as apprehension at being mischievously identified with the uncouth newcomers.

The reactions and later recollections of the East Europeans at the receiving end of the manifold philanthropic and educational pursuits were understandably mixed. Irving Howe quotes some contradictory statements on the activities of New York's Educational Alliance that are worth repeating:

> The memories of Eugene Lyons were bitter: "We were 'Americanized' about as gently as horses were broken in. In the whole crude process we sensed a disrespect for the alien traditions of our homes and came unconsciously to resent and despise these traditions, good and bad alike, because they seemed insuperable barriers between ourselves and our adopted land."
>
> The memories of Morris Raphael Cohen were warm: "It was [at the Alliance] that my father and mother went regularly to hear the Rev. Masliansky preach in Yiddish. It was there that I drew books from the Aguilar Free Library and began to read English. . . . A window of my life opening on the soul-strengthening vista of humanity will always be dedicated to the Educational Alliance."

Howe concludes that both types of reminiscences were valid:

> The German Jews, intent on seeing that the noses of those East Side brats were wiped clean, surely proved themselves to be insufferable. . . . Yet, in

a way, the latter were right: physical exercise and hygiene were essential to the well-being of their "coreligionists," and somehow, through prodding and patronizing, they had to be convinced of this. The East European Jews felt free to release their bile because they knew that finally the German Jews would not abandon them, and the German Jews kept on with their good works even while reflecting on the boorishness of their coreligionists.[46]

Writing from the vantage point of the East European immigrants, Elias Tcherikower's evaluation sounds less lenient:

Even with great sums at their disposal, the leadership of established American Jewry failed in its proposed resolution of the problem of the integration of East European Jewry into American society. Control, colonization, distribution, direction—all had proven bankrupt; direct philanthropy was to prevail. The masses of immigrants, with their own social and cultural needs and aspirations, went their own way.[47]

In retrospect they would have had to find "their own way" in any case. Philanthropy and benevolent guidance could, and did, smooth the first steps of the immigrants and facilitate their first efforts of orientation and adjustment. But the sheer numbers of new immigrants, soon followed by a remarkable host of young intellectuals, called for an autonomous development. Concentrating mainly in New York and a few other big cities, the East European Jews started to establish their own framework of social and cultural institutions, largely independent of the existing Jewish establishment. The separation of American Jewry into two distinctively different, although never entirely separate, groups was, at least for several decades, inevitable.

The Two Communities

It is doubtful whether the Americanized German Jews, under whatever circumstances, could have been expected to absorb a mass immigration so utterly different from themselves. Thirty or even fifty years before, they—or their elders—had come to America from an economically and politically disadvantaged, but at the time already slowly advancing, Jewish society. Most of them had the advantage of an at least elementary secular education. The background and composition of the East European Jews was extremely different. The first immigrants of the 1880s arrived as destitute fugitives, fleeing the horrors of the pogroms, and this situation was repeated in 1890 and 1905. The hopelessly deteriorating economic conditions of overcrowded cities and small towns of Russia and Galicia were probably even more compelling reasons to seek a new homeland. Economic backwardness combined with the entrenched Judeophobia of the population, which was deliberately manipulated by hostile governments, to make life unbearable. The pauperization of Russian Jewry had begun decades before its political crisis.[48] Therefore, most of the immigrants were dependent on charitable organizations for the cost of their passage.

While most early German-Jewish immigrants had been unmarried youngsters, many now came across with their families. Accordingly the ratio of able-bodied providers to the total number of immigrants was relatively low. But even more important is the fact that between 1899 and 1914 some 63 to 66 percent of all employed immigrants were classified as industrial workers, with only 5.5 to 10 percent in commerce.[49] To what degree these statistics resulted from deliberately misleading information given on disembarkation is hard to decide. Most of those who registered as "qualified workers" hardly knew any elementary crafts when they arrived, but most of them were nevertheless on their way to becoming "wedded to the 'Katrinka' [sewing machine]."[50] They started their economic life in the new homeland in the needle trades, working in sweatshops and loft factories, or at their homes, for the rapidly expanding garment industry, which was owned and developed mainly by German Jews. Many of their landlords in the overcrowded ghettos of New York and other big cities were also German Jews. In this way the clash of mentalities and cultural patterns attained from the very beginning the character of a social-class conflict.

New York City, the main port of entry, and where the greater part of the Jewish immigrants preferred to stay, was the center for the manufacture of ready-made clothing. German-Jewish entrepreneurs had been in the forefront of this expanding industry. In 1885 an estimated 97 percent of all garment factories of New York City were owned mostly by German Jews. From mid-century on German Jews had employed Irish, English, and German Gentiles. After 1880 the majority of their workers were East European Jews. In the words of an early trade-union leader: "The early class struggles in the modern clothing industry in New York were *Jewish* class struggles; both masters and men were of the Hebrew race."[51]

Many immigrants may have chosen this kind of work exactly because the owners were Jews who allowed them to work on Sunday instead of Saturday, or because they expected better treatment from their own kind. But this did not reduce the tension of conflicting interests. In an industry composed of a great number of small enterprises, competition was tough. The increasing supply of labor, available at almost any price, kept wages low, and they tended to fall even more. Working conditions were almost unbearable, and the exploitation of women and children working in the home was practically unrestricted by law or sanitary inspection. The picture has been painted many times and has often been exaggerated, but the prevailing reality was harsh by any standard.

It was, however, incomparably better than in the old country, and for a time this comparison may have dominated the newcomers' attitude toward their new homes. A contemporary immigrant guidebook claimed that the Jew "aspired to bread and pickles, earned 50 cents a day, spent 10 cents for coffee and bagels and saved 40 cents . . . . and writes home that America is a land of gold and silver."[52] But these sentiments soon gave way to a different set of values. In the words of a Senate committee's report, "they soon become Americans and want to live as they see others live, and then they find that they cannot make money enough to do that at the wages which they were first willing to accept."[53] When more and more immigrants entered the industry and crowded into loft factories instead of working at their homes, the first militant unions emerged, guided by the young intellectuals who had brought their radical ideologies with them from Russia.

The early American labor movement, led by Samuel Gompers, himself an English Jew, was slow to represent the interests of this newly arrived proletariat. Faced with the flood of a wage-depressing new labor supply, the movement showed restrictionist tendencies that were a quite natural reaction. Once the new immigrants arrived and invaded the shops and factories, they had, of course, no choice but to try to organize them within their own ranks, but they were poorly equipped for the task. Besides their narrow-minded restrictionism, the xenophobic nativism and anti-Semitic prejudices of many union members repelled the Jewish workers, who, instead, established their own organizations. Eventually, however, they united in large and multifaceted organizations like the Amalgamated Clothing Workers Union and the International Ladies Garment Workers' Union (ILGWU).

The United Hebrew Trades, founded in 1888, included by 1910 some ninety unions, representing a membership of 100,000, which during World War I grew to a quarter of a million members. Although most of the largest unions later became parts of the American Federation of Labor (AFL), their radical vocabulary, brought from Russia by some activists of Russian and Jewish socialist parties, at first estranged them from the established union leadership. But eventually the Jewish unions played an important role in the development of a pragmatic and down-to-earth trade unionism in America. Salo W. Baron has ascribed this "major Jewish contribution to the American labor movement, and American society as a whole," to the East European Jewish heritage. The traditions of social justice "enjoined by Bible and Talmud" and of self-governing Jewish communities called for peaceful cooperation between employers and workers.

> Although class struggle was far from absent from the old ghettos, the communal machinery, abetted by public opinion, for the most part succeeded in blunting the sharpness of controversies. . . . With the general instability of Jewish wealth and the solidarity generated by outside hostilities, Jews were also prone to deal with one another on a more egalitarian basis. Transplanted to America, these psychological attitudes generated a certain social equilibrium, even a measure of solidarity between management and workers.[54]

Be this as it may, apprehension of the Jewish situation in America, where anti-Semitic sentiments were becoming increasingly public, certainly affected both sides of the conflict. This awareness of a common interest uniting East European Jewish workers with their German-Jewish capitalist "exploiters" became especially evident during the "Great Revolt" in the garment industries of New York and Chicago in 1909–11. Led by the International Ladies Garment Workers Union some 20,000 dressmakers went on a strike that lasted from November 1909 till February 1910. In July 1910 60,000 cloakmakers affiliated with the Amalgamated Clothing Workers of America stopped work for over six weeks. They were followed several months later by some 8,000 workers of the world's largest men's clothing factory, Hart, Schaffner, and Marx in Chicago, in a strike lasting four full months.

These labor conflicts aroused a great deal of public attention. Unfavorable comments were aimed at both the employers and the striking unionists, and they did not forget to mention that most of the antagonists on both sides were Jews. Fearing that "a prolongation of the strike would entail considerable injury to the Jewish community at large," the German-Jewish leadership of the American Jewish Committee took the initiative of arbitration. The idea was actually not a new one in these circles. Jacob Schiff is quoted to have asked already in 1897 whether it might not be "possible that representatives of workers, contractors, and manufacturers meet to discuss ways and means in which a better condition of affairs could permanently be brought about?" There were rumors that Schiff used to contribute anonymously to relief funds for striking workers and even to union treasuries.[55]

Now it was Louis Marshall who succeeded in convincing the conflicting parties to invite judge Louis Brandeis from Boston to mediate a compromise. The outcome was the famous "Protocol of Peace" that ended the strike of July 1910 in New York and served as the lasting model for the arbitration of the Chicago and later conflicts. The nucleus of the agreement was the establishment of joint commissions, on the basis of parity, to settle issues of wages and sanitary conditions, and other grievances. Prominent Jewish community leaders acceptable to both sides were to hold the decisive vote in case of disagreement. "To be sure, the protocol broke down, was repaired, and broke down again after some years. But most scholars agree that its influence was lasting."[56]

Whatever its influence on the development of American trade unionism, the Jewish labor movement became for a considerable time the single most important vehicle of Americanization for the immigrants. Through it the East European Jewish immigrant workers "expressed their values and transmitted their traditions" to their new homeland.[57] The inevitable result of this process was the emergence of a distinctively East European Jewish community increasingly independent of the established German-Jewish institutions. Their common faith and the prejudiced stereotypes of the Gentile environment were instrumental in convincing both sides to negotiate and settle social and cultural conflicts inside the Jewish camp. German-Jewish capitalists and Russian-Jewish proletarians agreed to speak with one another, even if they did not love one another.

With the increasing flood of immigration, the Americanized German Jews became a relatively ever-smaller, although still powerful, minority inside the Jewish ethnic group. The Russian, Polish, and Rumanian Jews indeed "went their own way." Gaining more economic security, quick to adapt to the American scene and eager to escape from the fold of patronizing philanthropy, they established their own congregations and mutual aid institutions. With the arrival of an impressive group of intellectuals, authors and artists in both Yiddish and Hebrew, a secular Jewish culture reflecting all shades of the political and ideological convictions brought over from Europe separated the new Jewish community ever more from the earlier-established institutions. "The newcomer would now sooner worship on Sunday to the accompaniment of the temple's organ, than the native would be found downtown on his way to the Yiddish theater. They seemed almost to inhabit two distinct communities."[58]

New York City remained the center of the cultural and institutional life of both communities. Its Jewish population grew from an estimated 80,000 in 1870 to almost half a million in 1915. It constituted close to 28 percent of the city's total population, and almost one-half of all Jews living in the United States. Between 70 and 90 percent of all East European immigrants crowded, at least for some time, into the downtown ghettos of Manhattan, often replacing the successful German Jews who had moved further north not long before. This development was not confined to New York alone. The phenomenon of two distinct Jewish communities in separate residential quarters, each conserving its own long-lasting social and cultural milieu, is found repeated wherever the East European immigrants chose to settle in great numbers.

After New York City, Chicago is probably the best example of this process. Its Jewish community started relatively early, with settlers from Bavaria and the Rhenish Palatinate establishing a congregation in 1846 and their own synagogue in 1815. In 1860, the estimated 1,500 Jews of Chicago already constituted some 10 percent of the total population, and by 1880 the community had grown to around 10,000. But already at that time many of the more recently arrived Jews were *Ostjuden*, the "eastern Jews," from the formerly Polish parts of Prussia, from Galicia, and from Russian Poland. An Orthodox Russian congregation was established in the less prosperous neighborhood of the city in 1875. The fire of 1874 is recorded to have destroyed the home of many poor Polish and Russian Jews. Relief is said to have been offered them grudgingly, after a passionate appeal by Rabbi Liebmann Adler of the German congregation.[59]

As the Russian-Polish Jewish community of Chicago advanced in numbers and economic standing, it created its own congregations and associations. In 1881 Russian Jews, following the American example, founded a fraternal lodge and asked to be admitted to the local B'nai B'rith Grand Lodge, which consisted at the time of thirty-eighty German-Jewish lodges. After a hefty debate the application was denied by majority rule, causing an unforeseen reaction in the Jewish and non-Jewish press. The Russian lodge was eventually admitted to the national organization by the veto of its Grand Lodges of New York and other East Coast cities, but this early example of antagonism between the two segments of American Jewry gained wide attention. Ludwig Philippson accorded it a leader in his paper, quoting "some American newspaper" that had said of the German Jews in America that they "wish to prove to Prince Bismark that they care more for their Germandom than for their Judaism." Philippson went on to express his hope that the crisis might soon be solved by mutual agreement. "It would indeed be a bad spectacle, performed, of all places, in free America, while in German communities like Vienna a serious split between German and Polish Jews has never occurred. The present generation knows that already in the next . . . the differences between the native Jews and the Polish new arrivals will disappear."[60]

Observers on the spot were less optimistic. Early in 1881 Vilna-born Henry Gersoni (Zvi-Hirsch Gershoni), the editor of Chicago's *Jewish Advance,* reprinted some of his editorials in a forty-page brochure titled *Jew against Jew,* which depicted the current conflict in a broader historical perspective. Comparing the alleged hostility toward the Polish Jews of the German-Jewish historian Heinrich Graetz with the anti-Semitic tirades of the German historian Heinrich Treitschke, Gersoni concluded that prejudices like those of "congregations of Germany against the Jews of Russia and Poland . . . exist almost everywhere." Recounting the denial of a charter to the B'nai B'rith lodge in Chicago, he concluded: "The consequences of these prejudices against the Pollack are seen and felt most keenly in America. . . . The Pollack and the German Israelite regard each other as strangers, and yet there is an infathomable feeling of bitterness among them, because they cannot help admitting that they are both Jews after all."[61]

The more traditionalist—and less pronouncedly German—Jewish circles welcomed the East Europeans with more sympathy and understanding. The *Occident* praised the Polish and Russian Jews of Chicago for their Jewish knowledge and religious observance, as well as for their communal and educational achievements: "The masses are illiterate, if one disregards their Judaistic knowledge. . . . But some can be found who have studied at European universities and have acquired a high grade of general culture and training, proving that not every Jew coming from Eastern Europe is an ignorant Pollack." At the time there were already four main Polish congregations in Chicago, in addition to "a host of smaller congregations with their own "*Rabbanim* and *Hazzanim*. . . . Our Polish Jews deserve appreciation . . . for what they perform for the poor children. There are in this city [two] Hebrew free-schools, maintained almost exclusively by the Poles themselves, and attended by many children."[62] Three years later we learn in another report from Chicago that

not only is the Russian-Jewish element growing in the United States from day to day, it also consolidates itself as its own permanent corporation. Beside its own congregations, synagogues or prayer rooms, it cultivates a tendency of exclusiveness, brought over from the old home. This seems evident from a recent urgent circular written in *Jargon* [Yiddish] calling for the establishment of a separate hospital for the Russian-Polish emigrants. They are guided by the mistrust of how the ritual food-laws are observed in other Jewish hospitals. . . . A review of the city's synagogues and prayer-rooms proves how differently the local Jewry is composed. Only one of them belongs to the radical Reform, six are conservative, fifteen orthodox, one ultra-orthodox, and two Hasidic. Beside them we have 12 to 15 *minyanim*. . . . If one believes, following the statements in the American Jewish press, that radical Reform has the greatest support among the present Jewish population of America, this careful review proves how misleading this opinion is. The orthodox trend is still very strongly represented, next come mainly the conservatives, i.e., the moderate Reform following the example of many Jewish communities in Germany.[63]

The statement concerning religious affiliation is especially significant. Two years later Chicago's Jewish Relief Society published a protest
against the

> mass import of indigent Russian Jews . . . of whom the beautiful garden-
> city already contains more than can be mastered by the whole of Jewish
> philanthropy. These people are unable to acclimatize because, wherever
> they are found in greater numbers, they establish closed congregations, and
> are reluctant to amalgamate with other elements of the population.[64]

The president of Chicago's Jewish preparatory school also complained
that the Russian-Jewish immigrant population, numbering over 20,000
souls in 1895, "has settled in an almost closed quarter of our town. The
immigrants have become American citizens, but they still communicate
in a foreign hybrid language . . . Our school has set itself the systematic,
though patient, eradication of this *Jargon*."[65] What emerges from these
utterances is the picture of a minority of Americanized German-Jewish
notables who, even at this late date, were unable to accept the existence
of an autonomous East European Jewish society outside their sphere
of influence.

The same or similar developments took place wherever a substantial
East European Jewish community assembled. In Detroit, relations between the German and the more orthodox Polish Jews were, up to the
1870s, quite cordial, despite the evident paternalism of the Germans. As
long as the whole community was small, the need for cooperation in
philanthropic and religious matters, and the virtually common cultural
background of "Bavarians" and "Poseners," prevented the kind of rancor
that was to characterize later relations between these two segments of
the Jewish community. But with the massive influx of Russian-Polish Jews
after 1880 the rift deepened along clear social lines. By 1900 it had evidently split the community into two, according to its social and residential
stratification, as well as its religious and cultural activities. Some cooperation continued to exist, but social, economic, and religious differences
gained the upper hand. Jewish charity was controlled by affluent German
Jews who had little sympathy for the orthodox Russian Jews. The latter,
on their side, tried to do without this assistance. "The few attempts at
bridging the social barriers between German and Russian Jews failed to
achieve the desired results, and the majority of the city's German Jews
refused to associate with the immigrants. The Jews of Detroit, for all
intents and purposes, formed two separate communities at the outbreak
of World War I."[66]

Over one-half of the 600 Jews who lived in Atlanta, Georgia, in 1880 were Germans or their American-born descendants. By 1900 the Jewish community of the "Gate City" had grown to 2,000, to again double in 1910. The reaction of the established community to the new immigrants followed the described pattern, with an additional, specifically Southern antagonism toward any deviation from the norms and modes of the Protestant environment. Atlanta's German Jews took part in every organized act of expressing sympathy for the Russian Jews. They provided them with material assistance and endeavored to help them get settled and Americanize themselves. In the words of one of their prominent citizens: "Our duty does not rest with saving them from starvation, we must raise them from intellectual and physical destitution and decay, teach them and enlighten them. . . . Have mercy upon him and teach him to become like you." Before long, however, the East European Jews of Atlanta, like Jews elsewhere, began to free themselves of this condescending patronage and to establish their own congregations and institutions. In 1896 their spokesmen declared publicly that "we need not cling to the apron strings forever. . . . Let us work our way to prosperity and American citizenship in our own humble way."[67]

The German Jews of Atlanta, like many older Jewish communities in the South or Midwest, never became such a tiny minority inside the Jewish group as those of New York, Chicago, or Detroit. In Atlanta their numbers and wealth enabled the German Jews to maintain their own institutions. Traditions of religious worship and social and cultural pursuits were preserved beside, and to some extent outside, the emerging new mainstream of Jewish community life. From around the turn of the century on, the division of American Jewry into two communities became an established fact. The East European Jews, led by their own leaders, be they Orthodox rabbis, radical socialists, or ardent Zionists, indeed "went their own way." Culturally they could depend on a host of authentic and gifted writers and artists, and on their Yiddish theater and press.

The Americanized German Jews soon gave up their intention of dispersing the stream of the millions of new immigrants and of reforming the East European Jews in their own image. They did not totally shed the responsibility of leadership, but they certainly soon recognized its limits. In the public and political sphere a tenuous mode of cooperation and joint leadership were eventually established. In the sphere of social and cultural institutions and personal relations, the division proved to be of more persistent longevity. For many decades most Jews of German origin in the United States retreated into their own social shell, isolated by a tradition of condescension toward, and reciprocated contempt from, the majority of American Jewry.

Preserving the Clan

In 1966 the Jewish community of Kansas City, Missouri, celebrated its centennial with a series of lectures on the community's history. One of the lecturers pondered the alternatives open to the "Germans," who on the eve of World War I were "swamped by overwhelming numbers" of East European Jews: "(1) to merge with the new immigrants; (2) to shore up the wall of separation between the 'German' and 'Russian' communities; or (3) to sever ties with the Jewish community." His conclusion was that

> there were few if any serious attempts to maintain separate institutions, few decisions to leave the Jewish community (although a rather substantial drift from the community), and a general acceptance of the principle of merger, after the new immigrants achieved their own success and became less foreign. This came later, however. Nineteen hundred seventeen may be taken as a year in which the large majority of the "German" Jews found themselves adrift, having lost their sense of direction and their qualifications for communal leadership.

Kansas City was a relatively small and late-established community that had grown, partly through the efforts of the Industrial Removal Office, from an estimated 1,000 adults in 1890 to some 5,000 in 1914. The quoted statement may well describe local conditions. Yet in larger and older communities, attempts to maintain separate institutions were not only made, but made effectively and extended nationwide. Religious affiliation was at the time still the main route for affirming Jewish identity, and therefore the efforts of the Germans to maintain and develop their own exclusive institutions concentrated first and foremost on preserving the style and character of their congregations. The perceptive speaker in Kansas City actually presumed as much, wondering "about a possible interplay of cause and effect. Could it be that the older residents . . . having debated the subject for years, moved toward radical Reform in the 1880's as a means of establishing clearer lines of separation between themselves and the refugees from czarist rule?"[68]

Recent research substantiates these claims. In the 1880s, or—more precisely—with the adoption of the Pittsburgh Platform in 1885, Reform Judaism "came to represent the particular religious affiliation of Ameri-

can Jews of German descent, whether of the first, second, or third generation. Reform temples served as citadels of an Americanized Judaism,
practiced by men and women whose socioeconomic status and German
cultural heritage set them apart from the multitude of their coreligionists
arriving from eastern Europe."[69]

Under the impact of the new immigration, Reform Judaism soon lost
its preeminence. Already after the first decade of the mass immigration
from Eastern Europe, the governmental census of 1890 counted 316 Orthodox congregations against 217 of Reform. True, the Reform reported
more permanent synagogue buildings with greater seating capacity, but,
on the other hand, a large number of smaller and poorer Orthodox congregations remained outside the census. In New York the reported membership of Orthodox congregations was already almost double the number
of the Reform communicants.[70]

Ten years later the organized members of Reform congregations
counted no more than some 40,000 out of the estimated one million
American Jews, and no more than 10 percent of the 1,700 officially
recorded synagogues. Even in the Midwest, the stronghold of German
Reform Judaism, Reform congregations now constituted a minority. The
German Jews had lost their hegemony, first demographically, now also in
the religious sphere and in community leadership. Their reaction was
typical: in order to set themselves distinctly apart from the uncouth
masses disgorged in ever-increasing numbers from the steerage of ships
reaching New York, the impetus of Reform ideology and practice now
oscillated to its most radical extremes. The Pittsburgh Platform marked
the abandonment of the Reform movement's attempts to establish itself
as the generally recognized ritual and creed of American Judaism. From
now on it grudgingly accepted its role as a minority, one of the "branches"
of American Judaism, "less divided internally, but also further from Jews
outside it."[71]

The definition of principles and religious practice was the realm of
the ideologists, of rabbis and educated lay leaders. For the masses of
congregation members, the Reform "temples" and their cultural and social associations assumed ever more the character of an anxiously
guarded status symbol. New York's Temple Emanu-El, the prestigious
meeting place of the German financial aristocracy, was the exclusive sum-
mit of the social pyramid, almost inpenetrable to any East European Jew.
The same hierarchical pattern was found repeated in every larger Jewish
community. In a way, the emergence of the Conservative movement in
the late 1880s was a reaction not only to the extreme religious radicalism
of the Reform, but also to the snobbery of the German-Jewish upper
bourgeoisie as it was expressed in religious life.[72]

If the German Jews, retreating into their own Reform seclusion, reluctantly gave up their claim to religious leadership, they were far from doing so in the sphere of political representation. The emergence of open anti-Semitic social discrimination and journalistic invective had started before the mass immigration from Eastern Europe and demanded a response from the existing Jewish establishment. The German-Jewish community leaders stood up to this necessity in their own way, leaning on their prior experience and applying the leverage of their economic positions and personal connections. As we have seen, one of the issues was the fight against restrictionist policies and practices, where anti-Jewish prejudice often played a scarcely disguised role. The methods and tactics of these actions, resembling the age-honored tradition of the earlier German court Jews, were not always agreeable to the spokesmen of the new immigrants, but they had to admit that for the time being they could not dispense with the contributions of such highly influential men like Jacob Schiff, Judge Sulzberger, or Louis Marshall.

The American Jewish Committee was initiated in 1905 by the "Wanderers," a small group of German-Jewish lay leaders who used to meet unofficially in private homes. In February 1906 the new organization was established as an exclusive body of no more than 60 carefully selected individuals. (Only in 1931 was the number extended to 350.) Responding to some critics, Louis Marshall conceded the undemocratic character of the Committee, but explained it as a temporary necessity, in order to avoid "indiscreet, hot-headed, and ill-considered oratory, which might find its way into the headlines of the daily newspapers inflicting untold injury upon the Jewish cause."[73] In the end, the American Jewish Committee gained the guarded confidence and cooperation of the East European Jewish population and their leaders in New York and other locations both with its successes and with the readiness of its leaders to compromise. It was the major representative Jewish defense organization, fighting against infractions of the religious and civil rights of Jews in the United States and other parts of the world, up to the establishment of the Anti-Defamation League in 1913 and the American Jewish Congress in 1920.

One main issue of political discord between the German and East European Jews was their respective attitudes toward Zionism. In 1897 the Central Conference of American Rabbis (CCAR), the representative body of the Reform movement headed by Isaac M. Wise, adopted a resolution of disapproval "of any attempt for the establishment of a Jewish state . . . [which] do[es] not benefit, but infinitely harm our Jewish brethren where they are still persecuted." Whether or not the resolution was coordinated with, or influenced by, a similar "Protest" published at about the same time by German rabbis, it certainly resembled the latter's arguments and motivation, which were more political then religious. Both documents were issued before the assembling of the first Zionist Congress, and both condemned the contradiction between Zionism and the messianic mission of the Jewish people. Both placed even more emphasis on the alleged anti-patriotism of the Zionists' aim. The German "Protest" declared it to be the obligation of all Jews to serve "the national interests of their fatherland with all their force." The resolution of the CCAR condemned Zionism for "confirming the assertion of their enemies that the Jews are foreigners in the countries in which they are at home, and of which they are everywhere the most loyal and patriotic citizens."[74]

Although some prominent Reform rabbis became ardent supporters of Zionism, most German Jews did not follow them, and the movement as such did at first not tolerate such support. When Kaufmann Kohler became president of Hebrew Union College in 1903 Jewish nationalism in any form was barred from the classroom, although some Zionist teachers remained members of the faculty.[75] Very similar to its situation in Germany Zionism in the United States gained little sympathy and even evoked violent opposition among the assimilated and socially advanced Jews. In both countries most of the movement's supporters came from the ranks of the *Ostjuden.* It therefore became a central issue of discord between the two communities on the national, as well as on the local level, where the public argument in the press and official statements were generally more pronounced, or less restrained. In 1902, when the Zionists gained a strong foothold among the Orthodox working-class Jews of Detroit, the *Jewish American* voiced the opposition of the city's German-Jewish elite in undisguisedly hostile terms: "It is eternally untrue that the Jew is a man without a country. He has found his Canaan in America. . . . All talk of Zionism in a national sense by American Jews is nothing short of arch treason to the best government on earth and should so be dealt with."[76]

Political representation and philanthropy nevertheless demanded a minimum of cooperation. Religious affiliation was a matter of individual decisions and beliefs. Even the most radical Reform temple would not deny membership to an East European Jew who was able and willing to pay dues. The places where the German Jews were absolutely among themselves, and consistently guarded their exclusiveness, were the various secular associations of social contact, recreation, and amusement such as lodges, clubs, and literary circles. When the less Germanized Jews from Polish Prussia arrived, they either founded their own clubs and associations or were admitted to those of the "Bavarians" in the course of their "Americanization." The common background and language, and the relatively small size of their communities, enabled this mutual rapprochement before the start of the East European mass immigration. After 1880, when the German Jews found themselves in the position of a diminishing minority, these organizations became fortresses of social seclusion.

B'nai B'rith was the earliest and most important of these associations. The order was founded in 1843 in New York by a small group of German Jews who had been repelled by Christian fraternal lodges like the Odd Fellows. Following the American example, the order organized in district and national bodies, and introduced similar secret rituals and vestments, but used Hebrew words and titles in its ceremonies. But before long B'nai B'rith became a serious and public-minded organization of mutual aid and philanthropy, taking part in every Jewish communal activity. At the turn of the century it participated with the Baron de Hirsch Fund in the efforts of the Industrial Removal Office. In 1913 the order established the Anti-Defamation League to fight anti-Semitic discrimination and propaganda.

Despite the order's ideological commitment to the unity of all Jewish people, communities, and organizations, in practice its rules and procedures prolonged the exclusion of East European Jews. Individual membership, conceived as an elective status symbol reserved for the "best elements" of the Jewish community, was rarely granted to them. Because of this, and because East European Jews also preferred to be among themselves, they soon established their own lodges, but even then their admission to the district Grand Lodges sometimes met with difficulties, as in the above mentioned case of Chicago in 1881.[77]

In earlier days Jews who had attained wealth and position were refused entry into the prestigious Anglo-Saxon clubs of New York and other cities. Only a few of the *nouveaux riches* were at the time regarded as being of "clubbable disposition." After the Civil War, when wealth became a generally recognized substitute for nobility in high society, Jews who tried to be admitted were in most cases blackballed. One famous case was the futile attempt of Jesse Seligman in 1893 to be accepted by the Union League Club of New York. Even *The Nation,* a generally liberal paper, commented on this occasion in favor of the club members' negative vote:

> A club is simply an extension of a private dwelling. The right to select his guests and associates for reasons best known to himself is one which every man carries to his club. . . . The part of good taste and good manners is to avoid fighting one's way into clubs in which one's presence would be for any reason objectionable to any portion of the company.[78]

Actually, Jews had rarely attempted to "fight their way into" elite WASP organizations. The German Jews had already many years before silently given up seeking admittance to these clubs. Many had instead joined German clubs and associations. Here they were generally more welcome, at least before the 1870s, and felt more at home. They had at the same time also established their own Jewish social clubs, which they now anxiously guarded against the influx of the new immigrants. In doing so, the German Jews adopted the same arguments of privacy and exclusiveness formerly used to justify their own exclusion. "It is a well-known fact," commented the *Jewish Messenger* in 1886, "that German is the language of these clubs, from the *'Harmonie'* with its sumptuous mansion on 42nd street, to the *'Progress'* in its less pretentious quarters on 23rd street."[79]

The role of these organizations as bastions of deliberate German-Jewish exclusiveness is found repeated in almost every Jewish community. In Atlanta, Georgia, the hitherto prestigious Concordia was succeeded in 1905 by the Standard Club. This was defined as a "high-class social club . . . devoted to entertainments of high order," and its members consisted solely of the city's German-Jewish elite. It was highly selective in admitting members, limiting their number to no more than 150. Besides it, a number of similar organizations were open to younger and less affluent German Jews. Women's societies, some of them no less exclusive, held weekly "Kaffee-Klatsches" and regular card-playing and literary meetings, and engaged in philanthropic endeavors. Teenagers formed their own societies, pursuing all kinds of entertainments, balls, picnics, dramatic plays, and debut parties. The aim of these social meetings and recreational activities was to promote intragroup marriages within German-Jewish society.[80]

A similar development took place at about the same time in Boston. Although the Boston community was somewhat younger, and although the largest group of its German-Jewish founders had come from Prussian Poland, many of them had gained considerable wealth before the onslaught of the Russian immigrants. Their Elysium Club was recorded in a Boston handbook of 1889 to consist of "80 of the wealthiest Hebrews in Boston," regarded as the "inner circle" of the city's Jewish community. They were a close-knit group of wealthy German-Jewish merchants who had come to Boston some decades ago and considered themselves to be of the oldest stock. Even without a formal organization they would constitute a 'club' of sorts through their intra-marriage connections." Founded because of the inability to be admitted into the circles of Boston's elite Gentile society, the club was "as much a reaction against Christian social anti-Semitism as it was a barrier against Russian Jews."[81]

The connection between anti-Semitism and the German Jews' efforts to retire into their own clannish shell was evident not only in Boston.

This is not the place to elaborate on the development of American anti-Semitism, whether it was caused, or intensified, by the Gentiles' reaction to the alien bearing of the new immigrants, or to the ostentatious assertiveness of the German-Jewish *nouveaux riches*. Both arguments have been brought forward in still unresolved debates, and both have their merits.[82] It is, however, clear that the fear of anti-Semitism that had shown its face during the Civil War and again in the 1870s was very much on the minds of the German Jews.

An unsigned "private communication" from New York expressed the writer's opinion that

> many generations would have to pass before the numerous and growing masses of Polish and Russian immigrants will adjust to this land and people. . . . The American population distinguishes them from their resident coreligionists and observes them with not exactly friendly or respectful eyes. Let us hope that this will not awake general anti-Semitic sentiments.[83]

These fears may have been exaggerated but, although social anti-Semitism had made itself felt well before the start of the mass immigration, not entirely unfounded. Once anti-Semitism openly appeared on the American scene, the new immigrants "were a potential challenge to the security of American Jews. . . . The traits of the East European Jews which many Americans found so repulsive were likely to influence their opinions of the established Jewish community as well."[84]

Paradoxically, it was the same apprehension of growing anti-Semitism that eventually worked against a total split between the two communities. The Anti-Defamation League founded in 1913 by B'nai B'rith united all parts of American Jewry in the fight against anti-Jewish discrimination and slander. The Jewish press of all political, social, or religious shades mobilized a unanimous Jewish front against anti-Semitic invective. The same *Jewish American* of Detroit that had so viciously condemned Zionism felt compelled to stand up against those "of our newspapers [who] insist, despite correction and rebuke and threat, to point out the religion of every Jew who happens to get into trouble." But the paper still insisted that "the term Jew is connotative of his religion only and has nothing to do with nationality."[85]

Some years later it sounded a different note. The spokesmen of the German Jews of Detroit had apparently come to realize the futility of their attempts to prove their American loyalty by avoiding any close association with international Jewish causes. This disillusionment was clearly expressed in the *Jewish American*'s appeal of 1906: "Let us be Jews, live like Jews, worship like Jews. Let us prove to the world that we are endowed with sufficient moral courage to face whatever of discredit all non-Jews cast in our way."[86]

This may indicate a growing awareness of ethnic solidarity beyond merely denominational allegiance; on the level of social relations, however, German-Jewish clannishness persisted for many more years. Contrary to what one would expect, the differences did not diminish with the advancing process of Americanization of both groups. An analysis of membership lists of lodges and other social clubs in Portland, Oregon, surprisingly demonstrates the emergence of "a new sense of elite status among the children of the Germans. . . . The elite of German descent and the newcomers from Eastern Europe became separated more than previous subgroups had been." With the progressive acculturation of the second generation of East Europeans, socioeconomic diversity seems to have played an even more important role than cultural differences had previously. Even in small Jewish communities it separated the two groups residentially, as well as in their occupational distribution. Social clubs and lodges, established in Portland in the 1890s by the native-born descendants of both German and Russian Jews, remained strictly separated, "a division that lasted for an additional half century."[87]

For how long it really lasted may be a matter for debate. In pure socioeconomic terms it took over seventy years and two world wars "to raise the East European Jews—the immigrants of 1880–1924, their children and grandchildren—more or less to the level achieved by the German Jews in 1880." Nathan Glazer was cautious even in 1955 to underline that the "homogeneous character of the Jewish communities is beyond dispute" only outside of New York City.[88] Be this as it may, it was certainly still far from being accomplished anywhere in 1914. We may, however, believe that in general the social barriers separating the "two communities" had already begun to crumble.

In which way the arrival of new Jewish refugees and immigrants in the 1930s and after the Holocaust influenced the social texture or cultural identity of American Jewry is beyond the scope of this book. But in one way or other, German-Jewish group characteristics demonstrated an astonishing longevity and perseverance, distinguishable even in our days in whatever "Americanized" mutation.

Conclusion

Continuity in Separation

Throughout our story we have treated the German-Jewish immigrants to the United States as a branch of German Jewry. The legal and socioeconomic conditions in the German lands created the first impulse to seek overseas a substitute for the emancipation denied them at home. Later the situation of the Jews in Germany improved. Equality before the law was slowly and reluctantly granted. Many Jews in Germany considered their economic and educational achievements to be at least partial compensation for the remaining constraints of discrimination, social ostracism, and politically manipulated hostility. Yet at this time the previous emigration had already created its self-perpetuating momentum. The more the nineteenth century advanced, the more the "pull" factors of the immigration to the United States, and the chain-migration of families and whole communities, predominated. Jews continued to leave Germany and to come to America in considerable numbers all throughout the second half of the nineteenth century, a period regarded by historians as comprising the happiest decades in German-Jewish history.

How did the emigration influence the life and development of the majority of German Jews who stayed in Germany? Between 1820 and

1914 the emigration caused an unprecedented demographic drain. It was only thanks to the impressive increase in the German Jews' natural growth-rate up to 1860 that the total Jewish population did not decline in absolute terms. In some regions, such as Bavaria, the first and foremost source of immigrants, or in Hesse or Alsace-Lorraine, this is what indeed happened.[1] Later a part of the emigration loss was somewhat compensated by the in-migration of East European Jews. The demographic effect of the emigration was not confined to its direct and immediate influence. As most emigrants belonged to the younger, fertile age-groups, the birth-rate of the Jews in Germany declined dramatically during the second half of the century.[2]

Demographers and sociologists have explained this decline in the birthrate as a result of the socioeconomic ascent of a large part of German Jewry into the urban middle class. In my opinion, the process of the rising age-structure of Germany's Jewish population, a clear result of the emigration, was actually far more responsible for it.[3] The German Jews in America were certainly no less "urban" or "middle-class" but rather more so. Yet according to all existing evidence many of them raised large families until late in the nineteenth century. The only statistical and demographic study of American Jewry ever made by the U.S. government was published in 1890. It recorded an average of five children in a sample of 10,000 families, most of them immigrants from Germany during 1850–70.[4]

The second important result of the emigration was the depopulation of many rural Jewish communities. The urbanization of German Jewry by internal migration from villages to the large cities was a much slower and later process than is commonly assumed.[5] But in many villages in Bavaria, Württemberg, and other parts of Germany, where the Jews sometimes constituted up to one-half or more of the general population, communities dwindled to one or two dozens of mostly old people as a result of the emigration. Starting from the 1830s, Jewish publications and spokesmen showed concern about these shrinking communities that were no longer able to uphold religious worship and education.[6]

The next important influence of the emigration is to be sought in the economic sphere. From about 1815 on, the average per-capita income and the property holdings of the German Jews rose in an impressive way, relatively much more than those of the general population. The Jews' traditional concentration in small commerce and money-lending, for centuries detrimental to their economic and social position, worked to their advantage in the era of rapid demographic growth and an expanding market economy. The result was the economic improvement of almost all German Jews relative to their former situation and compared with the general populace. No less impressive was what I conceive as a process of gradual equalization of both income and property within the German-Jewish group.[7]

How can this be connected to the emigration? The explanation lies in the group-specific occupational structure and economic conduct of the German Jews: their concentration in a limited range of branches inside the commercial sector, and their persistent preference for self-employed independence. Unable or unwilling to change their occupations, the Jews crowded into the retail or wholesale trade of garments and household wares in towns, and of cattle and other agricultural products in the villages. Only some of them ventured at a later stage into manufacturing, mostly within these same branches. The emigration of a great number of younger and, as we may assume, often more enterprising Jews cleared the field by reducing competition for a limited range of opportunities in the old homeland. This enabled most Jews to improve their position. On the other hand, the emigration of the poorer strata, while the elite at the top was still small and had not yet accumulated a great amount of capital, probably explains the trend of slow equalization of average incomes between 1850 and 1890.[8]

The probably most surprising phenomenon is the many-sided and supra-generational similarity of the economic and sociocultural development of German Jews on both sides of the ocean. If we compare the immigrant group in America with the majority of German Jews who stayed behind, the persistence of typical, group-characteristic traits is indeed intriguing. *Plus ça change—plus c'est la même chose!* This was to be expected for the start of the immigration, its first wave, and even the first generation of proper immigrants. But how are we to explain the fact that this continuity is clearly discernible during the whole of the nineteenth century, among the later generations of their American-born descendants? and this in an era of immense and structural economic, legal, and political developments? In Germany, industrialization brought about some very significant changes in the legal position of the Jews, in their social situation, and in their internal religious and cultural life. At the same time, developments in America were also tremendous, but very different from those in Germany. German Jews in both countries were, of course, affected by these upheavals. They reacted and adjusted to the changing conditions. But despite significant environmental differences, they did so more or less in the same manner, and moved in the same direction.

It was initially only natural that the economic pursuits of the newcomers should resemble what they or their elders did and continued to do in Germany. People always tend to support themselves doing what they are used to doing, and what they know best how to do. Much less self-evident is the basic inflexibility of occupational structures and economic conduct, including the similarities of developments and adjustment, in the United States as compared with Germany, over many decades and generations. Taking into account the different legal and economic conditions and developments, one would expect to find very different occupational and economic adjustments, as German Jews on both sides of the ocean tried to make the best of expanding opportunities.

But this is apparently not what happened. Here and there small peddlers and tradesmen improved their economic and social situation. They became store-owners and merchants, but both groups remained predominantly in the same lines of business: garments and household goods, with a sprinkling of food and tobacco. Here and there the majority of those who ventured into manufacturing remained in the same branches. Here and there they continued to give preference to independent self-employment. In both countries they became pioneers of the department stores, and German-Jewish entrepreneurs often copied the American example. And in both countries the most fortunate and successful became bankers, although only in America were so many of them *nouveaux riches:* most of the Jewish private bankers in Germany, who were descendants of the court Jews of the eighteenth century, represented "old money." Some of them also set up branches of their banks in the United States and settled there eventually, but most German-Jewish bankers in America had started from scratch.

It is hard to establish for exactly how long these trends predominated in America. In Germany, where we have reliable quantitative sources, we know that they lasted to the very end of Jewish life in that country. There are, however, strong indications of their persistence also in the United States. It is my impression that even more of the native-born sons and grandsons of German Jews continued in the footsteps of their elders than in Germany. The reason was probably that here the ideological or social stigma that stuck to commercial enterprise in Imperial Germany was almost totally absent. American-born youths saw no reason to abstain from taking over the family business and improving it, even after finishing colleges and universities. University degrees and the professions seem to have played a much more important role as instruments of social and economic ascent for Jews of East European origin. Only after the turn of the century did a greater part of German-Jewish descendants strive to become doctors, lawyers, or university professors, while the majority still preferred to remain in business. Again, the parallels with the assimilated Jews in the old homeland are striking.

If this is true, how can we explain it? I do not believe that it proves some genetic or racial talent of Jews for trade and commerce, prevailing everywhere and through the ages. That thesis has been argued and repeated by anti-Semites since the last century, and granted "academic legitimacy" by Werner Sombart's widely distributed and translated *Die Juden und das Wirtschaftsleben* (published in 1911 and known in America under the title *The Jews and Modern Capitalism*).[9] What this pattern does prove is the persistence and longevity of group-characteristic traits of minorities under changing conditions and even geographic relocation. As Simon Kuznets has persuasively demonstrated, deviations from the overall occupational composition and the economic behavior of the majority are not "anomalies" but rather the "normal" condition of every small and permanent minority everywhere.[10]

The case of the German Jews proves that these deviations persisted not only in the economic sphere. On both sides of the ocean, sociological and cultural features of the German-Jewish group or subgroup remained distinct for a long time. They also showed a high grade of similarity. Jews of German descent soon spoke English even within the family, but their cultural and behavioral patterns were not very different from those of nineteenth-century Jews in Germany. Both had become preponderantly middle-class societies, assuming and maintaining essentially the same values of the educated bourgeoisie. Not content just to imitate the habits and mores of the German *Bildungsbürgertum* (educated bourgeoisie), the German Jews developed their own special brand of middle-class culture, distinct in communal organization and philanthropy, as in leisure-time recreation and family life.[11] Educational goals and political alignment were as much influenced by these group-specific trends as the daily life in the home or the position and self-assertion of Jewish women. And despite considerable environmental differences in America, the similarity in group-characteristic traits remained remarkable.

For how long did these and other group-specific traits of the German-Jewish subgroup persist in America? To my knowledge, a systematic and reliable investigation of this question is still outstanding, and widely differing speculation abounds. At first sight, judging rather intuitively from family histories and unprocessed genealogical data, I would say that in addition to economic pursuits and religious affiliation, group-specific patterns in residence and marriage prevailed for a considerable time. Differences of outlook, of cultural and political attitudes, between the German minority and the majority of American Jews can probably be distinguished to our very day, despite an evident process of social rapprochement and interrelation. In this, too, the German Jews in America behaved essentially like their kinfolk in Germany.

In Germany, of course, the proportions were reversed: at no time did the *Ostjuden* constitute more than 20 percent of German Jewry. Yet at the early stages of the East European immigration, attitudes and actions, as well as fearful apprehensions, were similar. In Germany as in America the old Jewish establishment fought against the legal discrimination and persecution of the East European Jewish immigrants. In both countries material, charitable, and educational assistance was generously provided. At the same time, social contacts remained distant. Condescension and exclusiveness were predominant, and were met with the envious contempt of the *Ostjuden*. In both countries the fear of being identified with the newcomers in an always-expected outbreak of anti-Semitism played an important role in the development of mutual relations. In Germany this fear was by no means imaginary. On what real substance it was actually founded in America is still a matter of debate. In both cases the first serious stirrings of social and politial anti-Semitism preceded the mass immigration of Polish or Russian Jews.

These similarities, and the continuing mutual interaction between individuals and families, as well as between religious and cultural institutions in the old and the new country, justify in my opinion a perception of the major part of American Jewry up to 1880 as a branch of German Jewry. Later, when the German Jews in America had become a relatively small and secluded minority, this tradition and heritage were the primary source of a changing, but still specific, subculture in the mainstream of an emerging new American-Jewish identity.

World War I and After

The choice to stop our story in 1914 may be questioned as arbitrary. It was made because every story has to stop somewhere, but also because I believe that World War I marks an important turning point in the history of both German and American Jewry, as, of course, it does for the whole world.

Before the United States joined the Allied camp in 1917, some revival of German patriotism seems to have been felt in German-Jewish circles. Family and friendly connections in Germany, along with cultural nostalgia, caused some Jews to support isolationism. In 1914 Herman Eliassof published an essay on "German-American Jews" in the *Deutsch-Amerikanische Geschichtsblaetter,* stressing the "strong combination of Jewish ethics and German civil virtue" of the German-Jewish immigrants:

The first helped them to develop their religious life along the lines of new thought. The second inspired them to become useful American citizens. While they strove to Americanize themselves they still remained true Jews and loyal to their German culture, they fostered the German language in their homes and in their synagogues. They clung tenaciously to their Jewish ideals and to that German honesty of purpose, love of liberty, sturdiness and solidarity which has enabled all German-Americans to be counted among the best, the most useful and most patriotic American citizens.

This was written before the outbreak, and outside the context, of the war in Europe. But in 1916 the article was reprinted as a special pamphlet in English by the German-American Historical Society of Illinois. We do not know whether the author was asked for, or gave, his permission.[12]

German activities, both open and clandestine, to prevent America's entry into the war included special efforts to influence Jewish public opinion. These were not confined to the German-Jewish group that at that time already constituted a minority of American Jewry. German agents, including some German Jews, focused a probably more effective propaganda campaign on the East European Jews' hatred of the tsarist regime, than on the German Jews' diminishing love toward Imperial Germany. In February 1917 Nachman Syrkin unmasked the editor of the *American Jewish Chronicle,* one Dr. I. Straus. He had arrived in America two years earlier, together with Dr. Dernburg, an official German agent, with the explicit task of influencing Jewish public opinion. Syrkin accused Straus that "under the disguise of independent Jewish journalism he now leads a systematic propaganda campaign for the Central Empires, irrespective of its incompatibility with real Jewish interests . . glazing over German anti-Semitism." Significantly, the Jewish agent's main efforts were aimed at buying influence in the Yiddish press.[13]

As we have seen, the "German-Jewish nexus" in America had already started to dissolve some decades earlier. The American Jews and their institutions, albeit still strongly influenced by the German-Jewish leadership, were hardly affected by the impact of the war on the Gentile German's organizations and ethnic assertion. The American Jewish communal structure had gained in strength and self-confidence by the East European immigration.

Identification with the German world had enriched the nineteenth-century American Jew culturally, but only in rare cases had it eclipsed his Jewish loyalties. Now fully Americanized, with an established Jewish community behind him, and sensitized to the barriers that Western society still maintained against his integration, the German Jew was less dependent on, or infatuated with, his German heritage. Dual ethnicity among the American Jews had finally evaporated.[14]

There can be no doubt that the First World War was crucial in the emergence of a united, although not absolutely unified, American-Jewish community. This does not necessarily imply that, at least in the social and cultural sphere, the "German heritage" totally lost its influence. I believe that it still continued to play an important role in the internal life of American Jewry. True, the German language, and the cultural activities conducted in that language, almost disappeared from the Jewish public scene, to be renewed only with the influx of the next German-Jewish immigration in the 1930s. Patriotism and loyalties were no longer divided between the old and the new homeland. Concerted functions of different religious congregations, and the establishment of nonreligious Jewish associations and institutions, created a common framework of an American-Jewish community integrated both locally and nationwide. But inside this framework German-American Jews and their descendants continued to demonstrate some characteristic group cohesion.

After the war and throughout the balance of the twentieth century, Jewish history all over the world has been the scene of political, social, and ideological upheavals of revolutionary dimensions. American Jewry, although spared the most tragic consequences of these events, did not remain unaffected. After the dust of World War I had settled, Jewish immigration was renewed in quite considerable numbers, despite political and economic restrictions. In the 1920s it was mainly East European Jews who arrived in the United States. In the 1930s a new generation of German Jews, this time impoverished refugees from Nazi persecution, sought and found entry. During the interval of one generation or more in the course of German-Jewish migration, the differences between the two main centers of German Jewry had deepened. Different traits and outlooks were now probably far more characteristic than any similarities. Still, the earlier German-Jewish immigrants certainly played an important role in the immigration and absorption of the German refugees. In many cases they explicitly took upon themselves, by signing the legal affidavits required by the immigration authorities, the care of relatives or other Jews after their arrival in the United States. Later they assisted the newcomers in their first steps in the country.

These acts of solidarity, although not confined to American Jews of German origin, took up the chain that had connected the branches of German Jewry since the start of their migrations. Now, after the Holocaust, German Jews are no more than a small and diminishing subgroup of any country's Jewry. In fact, they had for many centuries been but a small minority of the Jewish people dispersed all over the world. Neverless, they had long played a disproportionately large role in Jewish life, in the socioeconomic and political as well as cultural domains. This explains to some extent the immense interest in the history of German Jewry, which has in recent years yielded a host of scholarly publications. My contribution comprises one small stone in a fascinating and multifaceted historical mosaic.

Abbreviations Used in Notes and Bibliography

AJA(a)   American Jewish Archives, Cincinnati.

AJA(p)   Periodical of the American Jewish Archives, Cincinnati, 1948–.

AJH   *American Jewish History,* published by the American Jewish Historical Society (under the former titles: *Publications of the American Jewish Historical Society [PAJHS]* and *American Jewish Historical Quarterly [AJHQ]*), 1910–.

AJHQ   See *AJH.*

AJH, Quanti- fication   *Quantification and the American Jewish Experience,* edited by Marc Lee Raphael. Special Issue *AJH* 72, no. 3 (March 1983).

AJS   *American Journal of Sociology.*

AJYB   *American Jewish Yearbook,* 1899–. Published by the Jewish Publication Society of America and American Jewish Committee (since 1909).

AZJ   *Allgemeine Zeitung des Judenthums.* Weekly, Leipzig, Bonn, Berlin, 1837–1922.

JSS   *Jewish Social Studies.* Publication of the Conference on Jewish Social Studies, 1939–.

PAJHS   See *AJH.*

YIVO   Institute for Jewish Research, New York.

YLBI   *Yearbook of the Leo Baeck Institute,* London, 1956–.

Notes

Preface

1. J. Lestschinsky, *Schicksal*, p. 42.
2. Jacob R. Marcus, *Studies in American Jewish History*, p. 9.
3. See especially: Naomi Cohen, *Encounter*; Michael A. Meyer, *Modernity;* Leon A. Jick, *Americanization of the Synagogue.*
4. Oscar Handlin, *Uprooted*, pp. 4–5, 268–73.

Introduction: The Old World and the New

1. Stefan Schwarz, *Juden in Bayern*, p. 176. The following outline, if not indicated otherwise, is based on this work and J. Toury, *Geschichte;* A. Prinz, *Juden im Deutschen Wirtschaftsleben;* Barkai, *Industrialisation;* Lestschinsky, *Schicksal;* Barkai, *Minderheit.*
2. Bartyś, "Grand Duchy," pp. 194f.; U. Schmelz, "Demographische Entwicklung," p. 38.
3. See R. Glanz, *Geschichte;* Chr. W. Dohm, pt. 2, 1783. See also, R. Rürup, *Emanzipation*, esp. pp. 13ff.; R. Michael, "Antijudaistische Tendenz," pp. 12–48.
4. Barkai, *Industrialisation*, pp. 124ff.; Toury, *Geschichte*, pp. 53, 60ff.
5. Meyer, *Modernity*, pp. 10ff.
6. Quoted in *AZJ* 3 (August 31, 1839).
7. Ibid. 18 (1853): 149.
8. Ibid. 10 (1846): 18f.
9. E. Wolf and M. Whiteman, *History*, p. 7.
10. S. Broches, *Jews in New England*, pp. 12f.; J. Marcus, *Colonial Jew*, pp. 1327ff.

11. Stern, p. 11. See also Marcus, *Colonial Jew*, p. 1329; Glanz, "Immigration," p. 82; H. Eliassof, *German American Jews*, p. 2; E. Hirshler, *Jews from Germany*, pp. 22f. On Jewish indentured servants, see Kisch, *White Labor Servitude*, pp. 31f. and passim.

12. Marcus, *Colonial Jew*, p. 1332.

13. Meyer, "Identity," p. 249.

14. Wolf and Whiteman, *History*, pp. 7, 225f.; see also Marcus, *Colonial Jew*, pp. 1333f.; Marcus, *On Love*, pp. 2ff.; Weinryb, "Immigration," pp. 4ff.

15. Cohen, *Encounter*, pp. 55f.

16. Hirshler, *Jews from Germany*, pp. 30f. On Salomon see also Wolf and Whiteman, *History* pp. 98f.

17. To quote some extremes: Lestschinsky, "Migrations," p. 1559 estimated 150,000 Jewish immigrants from Germany during the whole of the nineteenth century. On the other hand, Liebman Hersch ("Jewish Migration during the Last Hundred Years," in *The Jewish People Past and Present*, vol. I, New York, 1946, p. 408) arrived at no more than 50,000 German-Jewish immigrants between 1830 and 1870, to which he added another 10,000 of Western European countries but almost none for the time after 1870. Bruno Blau spoke of a quarter of million German Jews who came to the United States between 1830 and 1930. A more plausible estimate was presented by Joseph Jacobs in the *AJY* for 5675/1914 p. 345, who obviously included all immigrants from German-speaking countries in his figure of nearly 200,000 for 1881.

18. Quoted in Glanz, "Immigration," p. 81.

19. AJA(a), miscellaneous file, folder ME [main entry]-antisemitism II ("Coney Island and the Jews. A History of the Development and Success of This Famous Seaside Resort, together with a Full Account of the Recent Jewish Controversy," New York 1879, pp. 24f).

20. See the article of Lloyd P. Gartner in the *Encyclopaedia Judaica*, 3d printing (Jerusalem 1974), vol. 15, pp. 1556f.; see also Barkai, *Industrialisation*, pp. 146ff.

21. Schmelz, "Demographische Entwicklung," pp. 48 f.

22. See Reissner, *German-American Jews*, passim, Mack Walker, *Germany*, p. 7 and passim; F. Burgdörfer, "Migrations," pp. 319–89; W. Köllmann, "Bevölkerungsgeschichte," pp. 19ff.

23. K. J. Bade, "German Emigration," pp. 120f.; G. Hohorst, J. Kocka, G. A. Ritter, eds., *Arbeitsbuch*, p. 38.

24. Calculated from Hohorst et al., *Arbeitsbuch*, ibid., and Schmelz, "Demographische Entwicklung," pp. 48f.; see also Barkai, "Migrations," pp. 310f.

25. Köllmann, "Bevölkerungsgeschichte," pp. 30f.; Burgdörfer, "Migrations," pp. 341f.; see also Hauptstaatsarchiv Düsseldorf, Landratsamt Bonn, No. 62, emigration records 1860–1892, stating occupation, marital status, and destination.

26. G. Moltmann, "Auswanderung," p. 297. The conception of Jewish emigration as a substitute for delayed emancipation is put forward by Naomi W. Cohen, among others, in her recent work, as already indicated by her title, *Encounter with Emancipation*.

27. M. L. Raphael, *Columbus*, p. 1.

28. Research of Professor W. J. Parish, University of New Mexico, mentioned in the memoirs of Herman Wertheim of Carlsbad, New Mexico, November 1964, AJA, biographies file, p. 7.
29. As, for example, in J. S. Mesinger, *Peddlers and Merchants*; S. Hertzberg, *Strangers;* W. Toll, "Portland"; S. G. Mostov, "Cincinnati"; Mostov, "Boston"; Raphael, *Columbus,* see also *AJH,* Special Issue: *Quantification,* edited by M. L. Raphael, 72/3 (March 1983).
30. S. G. Mostov, "Dun and Bradstreet," *AJH/Quantification,* p. 333.
31. See Gartner, *Encyclopaedia Judaica* (3d printing), pp. 1596f.
32. Meyer, *Modernity,* p. 262.

Chapter 1: The First Wave

1. Walker, *Germany,* p. 20; Burgdörfer, "Migrations," pp. 33f.
2. Mostov, "Cincinnati," pp. 34f.
3. *AZJ,* March 30, 1839.
4. Glanz, "Bayer," p. 28; H. Engelbert, *Statistik,* p. 10; Toury, "Manual," p. 51.
5. Bartyś, "Grand Duchy," p. 201; M. Aschkewitz, *West-Preussen,* pp. 129f.; Mostov, "Cincinnati," p. 34.
6. *AZJ* 15 (1851): 383; 17 (1853): 317.
7. Birmingham, *"Our Crowd,"* p. 31.
8. *AZJ* 30/6 (1837).
9. Kober, "Württemberg," p. 21; for Bavaria, Toury, "Manual," p. 54; see also Mostov, "Cincinnati," pp. 24f.
10. Toury, "Manual," p. 55; Mostov, "Cincinnati," p. 44 (derived from Kober's data).
11. Glanz, "Mass Emigration," pp. 52f.
12. AJA(a), small collections: passenger list, ship *Howard,* Port of New York, 1839.
13. Mostov, "Boston," p. 18. Reference is to the statistical data found in tables 4 and 6.
14. *Israelitische Annalen* (1840): 73f., 9 (translated by the author).
15. *AZJ* 20/7 (1839): 347, quoted and translated by Glanz, "Source Material," p. 112.
16. *AZJ* 25/5 (1839): 256 (ibid.).
17. Quoted by Kohler, *German Jewish,* p. 96.
18. Stefan Rohrbacher, "From Württemberg to America." I wish to express my thanks to Mr. Rohrbacher of the Institut für Antisemitismusforschung in Berlin for letting me use his valuable data before the publication of his paper.
19. Kober, *German Jewish,* p. 21.
20. Glanz, "Mass Emigration," p. 52.
21. Kober, *German Jewish*; see, for example, the memoirs of Walter Frank, Marcus, *Memoirs,* vol. 1, pp. 303f; M. Richarz, *Jüdisches Leben,* vol. 1, pp. 189f.; Toury, *Geschichte,* pp. 49f.
22. Mostov, "Cincinnati," p. 50.
23. Leon Hühner, *Jews in Georgia in the Colonial Period,* quoted by Kohler, *German Jewish,* pp. 88f.

24. Marcus, *On Love*, pp. 42f. On the Hessian deserters, see also E. Hirshler, *Jews from Germany*, p. 31.
25. On the Heine brothers: B. Korn, *New Orleans*, pp. 179f. On Frederick Warburg: H. Reissner, "German American Jews," p. 61.
26. Korn, *New Orleans*, pp. 123f.
27. All quotations from Glanz, "Source Material," pp. 90ff., and in his translation: *AZJ* (1837): 267; (1839): 420; *Der Orient* (Leipzig, 1847): 42.
28. Lestchinsky, "Social Features," pp. 9f. (author's translation).
29. *AZJ* 28/9 (1839), quoted by Glanz, "Immigration," p. 89.
30. AJA(a), autobiography file, folder ME—Frank, Henry.
31. Quoted in *Der Israelit des neunzehnten Jahrhunderts* 1 (1839/40).
32. *AZJ* 6 (1842): 291ff.
33. *AZJ* 11 (1846): 23ff.
34. AJA(a), correspondence file, folder ME—Stern, Julius.
35. AJA(a), correspondence file, folder ME—Hirsch, Babette.
36. Marcus, *Memoirs*, vol. 2, p. 48.
37. Ibid., 3, pp. 24ff.
38. *AZJ* 17 (July 7, 1853): 343f.
39. Ibid., 18, p. 192.
40. M.U. Schappes, *Documentary History*, p. 159.
41. Reissner, "Ganstown," pp. 25f.
42. Toury, *Turmoil*, p. 24.
43. AJA(a), biographies file, folder ME—Stern, Morris.
44. Toury, *Turmoil*, p. 24.
45. G. Kisch, "Revolution," pp. 188f. and the document (in German) p. 199.
46. *Der Orient* (Leipzig, 1848): 221, quoted by Glanz, "Source Material," p. 96.
47. Reprinted in Kisch, "Revolution," pp. 209ff.; see also Glanz, "Source Material," pp. 102f.
48. Bertram W. Korn, "Forty-Eighters," pp. 4ff; see also, Hirshler, *Jews from Germany*, pp. 40f.
49. Korn, "Forty-Eighters," p. 16; see also Hirshler, *Jews from Germany*, pp. 44f.
50. *AZJ* 31 (1867): 800.
51. Reissner, p. 62.
52. *Krünitz Enzyklopädie* (Berlin 1784), p. 523, quoted by Glanz, "Source Material," p. 95.
53. *AZJ* (April 2, 1839): 159.
54. A document "releasing" a Jewish subject to the Hessian Grand Duchy in 1845 is preserved in AJA(a), miscellaneous file, folder ME—Rosenthal, Loeb.
55. *AZJ* 10 (1846): 509.
56. *AZJ* 18 (1854): 128.
57. Glanz, "Source Material," pp. 8, 117f.
58. Kisch, *White Labor*, pp. 30f., 38; the document is on pp. 42f., written in "Jewish-German" with Hebrew letters.
59. AJA(a), biographies file, folder ME—Hammerschlag, Sarah.
60. Greenberg, "Immigrant's Perception," pp. 311f.
61. Marcus, *Memoirs*, vol. 2, pp. 48f.
62. C. J. Latrobe, quoted in Glanz, "Source Material," p. 119.

Chapter 2: Exploring the Territory

1. Glanz, "Immigration," pp. 82f.; Cohen, *Encounter*, p. 173.
2. Richarz, *Jüdisches Leben*, vol. 1, pp. 473f.
3. Marcus, *Memoirs*, vol. 1, pp. 289ff.
4. Ibid., p. 373.
5. Ibid., vol. 2, p. 12.
6. B. D. Weinryb, "Immigration," pp. 388f.
7. AJA(a), correspondence file, folder ME—Stern, Julius.
8. AJA(a), autobiographies file, folder ME—Frank, Henry.
9. *AZJ* 14 (1850): 32.
10. Cohen, *Encounter*, p. 123.
11. Ibid., pp. 20f.
12. Maxwell Whiteman, "Notions," p. 307.
13. Glanz, *Judaica*, p. 105.
14. Reissner, *German American Jews*, p. 74.
15. Whiteman, "Notions," pp. 318f.
16. Ibid.
17. All quotations by Glanz, *Judaica*, pp. 331f.
18. Marcus, *Memoirs*, vol. 2, pp. 10ff.
19. Ibid., pp. 106f.
20. Ibid., vol. 1, pp. 7f.
21. Ibid., pp. 355f.
22. Gerstäcker, *Amerikanische Wald- und Stromgeschichten;* reprinted in *AZJ* 13 (1849): 649f.
23. Toury, *Geschichte*, pp. 69ff.; Barkai, *Minderheit*, pp. 35f.
24. *Occident* 22 (1855): 599.
25. Reprinted in Schappes, *Documentary History*, pp. 195f.; see also H. B. Grinstein, *New York*, pp. 115f.
26. Grinstein, ibid.
27. "Ein Judenstaatsplan aus den Jahren 1832–1845," in *Der Jude* (Berlin, 1923), pp. 471–85. I am indebted to Mrs. Hanna Nehab of Kibbutz Hazorea for bringing this article to my attention.
28. Handlin, *Adventure*, pp. 54f.
29. Ashkenazi, "Creoles," p. 263.
30. See *Encyc. Judaica*, vol. 15, pp. 1596f.
31. Reprinted in Schappes, *Documentary History*, pp. 217ff.
32. J. D. Sarna, "Missions," p. 246.
33. R. Ernst, *Immigrant Life*, pp. 84f.
34. Ibid., p. 77.
35. *Encyc. Judaica*, vol. 13, pp. 368–76.
36. M. Friedman, *Philadelphia*, pp. 125ff., 235f., and passim.
37. *Encyc. Judaica*, vol. 4, pp. 145–47.
38. Kliman, "Jewish Brahmins," pp. 69f., 78.
39. Mostov, "Boston," p. 11; see also E. D. Baltzell, et al., "Tale of Two Cities," pp. 290–313.
40. "Trail Blazers of the Trans-Mississippi West," *AJA(p)*, Special Issue, 8 (1956): 59.
41. Ibid., p. 61.
42. AJA(a), autobiographies file, folder ME—1910, Rosenwald, Emanuel.

43. Ibid., folder ME—Frank, Henry.
44. H. Goren, *New York Jews*, p. 26.
45. R. Levinson, "Gold Rush," pp. 19f.
46. Sarna, "Paradise," p. 1.
47. Mostov, "Dun and Bradstreet," pp. 340f.
48. Marcus, *Memoirs*, pp. 309f.
49. Ibid., pp. 343f.
50. Ibid.., pp. 11f.
51. *Encyc. Judaica*, vol. 11, pp. 517f.; Ashkenazi, "Creoles," pp. 255f.
52. AJA(a), small collections, Heyman family.
53. Marcus, *Memoirs*, vol. 2, pp. 47ff.
54. Ibid., pp. 287ff.
55. B. E. Supple, "Business Elite," p. 75.
56. *AZJ* 13 (1849): 651.
57. Handlin, *Adventure*, pp. 52f.

Chapter 3: Putting Down Roots

1. H. S. Linfield, *Statistics*, pp. 5, 9ff.
2. K. Roseman, "Jewish Population," pp. 9f.; *Encyc. Judaica*, vol. 15, p. 1596.
3. *AZJ* 11 (1846): 23.
4. Ibid., p. 596.
5. Here quoted from the English translation of 1956, reprinted 1975.
6. I. B. Benjamin, *Three Years*, vol. 1, pp. 64ff.
7. Ibid., pp. 282ff.
8. Roseman, "Jewish Population," p. 15.
9. Ibid., p. 284; L. Silver, "Jews in Albany," pp. 221ff.
10. Wolf and Whiteman, *History*, pp. 36ff.; Cohen, *Encounter*, pp. 173f.
11. I. M. Fein, *Baltimore*, pp. 25–36, 47f.; *AZJ* 14 (1850): 31f.
12. Quoted in *AZJ* 10 (1846): 503.
13. Benjamin, *Three Years*, vol. 1, pp. 305f.; *AZJ* 23 (1864): 118f.
14. Kliman, "Jewish Brahmins," p. 78.
15. Ibid., pp. 43f.; Mostov, "Boston," pp. 16f.
16. Benjamin, *Three Years*, vol. 1, pp. 285f.; *Encyc. Judaica*, vol. 4, pp. 1264ff.
17. *Encyc. Judaica*, vol. 13, pp. 568ff.; Marcus, *Memoirs*, vol. 3, pp. 8ff.
18. Benjamin, *Three Years*, vol. 1, p. 306.
19. Reprinted in Schappes, *Documentary History*, pp. 223ff.; see also Sarna, *Cincinnati*, p. 2f.
20. Mostov, "Cincinnati," p. 81, 72ff.; see also B. B. Brickner, "Jewish Community," pp. 12f.; Hirshler, *Jews from Germany*, pp. 37f.; Sarna, *Cincinnati*, p. 3.
21. K. Guth, *Oberfranken*, p. 345.
22. *AZJ* 8 (1844): 190.
23. Benjamin, *Three Years*, vol. 1, pp. 308f.
24. Cohen, *Encounter*, p. 41.
25. Gartner, *Cleveland*, pp. 8ff.
26. Benjamin, *Three Years*, vol. 1, pp. 280f.
27. Raphael, *Columbus*, pp. 14ff.
28. Benjamin, *Three Years*, vol. 1, p. 335; *Encyc. Judaica*, vol. 11, pp. 520f.

29. Ibid., 14, pp. 662f.; Isador Busch, The Jews in St. Louis, typescript in: AJA(a), histories file, ME—Busch, Isador; Benjamin, *Three Years*, vol. 1, p. 271.
30. *Encyc. Judaica*, vol. 5, pp. 410ff.; Benjamin, *Three Years*, vol. 1, p. 273; *Chicago Democrat* report reprinted in *AZJ* 15 (1851): 419.
31. L. Switchkow and L. Gartner, *Milwaukee*, pp. 11f.; Benjamin, *Three Years*, vol. 1, p. 275.
32. Benjamin, *Three Years*, p. 276; *Encyc. Judaica*, vol. 5, pp. 1566ff.
33. Ibid., vol. 8, p. 1362ff.; Marcus, *Memoirs*, vol. 3, pp. 5–8; *AZJ* 14 (1850): 158; on Kansas City: AJA(a), Histories file; J. P. Schultz, *Kansas City*, pp. 147ff.
34. Roseman, *Jewish Population*," p. 148.
35. Ashkenazi, "Creoles," pp. 18f., 170f.; Benjamin, *Three Years*, vol. 1, pp. 316f.
36. S. Hertzberg, *Strangers*, p. 27.
37. *Encyc. Judaica*, vol. 14, pp. 160–62; 16, pp. 162–64; Benjamin, *Three Years*, vol. 1, p. 306.
38. *Encyc. Judaica*, vol. 15, p. 1606.
39. Ibid., 2, pp. 505f.; *AZJ* 8 (1844): 471.
40. H. F. Schlam, "Houston," pp. 23f., 59; Linfield, *Statistics*, p. 39.
41. *Encyc. Judaica*, vol. 12, pp. 1017–18, 1037–39; AJA(a), autobiographies file, ME—Rosenwald, Emanuel; *AZJ* 72 (1908): 384; Linfield, *Statistics*, pp. 4, 57.
42. *Encyc. Judaica*, vol. 5, pp. 753–54.
43. Ibid., 10, pp. 738–39; Schultz, *Kansas City*, p. 202.
44. *Encyc. Judaica*, vol. 14, p. 1605; Levinson, "Gold Rush," pp. 10f.
45. AJA(a), California collection, box 2802, ME—Bruml family.
46. Glanz, *Judaica*, p. 315, gives the number 5,000, i.e., 10 percent of the population. The higher estimates stem from the *True Pacific Messenger*, reprinted in *AZJ* 25 (1861): 302. Rabbi Julius Eckmann estimated 7,000 Jews in 1856 (*AZJ* 20, p. 174).
47. *Encyc. Judaica*, vol. 14, pp. 833–35; Benjamin, *Three Years*, vol. 1, pp. 205ff.
48. Benjamin, *Three Years*, vol. 2, pp. 9f.; *Encyc. Judaica*, vol. 14, pp. 598–99.
49. Ibid., vol. 5, pp. 56–60; 14, pp. 829–30; Benjamin, *Three Years*, vol. 2, passim.
50. M. Vorspan and L. Gartner, *Los Angeles*, pp. 19f.; Benjamin, *Three Years*, vol. 2, pp. 100f.
51. Toll, "Portland," p. 20,; Benjamin, *Three Years*, vol. 2, p. 163.
52. Ibid., p. 143.
53. Raphael, *Columbus*, p. 32.
54. Ann D. Michael, "Origins," p. 22.
55. Benjamin, *Three Years*, p. 64.
56. Grinstein, *New York*, p. 9.
57. Ibid., p. 33; J. S. Gurock, "On Rischin," p. 6; For similar developments see, Mostov, "Boston," p. 31; Raphael, *Columbus*, pp. 25–30; for Syracuse, New York: J. S. Mesinger, "Geography," pp. 359–64.
58. For the following see, Birmingham, *"Our Crowd,"* passim; Reissner, pp. 108–12; Frederick H. Brunner, "Juden als Bankiers," pp. 515–22; Kurt Grunwald, "Three Chapters," pp. 200–205.
59. *AZJ* 42 (1878): 599f.
60. Simon Kuznets, "Economic Structure," preliminary draft.
61. Mostov, "Cincinnati," pp. 127–33.

62. Mostov, "Boston," pp. 27f.; for Texas, Schlam, "Houston," pp. 30ff.; for California, Levinson, "Gold Rush," p. 52.
63. Mostov, "Boston," p. 27.
64. Gartner, *Cleveland,* pp. 17ff.; Levinson, "Gold Rush," pp. 45–52; Raphael, *Columbus,* p. 443.
65. Mostov, "Boston," table 13; Grinstein, *New York,* p. 128.
66. Kliman, "Jewish Brahmins," pp. 80ff. I wish to express my thanks to Mr. Kliman for providing me with a copy of his interesting study.
67. Mostov, "Cincinnati," p. 109; A. Tarshish, "Economic Life," p. 279. For detailed information on Charleston, Philadelphia, etc., see Roseman, "Jewish Population," pp. 95ff.; for Boston, Kliman, "Jewish Brahmins," p. 171 calculated 43 percent in clothing in 1850–60; for Milwaukee, Switchkow and Gartner, *Milwaukee,* pp. 12–15; see also Tarshish, *Economic Life,"* p. 280; for New York, Ernst, *Immigrant Life,* p. 77.
68. Matthews, *Pen and Ink,* p. 164, quoted in Glanz, *Judaica,* p. 127.
69. D. A. Gerber, *Anti-Semitism,* p. 208.
70. Mostov, "Cincinnati," pp. 114f.
71. Mostov, "Dun and Bradstreet," p. 342; Kliman, "Jewish Brahmins," p. 85; Cohen, *Encounter,* pp. 31ff.

Chapter 4: The Social Structure of an Emerging Community

1. *AZJ* 11 (1847): 741.
2. Gerber, *Anti-Semitism,* pp. 22f.; see also Sarna, "Mythical Jew," passim.
3. *AZJ* 14 (1850): 593; 17 (1853): 438.
4. *AZJ* 10/29 (1846); Cohen, *Encounter,* pp. 79ff.
5. Report in the *Sacramento Democratic State Journal,* quoted in Cohen, *Encounter,* p. 89.
6. *AZJ* 19 (1855): 287, 336.
7. Cohen, *Encounter,* pp. 79f.
8. *AZJ* 11 (1847): 742f.
9. Ibid. 19 (1855): 449.
10. Ibid. 15 (1851): 184; Cohen, *Encounter,* pp. 101–106.
11. *Die Deborah* 12 (1866): 122.
12. Cohen, *Encounter,* pp. 55f.
13. *Asmonean* 3 (1850): 109, quoted by Glanz, "Source Material," p. 136.
14. *Israelitische Wochenschrift* 5 (1874): 403, quoted in ibid., p. 137.
15. N. Glazer, *American Judaism,* p. 20.
16. Roseman, "Jewish Population," p. 20.
17. Fein, *Baltimore,* p. 23, passim.
18. Cohen, *Encounter,* p. 57; see also Weinryb, "Immigration," p. 13.
19. *AZJ* 10 (1846): 448f.
20. Glanz, "Bayer and Pollack," p. 32.
21. Bartyś, "Grand Duchy," p. 201.
22. Mesinger, "Geography," p. 362.
23. Grinstein, *New York,* pp. 171f.
24. *AZJ* 20 (1856): 173.
25. Ibid. 22 (1858): 192f.
26. Mesinger, "Geography," p. 363.

27. Mostov, "Cincinnati," p. 132, 218.
28. M. Sklare, *America's Jews*, p. 11; For more comprehensive evaluations see Steven E. Aschheim, *Brothers and Strangers;* Jack Wertheimer, *Unwelcome Strangers*. An interesting, still readable psychological approach is presented by Kurt Lewin, "Self-Hatred," pp. 219–32.
29. Handlin, *Adventure*, pp. 74f.
30. *AZJ* 11 (1847): 365.
31. Glazer, *American Judaism*, pp. 19f.
32. Ibid., pp. 53f.; Jick, *Americanization of the Synagogue*, pp. 54f.; Meyer, *Modernity*, pp. 228f.
33. Jick, *Americanization of the Synagogue*, p. 57.
34. Ibid., p. 17.
35. Glanz, *Judaica*, p. 220.
36. Wiener's report: *AZJ* 6 (1842): 295; Hochheimer's report: ibid. 14 (1850): 32.
37. Memoirs of Mayer Klein, quoted in Jick, *Americanization of the Synagogue*, p. 100.
38. Ibid., p. 57.
39. Handlin, *Adventure*, p. 76.
40. Ibid., p. 77; Cohen, *Encounter*, pp. 163f.; Fein, *Baltimore*, pp. 49f.; Glazer, *American Judaism*, pp. 32ff.
41. Cohen, *Encounter*, pp. 91ff.; Glazer, *American Judaism*, p. 34; Jick, *Americanization of the Synagogue*, p. 148.
42. Jick, ibid., 62f.; Cohen, ibid., pp. 186f.
43. Cohen, ibid., p. 218.
44. Jick, *Americanization of the Synagogue*, p. 19.
45. *AZJ* 27 (1863): 578; Jick, ibid., p. 105.
46. Cohen, *Encounter*, pp. 124ff.
47. Ibid., pp. 46ff.
48. Jick, *Americanization of the Synagogue*, pp. 112. See also Meyer, "Identity," pp. 252f.; *Encyc. Judaica*, vol. 4, pp. 1144ff.
49. *AZJ* 17 (1853): 17.
50. Ibid. 19 (1855): 271.
51. Handlin, *Adventure*, pp. 71f.; *Encyc. Judaica*, vol. 13, pp. 1050f.; *AZJ* 21 (1857): 148.
52. Jick, *Americanization of the Synagogue*, p. 113.

Chapter 5: Loyalties and Assertions

1. Cohen, *Encounter*, p. 131.
2. Korn, *Civil War*, p. 30.
3. Ibid., pp. 16f.; Cohen, *Encounter*, p. 135.
4. *AZJ* 25 (1861): 386ff.; Fein, *Baltimore*, p. 98.
5. Quoted in Korn, *Civil War*, pp. 23f.
6. Hirshler, *Jews from Germany*, p. 59.
7. *AZJ* 29 (1865): 170, 385, 574.
8. Korn, *Civil War*, pp. 121f.
9. *AZJ* 25 (1861): 266ff.
10. Ibid. 26 (1862): 445f.
11. Korn, *Civil War*, p. 251.

12. Hertzberg, *Strangers,* pp. 26f.
13. Korn, *Civil War,* p. 158.
14. *AZJ* 28 (1864): 198.
15. Cohen, *Encounter,* p. 148; L. Ruchames, "Abolitionists," pp. 506f.
16. Korn, *Civil War,* pp. 160ff.
17. Ibid., p. 173.
18. Ibid., p. 176.
19. Ibid., pp. 178f.
20. Ibid., p. 57. The following is based mainly on Korn, *Civil War,* pp. 56–97, unless other references are given.
21. Ibid., p. 62.
22. *AZJ* 26 (1862): 24.
23. Korn, *Civil War,* p. 73.
24. *AZJ* 26 (1862): 96.
25. Cohen, *Encounter,* p. 217f.
26. Korn, *Civil War,* p. 132.
27. *Jewish Messenger* 13, no. 3 (January 16, 1863): 20, quoted in ibid.
28. Korn, *Civil War,* p. 133.
29. Joakim Isaacs, "Ulysses S. Grant," p. 69.
30. Korn, *Civil War,* pp. 134–38.
31. Ibid., p. 138.

Chapter 6: The Second Wave, 1865–1914

1. Glanz, "Mass Emigration," p. 46.
2. See Glanz, "Immigration," pp. 81–99, originally published in Yiddish as *Geshikhte fun der Yidisher Arbeter-Bavegung in di Fareynikte Shtaten.* Many, but not all, of Glanz's essays on German-Jewish immigration are collected in his *Judaica Americana* of 1970.
3. *Encyc. Judaica,* vol. 15, p. 1596 (1820–1880. "Population, Immigration, and Settlement," by L. P. Gartner).
4. Schmelz, "Demographische Entwicklung," p. 48. These estimates are part of an extensive study based on what to my knowledge is the most comprehensive extant collection of demographical statistics on German Jewry in the nineteenth and twentieth centuries, at the Institute for Jewish Demography, Hebrew University, Jerusalem.
5. Barkai, *Industrialisation,* statistical appendix, pp. 146–49.
6. J. Jacobs, "Jewish Population," pp. 339ff.
7. German immigration calculated from Hohorst et al., *Arbeitsbuch,* vol. 1, p. 35; vol. 2, pp. 38f.; for Jewish percentage, see Jacobs, "Jewish Population," p. 344.
8. Meyer, "Identity," p. 248.
9. Toll, "Life Cycle," p. 311.
10. Richarz, *Jüdisches Leben,* vol. 2, pp. 236f.
11. AJA(a), documents files, immigrants and immigration.
12. Ibid., California collection, box 2802, file Adlai Goldschmidt.
13. Ibid., autobiographies collection, folder ME—Wile, Herman.
14. Ibid., biographies collection, folder ME—Seligberger, Sigmund.
15. Ibid., small collections, folders ME—Behrend, Jacob.

16. Stefi Jersch-Wenzel, "Geschichte," pp. 73ff.
17. Mostov, "Boston," p. 135.
18. Mostov, "Cincinnati," p. 78.
19. M. Gelfand, "Progress," p. 29.
20. Toury, *Geschichte*, p. 32.
21. J. Bartyś, "Grand Duchy," p. 202.
22. J. F. Harris, "Bavarians and Jews," p. 114.
23. *AZJ* 44 (1880): 824f.
24. Cohen, *Encounter,* pp. 39f.; for the census data, see Linfield, *Statistics,* p. 17 and table C.
25. Kliman, "Jewish Brahmins," pp. 258f.
26. AJA(a), biographies file, folder ME—Wertheim, Herman.
27. See *Encyc. Judaica,* vol. 15, pp. 1596ff. also for the following demographic data.
28. Kliman, "Jewish Brahmins," p. 78; Mostov, "Cincinnati," p. 5.
29. Vorspan and Gartner, *Los Angeles,* pp. 25ff.; Gelfand, "Progress," pp. 28ff.
30. Kliman, "Jewish Brahmins," p. 308.
31. Gurock, *Harlem,* pp. 6ff.
32. S. Berrol, "Image," p. 422; see also M. Rischin, *Promised City,* pp. 93f.
33. Berrol, "Image," p. 426.
34. *Menorah Journal,* Spring 1936 (AJA[a]), Nearprint collection, folder ME—Lasker, Morris.
35. AJA(a), California collection, box 2802.
36. Kliman, "Jewish Brahmins," p. 205.
37. Hertzberg, *Strangers,* pp. 153f.; Raphael, *Columbus,* pp. 48f.; for Boston, Kliman, "Jewish Brahmins," p. 100; Detroit, R. Rockaway, "Americanization," pp. 59f.; New York, Rischin, *Promised City,* p. 51; Los Angeles, Gelfand, "Progress," pp. 33ff.
38. Switchkow and Gartner, *Milwaukee,* p. 64.
39. Sklare, *America's Jews,* p. 11.
40. Hertzberg, *Strangers,* p. 59.
41. For America see Toll, "Life Cycle," pp. 314ff.; Kliman, "Jewish Brahmins," pp. 231ff. For Germany, see Schmelz, "Demographische Entwicklung," p. 42.
42. Rischin, *Promised City,* p. 53.
43. J. Lestschinsky, "Sotsiale Ponim" ("Social Features"), pp. 29f.
44. Glazer, "Social Characteristics," p. 3.
45. M. Kaplan, "Tradition," p. 12.
46. J. R. Marcus, *Woman,* vol. 2, pp. 129f.
47. Kaplan, "Tradition," p. 31.
48. Kaplan, "Love or Money," pp. 264ff.; see also letter of Menko Stern, above chapter 1, note 34.
49. AJA(a), correspondence file, ME—Lachman family.
50. Glanz, *Woman,* pp. 16f.
51. Calculated from Rohrbacher, "From Württemberg," pp. 161ff.
52. Kaplan, "Love or Money," p. 277.
53. Ibid., pp. 281f.
54. Marcus, *Woman,* vol. 2, pp. 190ff.
55. AJA(a) autobiographies collection, folder ME—Salomon, Anna.
56. C. Baum, *Jewish Woman,* p. 29.

57. Marcus, *Woman,* vol. 1, p. 26.
58. Ibid., vol. 2, p. 308.
59. Ibid., pp. 160ff.
60. Ibid., p. 36.
61. Ibid., pp. 38f.
62. Baum, *Jewish Woman,* p. 37.
63. Ibid., p. 30.
64. Ibid., p. 31.
65. Marcus, *Woman,* vol. 2, pp. 172f.
66. Glanz, *Woman,* pp. ix, 13f.
67. Marcus, *Woman,* vol. 2, pp. 420ff.
68. Ibid., vol. 1, pp. 32ff.
69. Both quotations from Baum, *Jewish Woman,* pp. 30f.
70. Ibid., p. 33f.
71. Beth S. Wenger, "Jewish Women," p. 26 and passim.

Chapter 7: Americanization Delayed

1. Malcolm H. Stern, "The 1870s" in Sarna, *Experience,* p. 31–32.
2. Melvin I. Urofsky, "Zionism," ibid., p. 215f.
3. Glazer, "Social Characteristics," p. 8f.
4. Ibid, p. 18.
5. AJA(a), Nearprint collection, folder ME—Lasker, Morris.
6. Ibid., correspondence file, folder ME—Reizenstein, Charles.
7. Quoted in Gartner, *Cleveland,* p. 9.
8. *Die Deborah* 6 (1860): 38.
9. Glanz, "Mass Emigration," p. 61.
10. Guth, *Oberfranken,* pp. 132, 285.
11. *AZJ* 18 (1854): 426.
12. *AZJ* 2/16.8 (1838).
13. Glazer, *American Judaism,* p. 35f; Meyer, *Modernity,* pp. 53ff., 228ff.
14. *AZJ* 5 (1841): 309; Cohen, *Encounter,* pp. 74, 175. Meyer, *Modernity,* pp. 233f.; Jick, *Americanization of the Synagogue,* pp. 82ff.
15. *AZJ* 6 (1842): 618.
16. Ibid. 7 (1843): 683; 17 (1853): 6.
17. Ibid. 19 (1855): 315.
18. Ibid. 18 (1854): 430.
19. Sarna, JPS, p. 5f.
20. Greenberg, "Immigrant's Perception," p. 308. See also, J. Sarna's comments in "A German-Jewish Immigrant's Perception of America, 1853–54," *AZH* 68 (1978): 206ff.
21. All quotations as translated by Greenberg, "Immigrant's Perception," pp. 322ff.
22. *Die Deborah,* no. 43 (June 12, 1857): 340f.
23. *Sinai* 2 (1858): 536.
24. *AZJ* 21 (1857): 297.
25. Ibid. 29 (1865): 405.
26. Ibid., p. 624.
27. Ibid., p. 656.

28. Ibid. 30 (1866): 10f.
29. Cohen, *Encounter,* p. 166.
30. *AZJ* 30 (1866): 202.
31. Ibid. 38 (1874): 877.
32. Meyer, "Identity," pp. 249, 251.
33. Bernard D. Weinryb, "Immigrants," pp. 125f.
34. *AZJ* 7 (1843): 478.
35. Ibid. 9 (1845): 408f.
36. See: Jick, *Americanization of the Synagogue,* pp. 95f.; Cohen, *Encounter,* pp. 164f.; Meyer, "Identity," pp. 256f.; Glazer, *American Judaism,* pp. 32f.; Meyer, *Modernity,* pp. 319f. The following leans heavily on this latest, most comprehensive history of the Reform movement.
37. Meyer, "Identity," pp. 254f.
38. Jick, *Americanization of the Synagogue,* pp. 121ff.
39. I. M. Wise, *Reminiscences,* quoted in ibid., pp. 155f.
40. Quoted by Glazer, *American Judaism,* p. 39.
41. Meyer, "Identity," p. 259; Meyer, *Modernity,* pp. 255ff.
42. *AZJ* 31 (1865): 94.
43. Quoted in *AZJ* 36 (1872): 44f.
44. I. M. Wise, "Ein Übelstand," in *Die Deborah* 10 (1864).
45. Quoted in *AZJ* 31 (1867): 95.
46. Ibid., p. 883.
47. Ibid., p. 559.
48. *Die Deborah* 14 (1868): 190.
49. R. Singerman, "Union List," vol. 2; Grinstein, *New York,* pp. 214ff.; *Encyc. Judaica,* vol. 13, pp. 1050ff.; Glanz, *Judaica,* p. 140. A full list of journals can be found in *Jüdisches Lexikon,* vol. 4, pp. 1105ff.
50. Switchkow and Gartner, *Milwaukee,* p. 127.
51. *AZJ* 14 (1850): 31.
52. Meyer, "Identity," p. 250.
53. Glanz, *Judaica,* pp. 142, 205.
54. Grinstein, *New York,* p. 205.
55. *Die Deborah* 16 (1871): 31.
56. *AZJ* 31 (1867): 758.
57. Ibid. 42 (1878): 10.
58. Ibid. 51 (1887): 100.
59. Ibid. 57 (1893): 18.
60. J. Goldtstein, "St. Louis," pp. 13ff.
61. Glanz, "Immigration," p. 86.
62. Nadel, "Race," p. 8.
63. Quoted by Glanz, *Judaica,* pp. 202ff., 250f., 258.
64. Marcus, *Colonial Jew,* vol. 3, pp. 1176f.
65. Cohen, *Encounter,* p. 21.
66. Mostov, "Cincinnati," pp. 84, 104.
67. Switchkow and Gartner, *Milwaukee,* pp. 26ff.
68. Ibid., p. 64.
69. Rockaway, "Americanization," pp. 6f.
70. Hertzberg, *Strangers,* pp. 76ff.
71. Quoted in *AZJ* 36 (1872): 417.
72. Nadel, "Race," pp. 18ff.

73. Ibid., p. 23.
74. Ibid., p. 12.
75. Rischin, *Promised City,* p. 95.
76. Meyer, "Identity," pp. 251f.
77. Marcus, *Memoirs,* vol. 2, p. 284.
78. Glanz, *Judaica,* p. 225.
79. Korn, *Civil War,* pp. 84f.
80. Benjamin, *Three Years,* vol. 1, pp. 240ff.
81. Glanz, *California,* pp. 36f.
82. Ibid., p. 104.
83. *Die Deborah* 10 (1864): 122.
84. Glanz, *Judaica,* p. 235; for a detailed treatment of the subject, see pp. 173ff.
85. Ibid., pp. 86f.
86. Esther E. Rawidowicz, "I. L. Chronik," pp. 137–47. I am indebted to Mrs. Cornelia Oesterreich for bringing this article to my attention.
87. *AZJ* 36 (1872): 754.
88. Quoted by Switchkow and Gartner, *Milwaukee,* pp. 111ff.
89. Ibid., p. 123.
90. Howard F. Sachs, "Seeking the Welfare," pp. 152f.
91. *AZJ* (1841): 14.
92. Ibid. 18 (1854): 314ff.
93. *Die Deborah* 2 (1856): 140.
94. *Sinai* 1 (1856): 156.
95. *Die Deborah* 10 (1865): 205.
96. *AZJ* 29 (1865): 202.
97. Tarshish, "Economic Life," pp. 284ff.
98. Glanz, *Judaica,* pp. 145f.
99. *AZJ* 36 (1872): 953ff.
100. Glanz, *Judaica,* p. 247.
101. Cohen, "Anti-Semitism," pp. 34ff.; Cohen, *Encounter,* p. 153.
102. Quoted by Switchkow and Gartner, *Milwaukee,* pp. 135f.
103. See Edward N. Sareth, *American Historians,* pp. 20ff.; Richard Hofstadter, *Social Darwinism,* pp. 148ff.
104. Glanz, *Judaica,* p. 207.
105. Theodor Lenke, *Geschichte,* passim; see also Glanz, *Judaica,* p. 230.
106. *AZJ* 21 (1857): 465.
107. Ibid. 36 (1872): 473.
108. *American Hebrew,* December 3, 1909, p. 135; January 3, 1913, p. 284.
109. Hirshler, *Jews from Germany,* p. 50f.
110. Cohen, *Encounter,* p. 61.
111. Reprinted in *AZJ* 45 (1881): 159.

Chapter 8: German and Other Jews

1. Glazer, "Social Characteristics," pp. 10f.; Kuznets, "Immigration," p. 39.
2. Glazer, ibid., p. 11; see also Lestschinsky, "Social Features," pp. 13ff.
3. Gurock, ed., *On Rischin,* p. 197f.; summarizing his discussion with Selma Berrol (ibid., pp. 142–62). See also Z. Szajkowski, "Reappraisal," passim.
4. Fein, *Baltimore,* pp. 147ff.

5. *Encyc. Judaica,* vol. 15, p. 1608.
6. *Israelitisches Wochenblatt* 1 (1870): 72, quoted in Glanz, "Source Material," pp. 155f.
7. *New York Herald,* September 27, 1869, quoted in Wischnitzer, *Dwell,* p. 31.
8. Wischnitzer, *Dwell,* p. 29.
9. Quoted in Schappes, *Documentary History,* pp. 538f.
10. *Israelitisches Wochenblatt,* 1 (1870): 248, quoted in Glanz, "Source Material," p. 156.
11. *AZJ* 36 (1872): 10.
12. Wischnitzer, *Dwell,* pp. 24ff.; Schappes, *Documentary History,* pp. 545ff., and notes pp. 728ff.
13. I. Howe, *World,* pp. 29f.
14. *AZJ* 45 (1881): 561.
15. Quoted in Howe, *World,* p. 31.
16. *AZJ* 45 (1881): 738f.
17. Ibid. 46 (1882): 110f.
18. Handlin, "Immigration," p. 39.
19. Howe, *World,* p. 31.
20. Quoted in Z. Szajkowski, "Attitude," p. 232.
21. Esther Panitz, "Polarity," pp. 114f., 121.
22. Fein, *Baltimore,* pp. 147ff.
23. Quoted in E. Tscherikower, *Labor,* p. 104.
24. Ibid., p. 105.
25. Howe, *World,* p. 32.
26. Tscherikower, *Labor,* p. 107.
27. Sajkowski, "Reappraisal," pp. 73ff.
28. Rischin, *Promised City,* pp. 98f.
29. *AZJ* 49 (1885): 98.
30. Selma Berrol, "Germans," p. 145; Rischin, *Promised City,* pp. 193f.
31. Rischin, *Promised City,* pp. 100f.
32. Cohen, *Encounter,* pp. 232f.
33. Melvin I. Urofsky, "Leadership," pp. 408f.
34. *AZJ* 55, no. 33 (1891).
35. Gartner, *Cleveland,* p. 105.
36. AJA(a), histories file, folder ME—Kansas City, Mo. Lecture of Morton I. Sosland, November 29, 1966.
37. Cohen, *Encounter,* pp. 322ff.
38. Vorspan and Gartner, *Los Angeles,* pp. 111f.
39. Tscherikower, *Labor,* p. 110.
40. *Jewish Exponent,* April 4, 1890.
41. Ibid., May 2, 1891.
42. Ibid., August 14, and November 6, 1891 (all quoted in Richard F. Address, "Reaction").
43. Cohen, *Encounter,* pp. 238ff.
44. Baron, *Steeled in Adversity,* pp. 286f.
45. Cohen, *Encounter,* p. 341.
46. Howe, *World,* pp. 234f.
47. Tscherikower, *Labor,* pp. 111f. For some more recent argument on this still controversial issue, see Selma C. Berrol, "Image," pp. 417–33; Myron Ber-

man, *Attitude;* Sheldon Morris Neuringer, *Immigration Policy,* and Jonathan Sarna's critical review in *AJH* 71 (1982): 403–407.

48. Lestschinsky, "Social Features," pp. 13f.; Kuznets, "Immigration," p. 120.
49. Kuznets, ibid., pp. 101ff.; Baron, *Steeled in Adversity,* pp. 296ff.
50. Handlin, *Adventure,* p. 92.
51. Isaac Markens, *New York,* pp. 139ff.; Howe, *World,* p. 82.
52. Howe, ibid., p. 298.
53. Rischin, *Promised City,* p. 67.
54. Baron, *Steeled in Adversity,* p. 301; see also Handlin, *Adventure,* p. 136; Lucy S. Dawidowicz, "Labor Movement," pp. 158–66.
55. Dawidowicz, ibid., p. 165.
56. Ibid., p. 163.
57. Ibid., p. 159.
58. Handlin, *Adventure,* p. 142.
59. *Encyc. Judaica,* vol. 5, pp. 410ff.; Jeffrey Langer, "White-Collar," pp. 18ff.
60. *AZJ* 45 (1881): 149f.
61. Henry Gersoni, "Jew against Jew," pp. 9, 13f., 29, 33.
62. *AZJ* 50 (1886): 347f.
63. Ibid., 53 (1889): 695.
64. Ibid., 55, no. 24 (1891).
65. Ibid., 59, no. 5 (1895).
66. Rockaway, "Americanization," p. 139.
67. Quoted in Hertzberg, *Strangers,"* pp. 188f.
68. Lecture of Howard F. Sachs, November 29, 1966, AJA(a), histories file, folder ME—Kansas City, Mo.
69. Meyer, *Modernity,* p. 264.
70. Baron, *Steeled in Adversity,* pp. 373f.
71. Meyer, *Modernity,* pp. 269f., 292.
72. Baron, *Steeled in Adversity,* p. 374.
73. Ibid., pp. 357f.
74. Quoted in ibid., p. 396.
75. Ibid.; Meyer, *Modernity,* p. 283.
76. Quoted in Rockaway, "Americanization," p. 136.
77. Cohen, *Encounter,* p. 51.
78. Quoted by Glanz, *Judaica,* p. 172.
79. Ibid., p. 181f.
80. Hertzberg, *Strangers,* pp. 174ff.
81. Kliman, "Jewish Brahmins," pp. 348ff.
82. See Higham, *Strangers,* pp. 25ff.; Higham, "Social Darwinism," pp. 6ff.; Higham, *Reinterpretation,* 567f.; For some more recent assessments, see David Gerber, *Anti-semitism,* pp. 23f.; Jonathan D. Sarna, "American Anti-Semitism," in Berger, *History and Hate,* pp. 121f.
83. *AZJ* 52 (1888): 556.
84. Cohen, "Anti-Semitism," p. 36.
85. *Jewish American,* May 30, 1902; quoted in Rockaway, "Americanization," p. 234.
86. Ibid., p. 236.

87. Toll, "Portland," pp. 31f.
88. Glazer, "Social Characteristics," pp. 25f.

Conclusion

1. Schmelz, "Demographische Entwicklung," pp. 37ff.; Barkai, "Industrialisation," pp. 146ff.; Schwarz, *Juden in Bayern*, p. 338.
2. See Heinrich Silbergleit, *Bevölkerungs*, pp. 14f.; Schmelz, "Demographische Entwicklung," pp. 44ff.
3. Schmelz, ibid., p. 55.
4. John S. Billings, "Vital Statistics," quoted in Glazer, "Social Characteristics," pp. 9f.
5. Barkai, *Minderheit*, pp. 20f.; Steven M. Lowenstein, "Rural Community," pp. 218–36.
6. Glanz, "Source Material," pp. 78ff.; Toury, *Geschichte*, pp. 142f.; see also Utz Jeggle, *Judendörfer*, and Guth, *Oberfranken*, passim.
7. Barkai, *Minderheit*, pp. 73ff.; Barkai, "Industrialisation," pp. 136ff.
8. See Arkadius Kahan, "General Survey: The Modern Era," pp. 94f.; see also Esra Bennathan's remarks in Barkai, "Industrialisation," pp. 153f.
9. Werner Sombart, *Wirtschaftsleben*.
10. See Kuznets, "Economic Structure"; and L. Finkelstein, idem, *Economic Structure*, passim.
11. See Shulamit Volkov, "Assimilation," pp. 373–87.
12. Herman Eliassof, *German-American Jews*, pp. 5f.
13. *American Hebrew*, February 2, 1917, pp. 410f.
14. Cohen, *Encounter*, pp. 62f.

Sources and Bibliography

(Where dissertations have been later published as books I usually prefer to quote from the original typescript versions, which are usually more detailed.)

I. Periodicals

American Hebrew. Weekly, New York, 1879–1956.
Allgemeine Zeitung des Judenthums. (AZJ). Weekly, Leipzig, Bonn, Berlin, 1837–1922.
The Asmonean. Weekly, New York, 1849–58.
Die Deborah. Weekly, Cincinnati, 1855–1903.
Israelitische Wochenschrift für die religiösen und sozialen Interessen des Judenthums. Weekly, Breslau, 1870–94.
Jewish Exponent. Weekly, Philadelphia, 1887.
Jewish Messenger. Weekly, New York, 1857–1903.
Der Jude. Periodical, Berlin, 1916–24.
Menorah Journal. Monthly, 1915–.
The Occident and American Jewish Advocate. Weekly, Philadelphia, 1843–68.
Der Orient. Weekly, Leipzig, 1840–51.
Sinai. Monthly (in German), Baltimore, 1856–62.

II. Books, Articles, Dissertations, and Archival Material

Address, Richard F. "The Reaction of the Philadelphia Anglo-Jewish Press to the Russian Immigrant Community: 1882–1892." AJA(a), miscellaneous file, folder ME, Address, Richard.
Aschheim, Steven E. *Brothers and Strangers: The East European Jews in German and German Jewish Consciousness, 1800–1923.* Madison, Wisc., 1982.

Aschkewitz, Max. *Zur Geschichte der Juden in West-Preussen.* Marburg, 1967.

Ashkenazi, Elliot. "Creoles of Jerusalem: Jewish Businessmen of Louisiana, 1840–1875." Ph.D. dissertation, George Washington University, 1983.

Aubin, H. and W. Zorn, eds. *Handbuch der deutschen Wirtschafts- und Sozialgeschichte,* vol. 2. Stuttgart, 1976.

Bade, K. J. "German Emigration to the United States and Continental Emigration to Germany in the Late Nineteenth and Early Twentieth Century," in *Labor Migration in the Atlantic Economies,* edited by D. Hoerder, pp. 117–42.

Baltzell, E. D., A. Glicksman, J. Litt. "The Jewish Communities of Philadelphia and Boston: A Tale of Two Cities," in *Jewish Life in Philadelphia, 1830–1940,* edited by Friedman, pp. 290-312.

Barkai, Avraham. "German-Jewish Migrations in the Nineteenth Century, 1830–1914." *YLBI* 30 (1985): 301–18.

———. "The German Jews at the Start of Industrialisation," in *Revolution and Evolution,* edited by Mosse et al., pp. 123–49.

———. *Jüdische Minderheit und Industrialisierung.* Tübingen, 1988.

Baron, Salo W. *Steeled in Adversity: Essays and Addresses on American Jewish Life,* edited by Jeanette M. Baron. Philadephia, 1971.

Bartyś, Julian. "The Grand Duchy of Poznan under Prussian Rule: Changes in the Economic Position of the Jewish Population, 1815–1848." *YLBI* 17 (1972): 191–204.

Baum, Charlotte, Paula Heyman, and Sonya Michel, eds. *The Jewish Woman in America.* New York, 1976.

Benjamin, Israel B. *Three Years in America, 1859–1862.* First German edition, Hanover, 1862; English translation, New York, 1959 and 1975.

Berger, David, ed. *History and Hate: The Dimensions of Anti-Semitism.* Philadelphia, New York, and Jerusalem, 1986.

Berman, Myron. *The Attitude of American Jewry towards East European Jewish Immigration.* New York, 1980.

Berrol, Selma C. "Germans versus Russians: An Update" in *On Rischin,* edited by Gurock.

———. "In Their Image: German Jews and the Americanization of the Ost-Juden in New York City." *New York History* 63 (1982): 417–33.

Billings, John S. "Vital Statistics of the Jews of the United States," Census Bulletin, December 1890. Quoted in Glazer, *Social Characteristics.*

Birmingham, Stephen. *"Our Crowd": The Great Jewish Families of New York.* New York, 1967.

Blau, Bruno. *Das Ende der Juden in Deutschland.* Congregation Beth-Hillel, New York, 1950.

Brickner, Barnett B., "The Jewish Community of Cincinnati: Historical and Descriptive 1817–1932." Ph.D. dissertation, University of Cincinnati, 1932.

Broches, S. *Jews in New England.* Vol. 1, *Historical Study of the Jews in Massachusetts (1650–1750).* New York, 1942.

Brunner, Frederick M. "Juden als Bankiers," in *In Zwei Welten: Festschrift für Siegfried Moses,* edited by Tramer, pp. 515–22.

Burgdörfer, Friedrich B. "Migrations Across the Frontier of Germany," in *International Migrations,* vol. 2, edited by Wilcox, pp. 313–89.

Busch, Isador. "The Jews in St. Louis." Typescript in AJA(a), histories file, ME Busch, Isador.

Cohen, Naomi W. "American Jewish Reactions to Anti-Semitism in Western Europe, 1875–1900." *American Academy for Jewish Research, Proceedings* 45 (Jerusalem 1978): 29–65.

––––––. *Encounter with Emancipation: The German Jews in the United States, 1830–1914.* Philadelphia, 1984.

Dawidowicz, Lucy S. "The Jewishness of the Jewish Labor Movement in the United States," in *A Bicentennial Festschrift for Jacob Raeder Marcus,* New York, 1976, repr. Sarna, *The American Jewish Experience.*

Decker, Peter R. *Fortunes and Failures: White Collar Mobility in Nineteenth Century San Francisco.* Cambridge, Mass., 1978.

Dohm, Chr. W. *Über die bürgerliche Verbesserung der Juden.* Berlin and Stettin, 1781; pt. 2, 1783.

Eliassof, Herman. *German American Jews.* (English translation reprinted from *Deutsch-Amerikanische Geschichtsblaetter* 14 [1914]). Chicago, 1916.

Encyclopaedia Judaica, editor in chief Cecil Roth. 3d printing. Jerusalem, 1974.

Engelbert, H. *Statistik des Judenthums im Deutschen Reich.* Frankfurt a.M., 1875.

Ernst, Robert. *Immigrant Life in New York City, 1825–1863.* New York, 1949.

Fein, Isaac M. *The Making of an American Jewish Community: The History of Baltimore Jewry, 1773–1920.* Philadelphia, 1971.

Fischer, W., J. Krengel, and J. Wietog, eds. *Sozialgeschichtliches Arbeitsbuch: Materialien zur Statistik,* vol. 1, *1815–1870.* Munich, 1982.

Friedman, Murray, ed. *Jewish Life in Philadelphia, 1830–1940.* Philadelphia, 1983.

Gartner, Lloyd P. "United States of America, 1820–1880: Population, Immigration and Settlement," in *Encyclopaedia Judaica,* vol. 15, pp. 1596ff.

––––––. *History of the Jews of Cleveland.* Cleveland, 1978.

Gelfand, Mitchell. "Progress and Prosperity: Social Mobility in Los Angeles in the Booming Eighties," in *the Jews of the West; The Metropolitan Years,* edited by M. Rischin, pp. 24–49. Berkeley, Calif., 1979.

Gerber, David A., ed. *Anti-Semitism in American History.* Urbana and Chicago, 1986.

Gersoni, Henry. "Jew against Jew." Chicago, 1881, AJA(a), miscellaneous file, folder ME Gersoni, Henry, pp. 9, 13f., 29, and 33.

Glanz, Rudolf. "The 'Bayer' and the 'Pollack' in America." *JSS* 17 (1955): 27–42. Reprinted in Glanz, *Studies in Judaica Americana,* pp. 187–202.

––––––. "The German Jewish Mass Emigration, 1820–1880." *AJA(p)* 22 (1970): 49–66.

––––––. "German Jews in New York City in the Nineteenth Century." *YIVO— Annual of Jewish Social Sciences* 11 (1956–57): 9–28. Reprinted in Glanz, *Studies in Judaica Americana,* pp. 122–51.

––––––. *Geschichte des niederen jüdischen Volkes in Deutschland. Eine Studie über historisches Gaunertum, Bettelwesen und Vagantentum.* New York, 1968.

––––––. "The Immigration of German Jews up to 1880." *YIVO—Annual of Jewish Social Sciences* 2–3 (1947): 81–99. Reprinted in Glanz, *Studies in Judaica Americana,* pp. 85–103.

––––––. *The Jewish Woman in America: Two Female Immigrant Generations, 1820–1929.* Vol. 2, *The German Jewish Woman.* New York, 1976.

––––––. *The Jews of California: From the Discovery of Gold until 1880.* New York, 1960.

———. "Source Material on the History of Jewish Immigration to the United States, 1800–1880." *YIVO—Annual of Jewish Social Sciences* 6 (1951): 73–156. Reprinted in Glanz, *Studies in Judaica Americana*, pp. 1–84.

———. *Studies in Judaica Americana*. New York, 1970.

Glazer, Nathan. *American Judaism*, 2d ed. Chicago, 1972.

———. "Social Characteristics of American Jews, 1654–1954." *AJYB* 56 (1955): 3–41.

Goldtstein, J. "St. Louis in the 1890s," AJA(a), box no. 2270b, pp. 13ff.

Goren, Arthur A. *New York Jews and the Quest for Community*. New York, 1970.

Greenberg, Gershon. "A German Jewish Immigrant's Perception of America, 1853–54." *AJHQ* 67 (1978): 307–41. (An annotated, somewhat shortened translation of the anonymous German original; *Deutsch-Amerikanische Skizzen für jüdische Auswanderer und Nichtauswanderer*. Leipzig, 1857.)

Grinstein, Hyman B. *The Rise of the Jewish Community of New York*. Philadelphia, 1945.

Gross, Nathan, ed. *Economic History of the Jews*. Jerusalem and New York, 1975.

Grunwald, Kurt, "Three Chapters of German-Jewish Banking History." *YLBI* 22 (1977): 200–205.

Gurock, Jeffrey S. *When Harlem Was Jewish, 1870–1930*. New York, 1979.

Gurock, J. S., ed. "On Rischin's *The Promised City* (Rereading and Reevaluating)." *AJH* 73 (1983): 113–204.

Guth, Klaus, et al., eds. *Jüdische Landgemeinden in Oberfranken (1800 – 1942): Ein historisch-topographisches Handbuch*. Bamberg, 1988.

Handlin, Oscar. *Adventure in Freedom: Three Hundred Years of Jewish Life in America*. New York, 1954.

———. *The Uprooted*, 2d ed. rev. Boston, 1973.

Handlin, Oscar, and Mary F. Handlin. "A Century of Jewish Immigration to the United States." *AJYB* 50 (1948–49): 1–84.

Harris, J. F. "Bavarians and Jews in Conflict in 1866: Neighbours and Enemies." *YLBI* 32 (1987): 103–17.

Hertzberg, Steven. "The Jews of Atlanta, 1865–1915." Ph.D. dissertation, University of Chicago, 1975. (Published version: *Strangers Within the Gate City*. Philadelphia, 1978).

Higham, John. *Anti-Semitism in the Gilded Age: A Reinterpretation*. Reprinted from *The Mississippi Valley Historical Review* 43 (1957): 559–78.

———. "Social Darwinism against Jews in America, 1830–1930." *PAJHS* 47 (1957): 1–33.

———. *Strangers in the Land: Patterns of American Nativism, 1860–1925*. New Brunswick, N.J., 1955.

Hirshler, Eric S., ed. *Jews from Germany in the United States*. New York, 1955.

Hoerder, D., ed. *Labor Migration in the Atlantic Economies: The European and North American Working Classes during the Period of Industrialization*. Westport, Conn., and London, 1985.

Hofstadter, Richard. *Social Darwinism in American Thought*. Philadelphia, 1945.

Hohorst, G., J. Kocka, and G. A. Ritter, eds. *Sozialgeschichtliches Arbeitsbuch: Materialien zur Statistik des Kaiserreichs*, vol. 2, *1870–1914*. Munich, 1978.

Howe, Irving. *World of Our Fathers*. New York, 1976.

Isaacs, Joakim. "Ulysses S. Grant and the Jews." Repr. in Sarna, *The American Jewish Experience*.

Jacobs, Joseph. "Jewish Population of the United States: Memoir of the Bureau of Jewish Statistics of the American Jewish Committee." *AJYB* (1914/15): 339ff.

Jeggle, Utz. *Judendörfer in Württemberg.* Tübingen, 1969.

Jersch-Wenzel, Stefi. "Zur Geschichte der jüdischen Bevölkerung in der Provinz Posen im 19. Jahrhundert," in *Juden im Ostmitteleuropa von der Emanzipation bis zum Ersten Weltkrieg,* edited by G. Rhode. Marburg on the Lahn, 1989.

Jick, Leon A. *The Americanization of the Synagogue.* Hanover, N.H., 1976.

Joseph, Samuel. *Jewish Immigration to the United States, 1881 to 1910.* New York, 1914.

Jüdisches Lexikon, 4 vols. Berlin, 1930.

Kahan, Arkadius. "General Survey: The Modern Period," in *Economic History of the Jews,* ed. Gross, pp. 55–104.

Kaplan, Marion A. "For Love or Money: The Marriage Strategies of Jews in Imperial Germany. *YLBI* 28 (1983): 263–300.

———. "Tradition and Transition: The Acculturation, Assimilation and Integration of Jews in Imperial Germany, A Gender Analysis." *YLBI* 27 (1982): 3–35.

Karp, Abraham J., ed. *The Jewish Experience in America,* vol. 3. New York, n.d.

Kisch, Guido. *German Jews in White Labor Servitude in America.* New York, 1937.

———. "The Revolution of 1848 and the Jewish 'On to America' Movement." *PAJHS* 38 (1948–49): 185–234.

Kliman, Burton S. "The Jewish Brahmins of Boston: A Study of the German Jewish Immigration Experience, 1860–1900." B.A. thesis, Brandeis University, 1978. Archive of the American Jewish Historical Society at Brandeis, Waltham, Massachusetts.

Kober, Adolf. "Jewish Emigration from Württemberg to the United States of America (1848–1855)," in *The Jewish Experience in America,* vol. 3, edited by Karp, pp. 1–25.

Kohler, Max J. *The German Jewish Migration to America. PAJHS* 9 (1901): 87–105.

Köllman, Wolfgang. "Bevölkerungsgeschichte, 1800–1970," in *Handbuch der deutschen Wirtschafts- und Sozialgeschichte,* vol. 2, edited by Aubin and Zorn, pp. 9–50.

Korn, Bertram W. *American Jewry and the Civil War.* Philadelphia, 1951.

———. *The Early Jews of New Orleans.* Waltham, Mass., 1969.

———. *Eventful Years and Experiences: Studies in Nineteenth Century American Jewish History.* Cincinnati, 1954.

———. "Jewish 'Forty-Eighters' in America." *AJA(p)* 2 (1949): 44ff.

Kuznets, Simon. "Economic Structure and Life of the Jews," in: Finkelstein, Louis, ed., *The Jews, Their History, Culture, and Religion.* New York, 1960. Quoted from the preliminary draft at the Mt. Scopus Library, Hebrew University, Jerusalem.

———. *Economic Structure of U.S. Jewry: Recent Trends.* Jerusalem, 1972.

———. "Immigration of Russian Jews to the United States: Background and Structure." *Perspectives of American History* 9 (1975): 35–124.

Langer, Jeffrey. "White-Collar Heritage: Occupational Mobility of the Jews in Chicago, 1860–1880." B.A. thesis, University of Illinois, 1976. AJA(a), small collections, pp. 18ff.

Latrobe, C. J. *The Rambler in North America, 1832–1833,* vol. 1. New York, 1835.

Lenke, Theodor. *Geschichte des Deutschtums in New York von 1848 bis 1891.* New York, 1891.

Lestschinsky, Jacob. "Jewish Migrations, 1840–1956," in *The Jews,* edited by Finkelstein, vol. 2, pp. 1536–96.

————. "Dos Sotsiale Ponim fun Amerikaner Yidentum" (The Social Features of American Jewry). *Yivo-Bleter* 17 (1941).

————. *Das wirtschaftliche Schicksal des deutschen Judentums.* Berlin, 1932.

————. "Jüdische Wanderungen im letzten Jahrhundert." *Welt-Wirtschafts-Archiv* 25 (1927): 69–87.

Levinson, R. "The Jews in the Californian Gold Rush." Ph.D. dissertation, University of Oregon, 1968.

Lewin, Kurt. "Self-Hatred among Jews." *Contemporary Jewish Record* 4, no. 3 (1941): 219–32.

Linfield, H. S. *Statistics of Jews and Jewish Organizations: Historical Review of Ten Censuses, 1850–1937.* New York, 1939.

Lowenstein, Steven M. "The Rural Community and the Urbanization of German Jewry." *Central European History* 13 (1980): 218–36.

Marcus, Jacob R. *The American Jewish Woman, 1654–1980,* vols. 1 and 2. New York and Cincinnati, 1981.

————. *The Colonial American Jew, 1492–1776,* 3 vols., continuously paginated. Detroit, 1970.

————. *On Love, Marriage, Children . . . and Death Too: Intimate Glimpses into the Lives of American Jews.* N.p., 1965.

————. *Memoirs of American Jews, 1775–1865,* vols. 1–3. Philadelphia, 1955.

————. *Studies in American Jewish History.* Cincinnati, 1969.

Matthews. *A Pen and Ink Panorama of New York City.* New York, 1853.

Mesinger, Jonathan S. *Peddlers and Merchants: The Geography of Work in a Nineteenth Century Jewish Community.* Syracuse, N.Y., 1977.

————. "Reconstructing the Social Geography of the Nineteenth Century Jewish Community from Primary Statistical Sources," in *AJH—Quantification,* edited by Raphael, pp. 354–68.

Meyer, Michael A. "German Jewish Identity in Nineteenth Century America," in *Toward Modernity: The European Jewish Model,* edited by Jacob Katz, pp. 247–67. New Brunswick, N.J., 1987.

————. *Response to Modernity: A History of the Reform Movement in Judaism.* New York and Oxford, 1988.

Michael, Ann D. "The Origins of the Jewish Community of Cincinnati, 1817–1860." M.A. thesis, University of Cincinnati, 1970, AJA(a), box 817; the California collection, box 280.

Michael, R. "Die antijudaistische Tendenz in Christian Wilhelm Dohm's Buch über die bürgerliche Verbesserung der Juden." *Bulletin des Leo Baeck Instituts* 77 (1987): 12–48.

Moltman, G. "Auswanderung als Revolutionsersatz?" in *Die Deutschen und die Revolution,* ed. M. Salewski, pp. 272–97. Göttingen, 1984.

Mosse, W., A. Paucker, and R. Rürup, ed. *Revolution and Evolution: 1848 in German Jewish History.* Tübingen, 1981.

Mostov, Stephen G. "Dun and Bradstreet Reports as a Source of Jewish Economic History: Cincinnati, 1840–1875," in *AJH—Quantification,* edited by Raphael, pp. 333–53.

————. "A 'Jerusalem' on the Ohio: The Social and Economic History of Cincinnati's Jewish Community, 1840–1875." Ph.D. dissertation, Brandeis University, 1981.

————. "A Sociological Portrait of German Jewish Immigrants in Boston: 1845–1861." *AJS Review* 3 (1978): 121–52.

Nadel, Stanley. "Jewish Race and German Soul in Nineteenth Century America." *AJH* 67 (1987): 6–26.

Neuringer, Sheldon Morris. *American Jewry and United States Immigration Policy, 1881–1953.* New York, 1980.

Panitz, Esther. "The Polarity of Jewish Attitudes toward Immigration." *AJHQ* (December 1963): 114f. and 121.

Prinz, Arthur. *Juden im Deutschen Wirtschaftsleben: Soziale und wirtschaftliche Struktur im Wandel, 1815–1914. Bearbeitet und herausgegeben v. Avraham Barkai.* Tübingen, 1984.

Raphael, Marc Lee. *Jews and Judaism in a Mid-Western Community: Columbus, Ohio, 1840–1975.* Columbus, 1979.

Rawidowicz, Esther E. "I. L. Chronik and his *zeichen der Zeit,"* in *The Chicago Pinkas,* edited by Simon Rawidowicz, pp. 137–47.

————, ed. *Quantification and the American Jewish Experience. AJH* Special Issue 72, no. 3 (March 1983).

Rawidowicz, Simon, ed. *The Chicago Pinkas.* Chicago, 1952.

Reissner, Hans G. "'Ganstown, USA'—A German Jewish Dream." *AJA(p)* 14 (1962): 20–31.

————. "The German American Jews (1800–1850)." *YLBI* 10 (1965): 57–116.

Rhode, G., ed. *Juden in Ostmitteleuropa von der Emanzipation bis zum Ersten Weltkrieg.* Marburg on the Lahn, 1989.

Richarz, Monika, ed. *Jüdisches Leben in Deutschland: Selbstzeugnisse zur Sozialgeschichte,* 3 vols. Stuttgart, 1976–82.

Rischin, Moses. *The Promised City: New York Jews, 1870–1914.* Cambridge, Mass., 1962.

Rockaway, Robert A. "From Americanization to Jewish Americanism: The Jews of Detroit, 1850–1914." Ph.D. dissertation, University of Michigan, 1970.

Rohrbacher, Stefan. "From Württemberg to America: A Nineteenth-Cenetury Jewish Village on Its Way to the New World." *AJA(p)* 41 (1989): 143–71.

Roseman, Kenneth. "The Jewish Population of America, 1850–1860: A Demographic Study of Four Cities." Ph.D. dissertation, Hebrew Union College—Jewish Institute of Religion, 1971.

Ruchames, Louis. "The Abolitionists and the Jews: Some Further Thoughts," in *A Bicentennial Festschrift for Jacob Raeder Marcus,* edited by Bertram W. Korn, pp. 505–15. New York, 1976.

Rürup, R. *Emanzipation und Antisemitismus: Studien zur "Judenfrage" der bürgerlichen Gesellschaft.* Göttingen, 1975.

Sachs, Howard F. "Seeking the Welfare of a City," in *Mid-America's Promise: A Profile of Kansas City Jewry,* edited by Joseph P. Schutz, pp. 147–82. Kansas City, 1982.

Salewski, M., ed. *Die Deutschen und die Revolution.* Göttingen, 1984.

Sareth, Edward N. *American Historians and European Immigrants, 1875–1925.* New York, 1965.

Sarna, Jonathan. "A Critical Review of Neuringer's *American Jewry."* *AJH* 71 (1982): 403–7.

————. "The Impact of Nineteenth Century Christian Missions on American Jews," in *Jewish Apostasy in the Modern World,* edited by Todd M. Endelman, pp. 232–54. New York and London, 1987.

————. "The 'Mythical Jew' and the 'Jew Next Door' in Nineteenth Century America," in *Anti-Semitism,* edited by Gerber, pp. 57–78.

————. "A Sort of Paradise for the Hebrews: The Lofty Vision of the Cincinnati Jews," in *The Jews of Cincinnati,* by Sarna and Nancy Klein, pp. 1–21.

Sarna, Jonathan D., and Nancy Klein. *The Jews of Cincinnati.* Cincinnati, 1989.

Schappes, Morris U. *A Documentary History of the Jews of the United States, 1654–1875.* New York, 1950.

Schlam, Helena F. "The Early Jews of Houston." M.A. thesis, Ohio State University, 1971, at AJA(a), community histories file.

Schmelz, Usiel O. "Die demographische Entwicklung der Juden in Deutschland von der Mitte des 19. Jahrhunderts bis 1933." *Zeitschrift für Bevölkerungswissenschaft* 8 (1982): 31–72.

Schultz, Joseph P., ed. *Mid-America's Promise: A Profile of Kansas City Jewry.* Kansas City, 1982.

Schwartz, Stefan. *Die Juden in Bayern im Wandel der Zeiten.* Munich, 1963.

Silbergleit, Heinrich. *Die Bevölkerungs- und Berufsverhältnisse im Deutschen Reich.* Berlin, 1930.

Silver, Louis, "The Jews in Albany, N.Y." *YIVO—Annual of Jewish Social Sciences* 9 (1954): 212–46.

Singerman, R. "Jewish Serials Published in the United States," in *Studies in Judaica Americana,* vol. 2. New York, Westport, Conn., and London, 1990.

Sklare, Marshall. *America's Jews.* New York, 1971.

Sombart, Werner. *Die Juden und das Wirtschaftsleben.* Leipzig, 1911.

Sozialgeschichtliches Arbeitsbuch. See Fischer et al., eds. (vol. 1); Hohorst et al., eds. (vol. 2).

Stern, Malcolm H. "The 1870s: American Jewry Comes of Age," in *The American Jewish Experience,* ed. Sarna, pp. 31–32.

Stern-Taeubler, Selma. "The Motivation of the German Jewish Emigration to America in the Post Mendelsonian Era," in *Essays in American Jewish History,* edited by Jacob R. Marcus, pp. 247–61. Cincinnati, 1958.

Supple, Barry E. "A Business Elite: German Jewish Financiers in Nineteenth Century New York," in *The American Jewish Experience,* edited by Sarna, pp. 73–86.

Switchkow, Louis J., and Lloyd P. Gartner. *The History of the Jews of Milwaukee.* Philadelphia, 1963.

Szajkowski, Zosa. "The Attitude of American Jews to East European Immigration (1881–1893)." *PAJHS* 40 (1951).

————. "The 'Yahudi' and the Immigrant: A Reappraisal." *AJHQ* 63 (1973): 13–44.

Tarshish, Allan. "The Economic Life of the American Jews in the Middle Nineteenth Century," in *Essays in American Jewish History,* edited by Jacob R. Marcus, pp. 247–61.Cincinnati, 1958.

————. "The Rise of American Judaism." Ph.D. dissertation, Hebrew Union College, 1937.

Toll, William. "The Female Life Cycle and the Measure of Jewish Social Change: Portland, Oregon, 1880–1930,"in *AJH—Quantification,* edited by Raphael, pp. 309–32.

————. *The Making of an Ethnic Minority Class: Portland Jewry over Four Generations*. New York, 1982.

Toury, Jacob. "Jewish Manual Labour and Emigration: Records from Some Bavarian Districts (1830–1957)." *YLBI* 16 (1971): 45–62.

————. *Soziale und politische Geschichte der Juden in Deutschland, 1847–1871*. Düsseldorf, 1977.

————. *Turmoil and Confusion in the Revolution of 1848* (in Hebrew). Merchavia, 1968.

Tramer, Hans, ed. *In Zwei Welten: Festschrift für Siegfried Moses*. Tel Aviv, 1962.

Tscherikower, Elias, ed. *The Early Jewish Labor Movement in the United States*. Translated and revised by A. Antonowsky. New York, 1961.

Urofsky, Marvin I. "American Jewish Leadership." *AJH* 70 (1980–81): 408f.

Volkov, Shulamit. "Erfolgreiche Assimilation oder Erfolg und Assimilation: Die deutsch-jüdische Familie im Kaiserreich," in *Wissenschaftskolleg Berlin, Jahrbuch II*, pp. 373–87. Berlin, 1983.

Vorspan, Max, and Lloyd P. Gartner. *History of the Jews of Los Angeles*. Philadelphia, 1970.

Walker, Mack. *Germany and the Emigration, 1816–1885*. Cambridge, Mass., 1964.

Weinryb, Bernard D. "Deutsch-Jüdische Wanderungen im 19. Jahrhundert." *Der Morgen* 10 (1934): 4–10.

————. "The German Jewish Immigrants to America: A Critical Evaluation," in *Jews from Germany in the United States*, edited by Hirshler, pp. 103–26.

————. "Jewish Immigration and Accommodation to America: Reseach, Trends, Problems." *PAJHS* 46 (1957): 388ff.

Wenger, B. S. "Jewish Women and Voluntarism: Beyond the Myth of Enablers." *American Jewish History* 79 (1989).

Wertheimer, Jack. *Unwelcome Strangers: East European Jews in Imperial Germany*. Oxford and New York, 1987.

Whiteman, Maxwell. "Notions, Dry Goods, and Clothing: An Introduction to the Study of the Cincinnati Peddler." *Jewish Quarterly Review* 53 (1962–63): 306–21.

Wilcox, Walter F., ed. *International Migrations*, vol. 2. New York, 1931.

Wischnitzer, Marc. *To Dwell in Safety*. Philadelphia, 1948.

Wolf, Edwin II, and Maxwell Whiteman. *The History of the Jews of Philadelphia from Colonial Times to the Age of Jackson*. Philadelphia, 1957.

Index

Italicized page numbers indicate illustrations.